D1601705

Autobiographical Memory

Theoretical and Applied Perspectives

AUTOBIOGRAPHICAL MEMORY

Theoretical and Applied Perspectives

Edited by

Charles P. Thompson
Kansas State University

Douglas J. Herrmann
Indiana State University

Darryl Bruce
St. Mary's University

J. Don Read
University of Lethbridge

David G. Payne
State University of New York, Binghamton

Michael P. Toglia
State University of New York, Cortland

LEA LAWRENCE ERLBAUM ASSOCIATES, PUBLISHERS
1998 Mahwah, New Jersey   London

Lawrence Erlbaum Associates, Inc., Publishers
10 Industrial Avenue
Mahwah, NJ 07430

Cover design by Kathryn Houghtaling

Library of Congress Cataloging-in-Publication Data

Autobiographical memory : theoretical and applied perspectives /
     edited by Charles P. Thompson ... [et al.].
       p. cm
     Companion volume to: Eyewitness memory.
     Includes bibliographical references and index.
     ISBN 0-8058-2075-2 (cloth).—ISBN 0-8058-
2795-1 (set)
     1. Autobiographical memory. I. Thompson, Char-
les P. II. Eyewitness memory.
BF378.A87A887   1997
153.1'13—dc21   97-11841
                             CIP

Contents

Preface   **vii**

PART 1: OVERVIEW AND GENERAL ISSUES

1   Autobiographical Memory: Themes and Variations   **3**
    Darryl Bruce and J. Don Read

2   The Relationship Between Basic Research and   **13**
    Applied Research in Memory and Cognition
    Douglas J. Herrmann

3   The Bounty of Everyday Memory   **29**
    Charles P. Thompson

PART 2: AUTOBIOGRAPHICAL MEMORY

4   Beginnings of a Theory of Autobiographical   **47**
    Remembering
    David C. Rubin

5   Loss and Distortion of Autobiographical Memory   **69**
    Content
    Harry P. Bahrick

6   Gendered Narratives: Elaboration, Structure, and   **79**
    Emotion in Parent–Child Reminiscing Across the
    Preschool Years
    Robyn Fivush

7   The Effects of Aging on Autobiographical Memory   **105**
    Gillian Cohen

8   Autobiographical Memory and Self-Narratives: A Tale   **125**
    of Two Stories
    John A. Robinson and Leslie R. Taylor

9   Remembering the Past in the Present: Verb Tense   **145**
    Shifts in Autobiographical Memory Narratives
    *David B. Pillemer, Amy B. Desrochers, and Caroline M.
    Ebanks*

10 What Is It Like to Remember? On Phenomenal   **163**
    Qualities of Memory
    Steen F. Larsen

Author Index   **191**

Subject Index   **197**

Preface

The first meeting of the Society for Applied Research in Memory and Cognition (SARMAC) was held in Vancouver in July 1995. Over 175 people attended the meeting, which featured more than 60 presentations, major invited addresses given by Steve Ceci and Dave Rubin, and presentations by SARMAC Chair Doug Herrmann and Chair-elect Chuck Thompson. We wanted to capture some of the excitement of the meeting with a book consisting of elaborations of some of the presentations. However, there were too many excellent presentations with the result that a single book would have been too lengthy and too expensive. Thus, we decided to publish companion volumes around the two related themes of autobiographical memory and eyewitness testimony. We hope that the chapters included in this volume will give the reader a feeling for what was a focused and exciting meeting.

ACKNOWLEGMENTS

Many people deserve credit for making that first meeting possible. Don Read was the chair of the Conference Organizing Committee and deserves the highest praise for his work. Darryl Bruce and Don Read organized special sessions on autobiographical memory and eyewitness testimony, respectively. David Payne and Mike Toglia co-chaired the program committee. Finally, John Yuille was the on-site organizer whose able assistant, Melissa Nisbet, seemed to be able to handle any emergency!

The 1995 meeting was a good kick-off for SARMAC. It is an energetic and growing organization that encourages participation by all those interested in practical applications of memory and cognition. If your research interests include (or have implications for) practical applications, contact Darryl Bruce, Don Read, Chuck Thompson, or Mike Toglia to get information on SARMAC. My e-mail address is chuckt@ksu.edu and I welcome your inquiries. We hope you enjoy the book!

—Charles P. Thompson

I

Overview and General Issues

1

Autobiographical Memory: Themes and Variations[1]

Darryl Bruce
Saint Mary's University

J. Don Read
University of Lethbridge

The organization of the first SARMAC conference around only two specifically identifiable research topics—autobiographical memory and eyewitness memory—may, at first blush, seem puzzling. The two areas, longtime staples on the menu of investigators of memory in more natural settings, differ on a variety of dimensions, perhaps most notably on their specific goals for scientific inquiry and application.

Yet these differences should not be exaggerated. For many questions about memory and cognition of interest to scientific psychology, there have been historical as well as rather arbitrary reasons for their assignment to the autobiographical or eyewitness memory fields. Both fields are highly active, are represented by substantial numbers of scientists, and continue to grow in size. In both areas, several separate scientific meetings dedicated to their respective interests have been held, numerous monographs published, and overlapping yet somewhat different journals established. To a significant extent, however, research in one area often serves as the basis for research

[1]As noted in the precise, some of the papers presented at the first SARMAC conference (Society for Applied Research in Memory and Cognition, Vancouver, 1985) were revised and extended for chapters in companion volumes on autobiographical memory and eyewitness memory. The two volumes are closely related, and this chapter describes how the same themes are expressed in both volumes. This chapter occurs in both volumes with slight changes in the title and text to make it appropriate for the volume in which it appears. Because it was truly coauthored, the order of authors also is reversed in the two volumes.

in the other. Most typically, work by eyewitness memory researchers has been stimulated by investigations of a more basic and theoretical nature in autobiographical memory.

Perhaps as a result of these differing historical orientations, this volume's seven autobiographical memory chapters generally focus on the qualities or types of recall from research participants, whereas the seven chapters in the eyewitness memory volume generally focus on the quantity (a concern for completeness) and accuracy of recall. This interest in the ultimate end product and its application within the legal process in general encourages eyewitness memory investigators to modify their testing procedures continually in an attempt to gain even more information from participants about an event. Indeed, several of the eyewitness memory chapters reflect such attempts.

In addition, the types of events to be recalled by participants in the two research environments have traditionally differed: Eyewitness memory participants have usually recalled very brief, recently witnessed, public (or staged) events, whereas individuals participating in autobiographical memory research have generally recalled private, personally significant, and personally selected events from remote memory, events for which accurate or complete public records have rarely existed. It is therefore not surprising that investigators of autobiographical memory have usually concentrated more on the quality than the quantity or veridicality of such reports.

In our review, research over the last decade has changed in such a way as to reflect more commonalties than differences between the two areas: For example, eyewitness researchers, prompted perhaps by the fact that a public record exists, have explored the recall of events that are both personal and autobiographically significant to the participants. Chapter 3 in the companion volume by Parker, Bahrick, Lundy, Fivush, and Levitt on children's recall of Hurricane Andrew well reflects this orientation. Investigation by Yuille and Daylen (chap. 8, companion volume) of the recall of single or repeated instances of traumatic experiences, even though not in the public domain or documented, also shows the long-standing concerning of traditional eyewitness researchers for the remembering of events of personal importance, a matter that for methodological and ethical reasons has been difficult to study. Both of these chapters could as easily fit with the field of autobiographical memory, but because the events described are either public or their recollection has legal implications, they find themselves on the eyewitness side of the ledger.

Similarly, this volume contains contributions that, if not central to the topic of eyewitness memory, at least have considerable relevance to it. For example, Bahrick's chapter 5 deals with the problem of distortions of memory, an issue of enormous moment to those concerned about recollections made in legal and clinical situations. Likewise, the observations described by Pillemer, Desrochers, and Ebanks (chap. 9) on verb tense shifts have implications for the authenticity of experiences reported in personal narratives and should thus be of interest to those working in clinical and legal contexts. Finally, Fivush's research (chap. 6) shows the close relation between the qualitative characteristics of autobiographical memory and their relevance to matters of eyewitness testimony.

THEMES AND VARIATIONS

From our perusal of the chapters in the autobiographical memory and eyewitness memory volumes, it appeared that each featured one or more of the following six themes: accuracy, affect, imagery, development, methods, and theory. We emphasize that we developed these themes after the fact; other readers may discover other themes. Nevertheless, these themes permit us to provide the reader with a framework for organizing the information to come and to introduce the chapters themselves. Here, then, is an indication of how the six themes or threads crop up in the various chapters.

Accuracy and Distortions of Memory in Children and Adults

Accuracy in remembering is a prominent theme of a number of chapters. Three on autobiographical memory touch on the problem. Bahrick's (chap. 5) particular interest is the basis for distortions in the recollection of one's grades in high school. If they are not accurately recalled, errors are usually inflations of the actual grades. The contribution by Pillemer et al. (chap. 9) examines shifts from the past to the present tense that sometimes occur in the recounting of a personal narrative. Such shifts may be an indicator of accuracy; that is, they may suggest that an individual is reporting something that was actually experienced rather than known secondhand or even fabricated. In his highly original essay, Larsen (chap. 10) explores the phenomenal qualities of memories and notes that assessing memory accuracy is really a matter of comparing one's original experience (not the objective event itself) with one's later recollection. The problem, as Larsen points out, lies in what we can know of our initial experience.

Four of the chapters in the companion eyewitness memory volume examine accuracy in the recollections of both children and adults. The exploration of the subject with children reflects an interest in cognitive development as well as the interface between psychology and the law. What is recalled by a child about a personally significant (and sometimes criminal) event is often critical to the legal process. For Ceci, Crossman, Gilstrap, and Scullin (chap. 2), the question is related to developmental differences in suggestibility between younger and older children across very different types of information, including bodily touching. For Walker and Hunt (chap. 4), on the other hand, the primary question is how we can better obtain from young children more complete recall of their experiences. Walker and Hunt point to a variety of specific interview techniques that psychologists have recommended for use with children as methods for bolstering recall. However, when evidence of their use is sought within actual forensic interviews with children, their presence is very rare indeed.

Concerning adults, Yarmey (chap. 7) and Read, Lindsay, and Nicholls (chap. 6) describe recent data concerned with accuracy of person identification following brief interactions between research participants and a target individual. Yarmey's chapter focuses on a number of specific identification techniques (e.g., showups) and bases of identification (e.g., faces, voices, and bodily movements), whereas Read et al.'s chapter evaluates the controversial relation between the accuracy of a participant's identification decision and the subjective confidence expressed in that decision. The results of the latter chapter demonstrate that the association between accuracy and confidence can be very strong. They also suggest that eyewitness memory research has generally been unsuccessful at incorporating those characteristics of real-world identifications that may set the stage for the observation of a substantial link between accuracy and confidence.

Affect, Emotion, and Memory

The relation of affect and emotion to memory is complex and any attempt on our part to summarize the situation would be well beyond the scope and purpose of our introductory essay. The reader may therefore wish to turn first to chapter 5 by Bahrick, which contains a useful review of some of the relevant literature as well as some pitfalls in conducting and interpreting research in the area. Bahrick proposes a number of ideas in his discussion, a chief one being that reconstructive memory processes lead to errors of recollection that engender positive affect.

A number of chapters in this memory volume report intriguing effects concerning emotion and memory. Pillemer et al. (chap. 9) show that a narrator's shift from the past to the present tense in recounting a past experience tends typically to occur at an emotional high point in the story. In her contribution, Fivush (chap. 6) notes certain adult gender differences in autobiographical memory reports (e.g., women's are generally more emotional than men's), and asks whether they might originate in differences in the way that mothers and fathers reminisce with their children over the preschool years. One of her many findings is that both parents used substantially more emotion words in reminiscing with their daughters than with their sons. In chapter 10, Larsen describes the results of an investigation of memory for emotional experiences. A particularly intriguing outcome was that when the focus of an emotion was an internal state (e.g., being joyful), the accompanying imagery was more somatic; when the focus was an external event (e.g., a holiday breakfast), the accompanying imagery was more visual. In a more theoretical vein, Rubin (chap. 4) sees affect as one of the major components of the process of autobiographical recollection.

Some of the eyewitness memory contributions also bear on the relation of affect and memory. One possibility is that it depends critically on the valence of the affect: When events generate positive affect, the relation is positive; when they generate negative affect, the relation is reversed. That is, it has been often argued that life events accompanied by strong negative affect or emotion are recalled with much greater difficulty than events accompanied by less emotional intensity. Consistent with the latter position are reports from individuals of "recovered" memories of events they claimed to have completely forgotten for several years, even decades. Parker et al. (chap. 3, companion volume) point to the complexity of the association between affect and memory and, in so doing, find support for both positions: Recall of a hurricane and its aftermath by children reflected a curvilinear, Yerkes–Dodson relation between emotion and recall. In a related way, Ceci et al.'s chapter 2 (companion volume) suggests that children are less willing to develop false beliefs about events that have negative rather than positive valence, although the effects of suggestive questioning in general were seen in the accounts of preschool and older children and across different domains of inquiry.

Like Parker et al., Yuille and Daylen (chap. 8, companion volume) are also concerned with events accompanied by negative emotion. They emphasize what they refer to as events of impact, and they restrict their interest to a subset of those that are traumatic. The authors make the important point that at this stage of our knowledge, in both eyewitness memory and autobiographical memory, the consequences of emotional events may be so idiosyncratic as to preclude the possibility of any generalizations about the relation between emotion and memory. Yuille and Daylen describe a variety of hypothetical patterns relating trauma to memory that may well provide useful direction to future researchers.

Imagery and Memory

If anything can be considered a defining aspect of autobiographical memory, it is imagery, especially visual imagery. Larsen's (chap. 10) investigation that we have just referred to yields helpful amplifying information. First, the imagery accompanying a personal recollection appears to be based at least partly on the original experience and not simply generated at the time of retrieval. Second, imagery of a visual nature is indeed prominent in autobiographical remembering, but if an internal emotion is being retrieved, then somatic imagery can be strongly in evidence. Pillemer et al.'s (chap. 9) analysis of changes from the past to the present tense in relating an episode from one's past may likewise underscore the central role of imagery in autobiographical memory. They suggest that such shifts may occur partly because the episode has a strong sensory representation in memory, and that the past is being perceived again. But whatever the implications of the findings of Larsen and Pillemer et al., Rubin (chap. 4) considers imagery, especially visual imagery, as a key component in recollecting one's personal past.

Within a series of five experiments designed to assess the boundary conditions and ages, if any, at which suggestive effects of misleading information occur with children, Ceci et al. (chap. 2, companion volume) also emphasize the centrality of visual imagery (or of repeatedly imagining an event) in the formation and retention of autobiographical memories, albeit false ones. For example, the children in Ceci et al.'s investigations were sometimes encouraged to develop a memory of an unusual (and nonexperienced) event by generating on 10 occasions a visual image of the event and their involvement with it. Although explanations other than the production of vivid imagery exist for the construction of what appear to be some firmly entrenched false autobiographical memories following successive applications of the researchers' instructions, imagination and imagery do seem likely candidates.

The potentially misleading consequences of mental imagery are also seen in Yarmey's (chap. 7, companion volume) study of participants whose estimates of the duration of their brief interactions with a target person were preceded by brief periods of mental rehearsal. As it turned out, the rehearsal manipulation reduced confidence ratings of the duration estimates, but an explanation for the effect is not obvious at this time. Finally, Yuille and Daylen (chap. 8, companion volume) suggest that the quality of the verbal report following a traumatic incident, including access to detailed imagery, is a joint function of the type of event experienced and the locus of a witness' attention (internal or external) during the event. Taken together, the eyewitness memory chapters frequently do consider imagery (visual or otherwise) as an important moderator and indicator of events in autobiographical memory, but the focus seems more on the measurement of imagery than on its function.

Development of Memory

A number of the authors in this volume are concerned to varying degrees with the development of memory. Fivush (chap. 6) concentrates on the preschool years and looks for variations in reminiscences during the period between daughters and sons on the one hand and mothers and fathers on the other. She finds that gender differences appear early on in autobiographical narratives. In comparison with boys, girls recalled more information, referred more to emotions (as mentioned earlier), and included more orientations (linkages to other events) and evaluations in their narratives. Fivush believes that parents may be contributing to this pattern because in conversing with their daughters, both mothers and fathers elaborated and confirmed more and used more emotion words.

Cohen (chap. 7) focuses on the later years of life and considers the changes that occur in both the character and function of autobiographical memories. One such change is that personal memories of older people sometimes become overgeneral. At other times, however, they retain their vivid and detailed nature, perhaps because they are personally important and are rehearsed. Cohen speculates that such memories maintain the individual's self-concept and sense of personal identity.

An important developmental question posed by Robinson and Taylor (chap. 8) is whether a reminiscence bump (heightened recall of autobiographical memories from the period spanning 10–30 years of age) would be obtained when participants—here, middle-aged women—gave narrative accounts of their lives. The authors observed such heightened recall, but more for experiences from the childhood and preadolescent years than from the adolescent years, suggesting that "the reminiscence bump reflects a feature of autobiographical memory at all levels of its hierarchical structure" (p. 132).

The chapters by Ceci et al. (chap. 2, companion volume) and Walker and Hunt (chap. 4, companion volume) easily fit with the developmental concerns of the autobiographical memory authors, albeit from a different perspective. For Ceci et al., the primary issue is whether a child's autobiographical memory can be substantially altered through suggestive techniques and whether, as some have suggested, there is an age beyond which children are less at risk. Further, Ceci and his associates explore the long-term fate of information suggested to and accepted by a child.

Walker and Hunt, on the other hand, take as a given the need to tailor interview practices according to the age of a child in recognition of the developmental differences between children and adult eyewitnesses in the recollection or description of autobiographical events. That is, the accurate and complete description of a witnessed event, like all autobiographical memories studied by both groups of researchers, results from an interaction between questioner and respondent and assumes their common understanding of the ground rules, language, and goals of the interview. Unfortunately, as Walker and Hunt demonstrate, although the goals may be common, age-appropriate language and rules were not evident in the majority of professional interviews they analyzed. Perhaps this lack best demonstrates the need for the application of research on cognition and memory to problems in the world beyond the laboratory.

Methods

Several chapters have implications for the methods used to investigate memory. Bahrick (chap. 5) not only raises several methodological problems in studying the influence of affect on memory, but he recommends research strategies for combatting them. In studying autobiographical memory in the aged person, Cohen (chap. 7) notes that the picture varies depending on whether such memories are self-selected (e.g., obtained by cueing with a word) or experimenter designated (e.g., asking the participant to recall a flashbulb memory event): Experimenter-designated memories show aging effects (less detail and accuracy in reports by older individuals); for self-selected memories, the general pattern is that there are no age differences in vividness and detail.

Three of the autobiographical memory chapters have the methodological commonality of asking individuals to give some kind of narrative account of their personal pasts. In this respect, they represent something of a departure from the more typical methods used to study autobiographical memory (see Cohen, chap. 7, for an overview). The most extensive use of the approach is by Robinson and Taylor (chap. 8). They obtained life narratives from the middle-aged participants in their study. The findings provide a wealth of information on the interplay between narrative forms and the reconstruction of one's past. Pillemer et al. (chap. 9), as we have previously indicated, emphasize the verb tense shifts that are sometimes a feature of the narrative structure of autobiographical recollections. Fivush (chap. 6) also focuses on narrative structure, but as it develops in preschoolers. She reports gender differences in the use of various narrative devices that show up very early in conversations between children and their parents. The investigations by Robinson and Taylor, Pillemer et al., and Fivush may make it more obvious to the reader why Rubin (chap. 4) holds narrative structure to be one of five essential components of autobiographical remembering.

An emphasis on methodology is also evident in the eyewitness memory chapters by Köhnken (chap. 5, companion volume) and of Walker and Hunt (chap. 4, companion volume). Both stress that for children and adults, respectively, interview techniques should enhance the accuracy and utility of testimony about life events. In Köhnken's case, the procedures are intended to be prescriptive and, for many specific components, are based on empirical work with the cognitive interview technique. For Walker and

Hunt, the goals of accuracy and completeness are the same, but specific techniques are recommended as a means of reducing the possibility of contamination of child witness accounts by interviews and other sources. One feature for which there is agreement across these two chapters is that an opportunity for the interviewee (whether adult or child) to provide at the outset an unstructured narrative account of the event or events in question is central to a complete and accurate recollection.

Theory

The most theoretical of the volume's chapters is by Rubin (chap. 4) who describes a theory of autobiographical recollection. Taking Marcel Proust's classic autobiographical recollections as prototypical, Rubin presents an account of remembering one's past that starts with an initial cue and then moves on to a slow search process that retrieves and integrates narrative, visual imagery, and affect components. Rubin also explores the underlying neurophysiological processing that may be involved.

Although no other chapter is as much concerned with theory as Rubin's, many have significant theoretical implications. Larsen (chap. 10), for example, would have us pay more attention to the phenomenal qualities of remembering—the subjective conscious experience associated with memory and recollection. He sets forth a framework that distinguishes three kinds of qualities: (a) *content qualities,* which are about the past experience itself; (b) *appearance qualities,* which have to do with the present experience and evaluation of the content qualities; and (c) *process qualities,* which concern how content and appearance qualities are cognitively produced.

At least three of the volume's chapters have implications for the structure of autobiographical memory: Robinson and Taylor's (chap. 8) consideration of self-narratives convinces them that autobiographical memory is organized at several levels, with self-narratives themselves perhaps being one type of organization. Pillemer et al. (chap. 9) argue that verb tense shifts also suggest multiple levels of representation, among them, personal memories that are expressed through images or emotions and those expressed via a narrative memory system. Cohen's (chap. 7) general explanation for the prevalence in older people of overgeneral autobiographical memories—ones that are imprecise and lacking in detail—is that autobiographical memory is hierarchically organized and that overgeneral memories are due to truncated retrieval at a level in the hierarchy that is too high for the retrieval of specific details.

With the exception of Yuille and Daylen (chap. 8, companion volume), the eyewitness memory authors have not concerned themselves with the construction of broad models of memory. This is not to say that the chapters are atheoretical. Several have hypothetical general relations between variables as their general concern. For example, for Read et al. (chap. 6, companion volume), the relation is between accuracy and confidence; for Ceci et al. (chap. 2, companion volume), between age and susceptibility to different types of misleading information; and for Parker et al. (chap. 3, companion volume), between level of arousal and recall memory. Of the autobiographical memory chapters, we believe the theoretical discussion provided by Larsen (chap. 10) to be most readily applicable to the eyewitness domain. In particular, it bears on questions concerning the assessment of the credibility of witnesses' statements.

CONCLUSIONS

Beyond the specific contributions of each chapter to the literature on autobiographical and eyewitness memory, what do we hope that the reader will come away with in general concerning the many basic and applied investigations of remembering discussed herein? At the very least, that autobiographical and eyewitness memory fields are thriving; that they are likely to remain center stage in the further investigation of memory in natural contexts; that although the autobiographical and eyewitness memory chapters have been segregated in these two volumes, the separation is often more arbitrary than real and that connections between the two areas abound; that the two research traditions are entirely mindful of fundamental laboratory methods, research, and theory, sometimes drawing their research inspirations from that quarter; and, perhaps finally, that the two fields, although driven largely by everyday memory concerns, can contribute to a more basic understanding of memory at both an empirical and a theoretical level.

2

The Relationship Between Basic Research and Applied Research in Memory and Cognition

Douglas J. Herrmann
Indiana State University

In recent years, many scientists, politicians, and bureaucrats have claimed that the progress of science has decreased (Brown, 1992; Holden, 1992; Marshall, 1992). Because the global economy has slowed down, less money has been available to spend for research. At the same time, researchers have been enjoined to increase progress in order to solve the world's problems.

Some have proposed that scientific progress has been impeded by inadequacies in basic research practices. According to this position, basic researchers have become preoccupied with artificial questions of little consequence to the world's problems. Alternatively, others have proposed that the scientific progress has been impeded by inadequacies in applied research. According to this position, applied researchers have become preoccupied with technological details and, as a result, have failed to develop the best possible applications.

However, it may be incorrect to blame either basic research or applied research. Instead, the progress of science may be impeded by less-than-optimal interactions between basic researchers and applied researchers. If basic–applied interactions are ineffective, there is little hope that applied researchers will be successful in applying basic research. Also, there is little hope that basic researchers will have the opportunity to learn from the successes and failures of applied attempts to use basic theory.

It will be seen in the following that the difficulties in basic–applied interaction in science generally, and therefore in cognitive psychology as well, are due to cultural factors (Herrmann & Raybeck, 1994, 1997). Interculturally, the enterprise of science is made up of two large cultures: the basic research culture and the applied research culture. Interpersonally, basic researchers get along well with other basic researchers; applied researchers get along well with other applied researchers. However, basic researchers and applied researchers interact infrequently. When their work requires them to interact with each other, their cultural differences often interfere with these interactions (Semmer, 1993).

IMPROVING THE COLLABORATION OF BASIC AND APPLIED RESEARCHERS

The primary purpose of this chapter is to analyze the current effectiveness of the basic–applied collaboration within cognitive psychology. This analysis advances conclusions about the philosophy of science as it pertains to the relationship of basic and applied research. These conclusions originate in the philosophy of science literature, discussions with many colleagues, and my own experience in basic and applied research. Most of the specific examples offered here come from cognitive psychology but, in my view, the conclusions apply to science generally.

In order to make critique of the basic–applied collaboration as clear as possible, I begin this chapter by characterizing the roles of basic researchers and applied researchers. Subsequently, two sources of problems for the basic–applied collaboration are discussed, including the development of multiple research cultures in the basic–applied communities and inaccurate perceptions that each camp has developed of the other research camp. Finally, I propose some specific steps basic and applied researchers can take as individuals and collectively to strengthen the basic and applied collaboration in cognitive psychology.

CHARACTERISTICS OF BASIC AND APPLIED RESEARCHERS

Basic researchers seek the fundamental principles of phenomena without concern for the possible use of such knowledge. Applied researchers seek to apply basic findings and basic theory to solving real-world problems (Gruneberg & Morris, 1992).

Most basic researchers work within academe. Most applied researchers work outside of academe, in business, industry, or government (Gruneberg, Morris, Sykes, & Herrmann, 1996). There are exceptions to these characterizations of basic and applied researchers. For example, some basic researchers work outside of academe in basic research institutes or "think tanks" and some applied researchers work in academe.

Basic researchers rarely make forays into applied research and applied researchers rarely are involved in the development of basic theory. Basic researchers who consult on applied problems are clearly more oriented toward applied work (at least at the time of the consulting) than those basic researchers who never get near applied research. However, consulting per se usually does not make a basic researcher into an applied researcher any more than making pronouncements about basic research makes an applied researcher into a basic researcher.

Basic and applied researchers tackle research in different ways. Basic researchers are typically very skilled at traditional experiments; applied researchers are very skilled at quasi-experiments and correlational analyses. Basic researchers and applied researchers consult literatures that are sometimes very different from each other (Herrmann & Gruneberg, 1993). In the final analysis, basic and applied researchers differ because they have different research objectives: either the identification of fundamental principles, regardless of potential application, or the determination of ways to adapt basic knowledge to solve a real-world problem.

PROBLEMS IN THE BASIC–APPLIED COLLABORATION

Multiple Cultures in Cognitive Psychology

Basic research and applied research are made up of subgroups. Until now, the subgroups have often gone unnoticed or at least undiscussed. Knowing what group one is in and what group one is talking to can help considerably in interactions with someone from the other group. Thus, it is important to scientific progress to appreciate the differences among these groups. Each research group is identified with a different kind of research. In cognitive psychology, these groups include the following, in addition to basic research.

Ecological Research. Applied cognitive psychology evolved primarily out of an interest in the *ecological* validity of basic memory research (Neisser, 1976, 1978a, 1978b). Many researchers recognized that ecological validity often provides a shortcut to basic theory that may be readily applied. For example, a basic theory of eyewitness memory has evolved more rapidly out of ecological research on staged crimes and other events than out of investigations on the recognition of faces (Searelman & Herrmann, 1994).

Clearly the call for ecological cognitive research has been met in recent years (see Gruneberg, Morris, & Sykes, 1978, 1987, and Herrmann, McEvoy, Hertzog, Hertel, & Johnson, 1996, for many excellent examples of this kind of research). However, ecological research needs to be distinguished from more than just basic research. In addition, basic research and ecological research need to be distinguished from applicable research and application research.

Applicable Research. Applicable research involves investigations that are ecologically valid and that suggest an application (Herrmann, 1995). For example, memory for staged or simulated events possesses ecological validity and in addition mimics the experience of eyewitnesses who may be called to testify in court (a real-world task to which memory theory may be applied). For example, because face recognition has been investigated in the context of staged crimes, it has been possible to make useful recommendations to police about lineups and mugbook procedures (Deffenbacher, 1996). Applicable research sometimes builds on ecologically valid investigations (Herrmann & Gruneberg, 1993) but it is not always possible to do so (Yuille & Cutshall, 1986). When no previous study comes close enough to the conditions of application, the first step in applied research is usually to conduct applicable research.

Application Research. Application research is specifically designed to yield information that bears on a potential product or service. Application research has been distinguished from laboratory research for centuries (Chapanis, 1967, 1986, 1988; Hoffman & Deffenbacher, 1992). Although application research is useful primarily to applied researchers and practitioners designing a product or a service, it can also be useful to basic researchers and ecological researchers as well (Gruneberg et al., 1996; Herrmann & Gruneberg, 1993; Hoffman & Deffenbacher, 1993).

Application findings can delineate the boundary conditions of phenomena in ways that basic research normally does not (Barber, 1988; Berger, Pezdek, & Banks, 1987). Successful applications provide society with compelling demonstrations of the power of basic research. Such demonstrations often channel funds to more basic research (Miller, 1995). For example, in science generally, the U.S. Space Program has often been held up as a model for how an applied project can stimulate increases in governmental support of basic research. An example of applied cognitive research that has increased opportunities for basic research can be found in the work of nonprofit testing organizations, such as the Educational

Testing Service. Such organizations have stimulated a great deal of basic research on the cognitive processes involved in taking the tests they administer and in the nature of college aptitude (Sternberg, 1992).

Impact of Multiple Cultures. Each of the four kinds of research (basic, ecological, applicable, and application) requires considerable knowledge, effort, and time. Consequently, the psychologists who do one kind of research tend to not get involved in the other kinds of research. Thus, cognitive psychology is made up of at least four subgroups (basic researchers, ecological researchers, applicable researchers, and application researchers), each with a different mission.

The growth of the cognitive discipline into different groups with different orientations can be viewed as a positive outcome in that it demonstrates that our science is evolving. However, this growth comes with some costs. Each of these groups look at the world in somewhat different ways and each of these groups know their own approach better than they know the approaches of the other groups (Herrmann & Raybeck, 1994, 1997). If the basic–applied collaboration is to work at its best, we will have to learn ways to overcome the cultural differences that limit access to these groups.

Misperceptions of the Other Research Camp

Roles in the Basic–Applied Relationship. The standard account of the relationship between basic and applied research was originally set forth by Sir Francis Bacon (1561–1626). As mentioned earlier, this account holds that basic and applied researchers collaborate in a cyclical manner. Basic researchers discover the fundamental principles. Applied researchers apply these principles until inadequacies in these principles are detected, at which point applied researchers communicate the inadequacies to the basic researchers. Basic researchers then investigate the inadequacies until they find a way to improve the original principle (Intons-Peterson, 1997; Munsterberg, 1914), and the cycle continues.

However, as described in detail later in this chapter, the standard account is no longer sufficient to describe the range of research activities of applied researchers. Specifically, modern applied researchers not only apply basic theories, but they also seek to develop theories that are pertinent to particular applications. Because the standard account does not recognize the theoretical role of modern applied researchers, these researchers sometimes feel that their work is misunderstood by researchers from other camps. The idea that applied researchers are merely the implementers of basic research ingenuity is regarded by some applied researchers as insulting because they feel that—like basic researchers—they too manifest ingenuity in their work.

This misperception of applied researchers as nontheoreticians acts as a barrier to communication between basic and applied researchers. Later in this chapter, I advance a new account of the basic–applied relationship that gives modern applied researchers credit for this theoretical work and thereby allows basic and applied researchers to meet each other on a level playing field.

Approaches to Science. Basic and applied researchers often appear to each other to hold fundamentally different views about philosophy of science (e.g., views pertaining to the discoverability of truth, the generalizability of basic principles, interpretation of basic principles, and inferential processes). Basic researchers and applied researchers also differ in the way they approach research; for example, in terms of research designs, reporting customs for null findings, the use of replication, and so on. Basic and applied researchers also engage in somewhat different statistical practices concerning imputation of data and the seriousness of Type I and Type II errors. (For more detail on these differences in scientific approach, see Herrmann & Raybeck, 1994, 1997).

Work Environments. The scientists who conduct research in academe, business, industry, or government might presume a comradery with each other. However, basic and applied researchers have very different work experiences. Basic and applied scientists attend separate meetings, publish in separate journals, seek funding from different agencies, have supervisors with widely different powers over researchers, and participate in contrasting systems that offer different rewards. Basic researchers in recent decades typically pride themselves on being specialists. In contrast, applied researchers are constantly shifted from one research topic to another, leading them to become generalists. Both groups can speak the same language but attach substantively different meanings to the terms they use.

Beliefs. It is sad but true that basic and applied researchers sometimes harbor negative beliefs about each other. Ask almost any basic or applied researcher and they will readily agree that such prejudices exist (Herrmann & Raybeck, 1994, 1996; Pedhazur & Schmelkin, 1991). The most conspicuous prejudices fall into six categories: those concerning the importance of research, competence, accountability, ethics, personal standards, and intelligence.

Table 2.1 lists examples of these prejudices from both the basic and the applied perspectives. An example of how prejudices can interfere with communication between basic and applied research may be found in the

TABLE 2.1
Prejudices Basic and Applied Researchers Hold About Each Other

Concerning the Importance of Research

Basic researchers sometimes regard their research as the more important because it deals with fundamental knowledge.

Applied researchers sometimes regard their research as the more important because it provides society with knowledge it can use.

Concerning Competence

Basic researchers sometimes believe that applied researchers are less competent at conducting research because applied research is less controlled than basic research.

Applied researchers sometimes believe that basic researchers are less competent at conducting research because drawing inferences from controlled research is much easier than drawing inferences from observational research.

Concerning Accountability

Basic researchers sometimes feel that applied researchers are irresponsible in that they do not try to apply basic research.

Applied researchers sometimes feel that basic researchers are irresponsible because no one holds them accountable for the quality of their basic research.

Concerning Ethics

Basic researchers sometimes regard applied researchers as unethical for accepting pay for doing research that others want done.

Applied researchers sometimes feel that basic researchers are corrupted by the incentives of grants and royalties for publishing.

Concerning Personal Standards

Basic researchers sometimes believe that applied researchers have low standards because they have chosen a career that involves dealing with the public.

Applied researchers often believe that basic researchers are snobs because they refuse to deal with the public.

Concerning Intelligence

Basic researchers sometimes brag that they are brighter than applied researchers because their research is tighter and theoretically richer than applied research.

Applied researchers sometimes brag that they are brighter because they are engaged in work that truly affects the world.

---

recent "my science is better than your science" debate (Banaji & Crowder, 1989; Gruneberg, Morris, & Sykes, 1991; Loftus, 1991; Neisser, 1978a). This debate revolved around whether or not everyday memory research or basic research was worth conducting. Instead of trying to determine what everyday memory (ecological and applicable) and basic research might offer each other, most of the participants in this debate attempted to illustrate how the other group was of little value.

However, it is not sensible to argue that applied science should or should not exist, as it is not sensible to argue that basic science should or should not exist (Baddeley, 1993). Most of the participants in the "my science is better than your science" debate were talking past each other, expressing more about the supposed superiority of their group than about the strengths and weaknesses of each group's methodologies. Had the participants in this debate been aware of each other's beliefs at the outset, they might have moved beyond the airing of prejudices to more substantive issues about the basic-applied collaboration. There are many important differences that deserve discussion: For example, should all researchers report their null hypothesis findings (applied researchers usually do, whereas basic researchers usually do not)? A related issue concerns whether the use of controls place restrictions on the generalizability of findings (basic research usually is highly controlled, whereas applied research usually is less controlled).

STRENGTHENING THE BASIC–APPLIED COLLABORATION IN COGNITIVE PSYCHOLOGY

Whenever two people presume they share similar experiences — where in fact the similarity is not real — miscommunication occurs. It is clear that basic researchers and applied researchers possess characteristics of which neither group is aware (Herrmann & Raybeck, 1994, 1997; Payne & Conrad, 1997; Payne, Conrad, & Hager, 1997; Schönflug, 1993a, 1993b). Hence, basic and applied researchers meet and talk many times without realizing the differences in scientific approach, in their work experiences, and in how these differences result in disparate views of the same phenomena.

If cognitive psychology is to improve its basic–applied collaboration, then means must be developed to foster more interaction between basic and applied psychologists. Getting applied researchers to interact with basic researchers will require more than just an attractive flyer (Gruneberg et al., 1996; Herrmann & Gruneberg, 1993). We must endeavor to understand the factors that dissuade applied psychologists from feeling comfortable with basic researchers with applied interests. To do so, ways must be developed to make contact with applied psychologists who are interested in cognition and invite them to engage in a meaningful dialogue that will benefit basic researchers and applied researchers alike.

Awareness of Multiple Cultures

To strengthen the basic–applied collaboration, communication channels need to be opened that will enable basic and applied researchers to learn about each other's culture. Perhaps the first step to be taken in improving communication is to label the multiple research cultures appropriately. For example, applicable research should not be presented as applied research (Herrmann, 1995; Herrmann & Gruneberg, 1993). Similarly, laboratory research should not be regarded as ecologically valid because the laboratory research anticipates or predicts phenomena in the real world. To be ecologically valid, the setting of research must mimic the real environment (Hoffman & Deffenbacher, 1993).

Scientific subcultures need to find ways to respect the other groups. Members of all groups tend to have pride in their own group and certainly group pride is helpful, especially in contact sports such as football or ice hockey. However, science is not (or at least it should not be) a contact sport. Regardless of what scientific group we belong to, we need to struggle against the tendency to view our group as the best, regardless of the evidence, and instead view all groups as equal until proven otherwise.

When basic researchers look down on applied researchers, or when applied researchers look down on basic researchers, the target of this disdain feels uncomfortable at best (Gruneberg et al., 1996; Herrmann & Raybeck, 1994, 1997). Obviously, prejudicial attitudes thwart the transfer of knowledge from basic to applied and vice versa. Without the proper regard of one camp for the other, effective transfer of knowledge cannot occur and the collaboration between basic and applied researchers will slow to a halt (Schönflug, 1993a, 1993b).

Correcting Misperceptions of the Other Camp

A Role for Applied Researchers in the Basic–Applied Relationship. I indicated earlier that modern applied researchers usually are not content to just implement the findings and principles of basic research. In addition, applied researchers seek to develop theories of applications that supplement basic theory as adapted for an application. Because the standard account does not fully describe the scientific role of applied researchers (developing a theory of particular applications), I propose in the following a revision of the standard account of the basic–applied relationship that addresses a new theoretical role that modern applied researchers have assumed. In order to specify clearly the nature of this new role of applied researchers, it is necessary to first describe the roles of basic and applied researchers that have been in effect until now.

Basic researchers employ what may be called the *common process strategy*. This strategy requires that a scientist identify through research those processes that are common to a set of tasks, situations, and subjects. For example, Tulving (1983) formulated the encoding specificity principle to apply to a wide range of materials and situations, which indeed it does (Searleman & Herrmann, 1994).

Once basic research has established a principle, applied researchers employ a *goodness-of-fit strategy*. This strategy requires that a scientist identify through research those procedures that permit successful application of basic theory. For example, one applied researcher (Wilson, 1987) decided to use imagery rehearsal techniques to improve the memory of head-injured patients. Knowing that these patients normally will not use the techniques spontaneously, the researcher had hospital staff prompt the patient to use the strategy that healthy people use on their own to prompt their memory. If the researcher had insisted on having the head-injured patients learn to prompt themselves as done by normal individuals, the patients would not have been able to make use of the technique. By adapting the technique to fit the basic knowledge of imagery in rehearsal, a successful application of this basic knowledge was achieved (Wilson, 1987).

In recent years applied researchers have found it necessary to adopt yet a third strategy in their research. As described already, applied researchers have found it necessary to extend, elaborate, and modify basic theory in order to develop a theory that uniquely describes the application of interest to the researcher. In seeking to develop *application theories*, applied researchers could not focus only on common processes and those variables that allow successful manipulation of common processes. In addition, applied researchers found it necessary to develop theoretical accounts of processes that were not common to all situations but that were essential to a successful application. This research strategy is called here the *essential process strategy*. Once essential processes have been identified for an application, the researcher may then use this knowledge in conjunction with basic research's knowledge of common processes to maximize an application's effectiveness (Herrmann, 1993).

The essential process strategy has proved useful in many application areas. For example, Mullin, Herrmann, and Searleman (1993) used this strategy when distinguishing between intrinsic and extrinsic memory variables. Memory strategies, such as rehearsal, intrinsically affect common processes of encoding and storage in long-term memory. Optimizing physical state, emotional state, and self-concept are essential to effective use of memory strategies because a poor physical state, mood, or self-concept may extrinsically dispose a person not to encode information or transfer it to long-term memory. Although extrinsic variables do not directly affect memory processes per se, these variables have to be optimized for people to make use of techniques for encoding and learning. Extrinsic variables concerning physical and emotional state have been shown to play an essential role in memory improvement (Herrmann & Palmisano, 1992; Herrmann & Searleman, 1990), memory training of the elderly (McEvoy & Moon, 1988; West, 1985), rehabilitation of head-injured individuals (Herrmann, 1993; Herrmann & Parenté, 1994; Parenté & Herrmann, 1996; see also Wilson, 1987, 1993), informal learning (Herrmann & Plude, 1996), and surveying the public for its recall of everyday events (Dippo & Herrmann, 1990).

Essential variables are limited in being application bound; that is, they are relevant to one application but may or may not be essential for other applications. For example, a person's "remembering" of medical appointments requires an explanation that goes beyond retention and recall to matters of compliance (Levy & Loftus, 1984). Compliance is essential to a full account of appointment remembering but is not essential to many other applications involving memory. For example, analysis and treatment of repressed memory requires the discovery of a trauma that presumably produced the repression (e.g., Loftus & Ketcham, 1991). Thus, a knowledge of memory processes that occur as a result of trauma is essential to applications dealing with repressed memory but not necessarily to many other applications of memory (e.g., medical appointments, medication adherence, advertising, air traffic control).

Although essential processes for one application may be irrelevant to another application, these processes may figure prominently in some other applications. For example, degrees of relaxation affect learning and remembering in memory training. Relaxation, whether it is achieved by training or by altering environmental comfort and attitudes, is essential to many applications areas and affects the efficiency, if not the accuracy, of memory performance in most memory tasks (Yesavage, Sheikh, & Lapp, 1989).

Learning About the Other Camp's Approach to Science, Work Environment, and Beliefs. Because basic and applied researchers work in different scientific cultures, it is valuable for members of each research camp to learn about professional differences in scientific assumptions, customs of work, and beliefs of members of the other research camp. In order for basic and applied researchers to interact productively, they need to explore differences in scientific and statistical practices in order to avoid misunderstandings in the analysis and interpretation of data. It is important that basic researchers and applied researchers come to recognize that, as specialists and generalists, they come from different perspectives. Additionally, we need to examine our beliefs about those in the other research camp and eliminate any prejudices we have about them.

Proactivity in Improving the Basic–Applied Collaboration

Basic researchers and applied researchers can come to collaborate more productively by becoming aware of the multiple cultures and by correcting misperceptions about these cultures. This increase in awareness can be achieved largely through reading, such as this chapter and other writings on this topic (Gruneberg & Morris, 1992; Gruneberg et al., 1996; Herrmann & Raybeck, 1994, 1997; Payne, Conrad, & Hager, 1997). However, if you agree that the basic-applied collaboration is a serious issue deserving of more than reading, I urge you to join my "make a friend in the other camp campaign." Cultural understanding comes quickest and best to those who have contact with a culture. Basic researchers would enhance their perspective on applied research if they would make at least one friend in the applied camp. For example, such a friendship would reveal to basic researchers conditions that influence the applicability of a basic principle. Alternatively, applied researchers would enhance their perspective on basic research if they too would make at least one friend in the basic camp. For example, such a friendship might help clarify for applied researchers ways to apply basic principles more effectively. Such a friendship would probably lead applied researchers to also make more and better use of basic theory.

CONCLUSION

Basic research and applied research have more to offer each other than they are currently offering (Schönflug, 1993a, 1993b). Basic research has created an abundance of basic theory that applied researchers have yet to apply. Alternatively, applied researchers have considerable experience with certain basic theories, experience that could suggest to basic researchers ways to improve these theories. Given these complementary rewards, basic researchers and applied researchers have a great deal to gain if they can substantially improve communication between themselves. If basic and applied researchers can learn to interact effectively under the same roof, such as the one provided by the Society for Applied Research on Memory and Cognition, it will accelerate the development of basic and applied cognitive research and set an example for other scientific disciplines to emulate.

ACKNOWLEDGMENTS

I thank Doug Raybeck for his many insights concerning differences in the basic culture and the applied culture. I am also indebted to Fred Conrad, Jared Jobe, Roger Long, Monroe Sirken, Doug Weldon, and especially Mike Gruneberg and David Payne for valuable discussions that guided the writing of this chapter.

REFERENCES

Baddeley, A. (1993). Holy war or wholly unnecessary? Some thoughts on the "conflict" between laboratory studies and everyday memory. In G. M. Davies & R. H. Logie (Eds.), *Memory in everyday life* (pp. 532–536). New York: North-Holland.

Banaji, M. R., & Crowder, R. G. (1989). The bankruptcy of everyday memory. *American Psychologist, 44*, 1185–1193.

Barber, D. (1988). *Applied cognitive psychology.* London: Methuen.

Berger, D. E., Pezdek, K., & Banks, W. P. (1987). *Applications of cognitive psychology: Problem solving, education, and computing.* Hillsdale, NJ: Lawrence Erlbaum Associates.

Brown, G. E. (1992). Commentary. *Science, 258*, 200–202.

Chapanis, A. (1967). The relevance of laboratory studies to practical situations. *Ergonomics, 10*, 557–577.

Chapanis, A. (1986). A psychology for our technological society: A tale of two laboratories. In S. H. Hulse & B. F. Green (Eds.), *One hundred years of psychological research in America* (pp. 52–70). Baltimore: Johns Hopkins University Press.

Chapanis, A. (1988). Some generalizations about generalization. *Human Factors, 30*, 253–267.

Deffenbacher, K. A. (1996). Eyewitness memory. In D. J. Herrmann, C. McEvoy, C. Hertzog, P. Hertel, & M. K. Johnson (Eds.), *Basic and applied memory research: Theory in context* (Vol. 1, pp. 421–438). Mahwah, NJ: Lawrence Erlbaum Associates.

Dippo, C. S., & Herrmann, D. J. (1990). *The Bureau of Labor Statistics' collection procedures research laboratory: Accomplishments and future directions* [Seminar on quality of federal data]. Washington, DC: Council of Professional Associations on Federal Statistics.

Gruneberg, M. M., Morris, P. E., & Sykes, R. (Eds.). (1978). *Practical aspects of memory.* New York: Academic Press.

Gruneberg, M.M., Morris, P.E., & Sykes, R. (Eds.). (1988). *Practical aspects of memory.* Hillsdale, NJ: Lawrence Erlbaum Associates.

Gruneberg, M. M., & Morris, P. E. (1992). Applying memory research. In M. M. Gruneberg & P. E. Morris (Eds.), *Aspects of memory* (Vol. 1, pp. 1–17). London: Routledge.

Gruneberg, M. M., Morris, P. E., & Sykes, R. N. (1991). The obituary on everyday memory and its practical applications is premature. *American Psychologist, 46*, 74–76.

Gruneberg, M. M., Morris, P. E., Sykes, R. N., & Herrmann, D. J. (1996). The practical application of memory research: Practical problems in the relationship between theory and practice. In D. J. Herrmann, C. McEvoy, C. Hertzog, P. Hertel, & M.K. Johnson (Eds.), *Basic and applied memory research: Theory in context* (Vol. 1, pp. 63–82). Mahwah, NJ: Lawrence Erlbaum Associates.

Herrmann, D. (1993, August). *Basic research contributions to memory improvement and rehabilitation.* Invited address to the American Psychological Association, Toronto.

Herrmann, D. J. (1995). Applied cognitive psychology versus applicable cognitive psychology [Review of the book *Cognitive Psychology Applied*]. *Applied Cognitive Psychology, 9*, 448–449.

Herrmann, D. J., & Gruneberg, M. J. (1993). The need to expand the horizons of the practical aspects of memory. *Applied Cognitive Psychology, 7*, 553–566.

Herrmann, D. J., McEvoy, C., Hertzog, C., Hertel, P., & Johnson, M. K. (Eds.). (1996). *Basic and applied memory research: Theory in context* (Vol. 1). Mahwah, NJ: Lawrence Erlbaum Associates.

Herrmann, D. J., & Palmisano, M. (1992). The facilitation of memory. In M. Gruneberg & P. Morris (Eds.), *Aspects of memory* (2nd ed., Vol. 1, pp. 147–167). London: Routledge.

Herrmann, D. J., & Parenté, R. (1994). A multi-modal approach to cognitive rehabilitation. *NeuroRehabilitation, 4*, 133–142.

Herrmann, D., & Plude, D. (1996). Museum memory. In J. Falk & L. Dierking (Eds.), *Public institutions for personal learning: The long-term impact of museums* (pp. 53–6). Washington, DC: American Association of Museums.

Herrmann, D., & Raybeck, D. (1994, August). *The relationship between basic and applied research cultures.* Paper presented at the third Practical Aspects of Memory Conference, College Park, MD.

Herrmann, D. J., & Raybeck, D. (1997). The relationship between basic and applied research cultures. In D. G. Payne & F. G. Conrad (Eds.), *Intersections in basic and applied memory research* (pp. 25–44). Mahwah, NJ: Lawrence Erlbaum Associates.

Herrmann, D. J., & Searleman, A. (1990). A multi-modal approach to memory improvement. In G. H. Bower (Ed.), *Advances in learning and motivation* (pp. 175–205). New York: Academic Press.

Hoffman, R. R., & Deffenbacher, K. A. (1992). A brief history of applied cognitive psychology. *Applied Cognitive Psychology, 6,* 1–48.

Hoffman, R. R., & Deffenbacher, K. A. (1993). An ecological sortie into the relations of basic and applied science: Recent turf wars in human factors and applied cognitive psychology. *Ecological Psychology, 5,* 315–352.

Holden, C. (1992). Commentary. *Science, 257,* 1867.

Intons-Peterson, M. J. (1997). How basic and applied research inform each other. In D. G. Payne & F. G. Conrad (Eds.), *Intersections in basic and applied memory research* (pp. 3–24). Mahwah, NJ: Lawrence Erlbaum Associates.

Levy, R. L., & Loftus, G. R. (1984). Compliance and memory. In J. E. Harris & P. E. Morris (Eds.), Everyday memory, actions, and absent-mindedness (pp. 93–112). London: Academic Press.

Loftus, E. F. (1991). The glitter of everyday memory . . . and the gold. *American Psychologist, 46,* 16–18.

Loftus, E., & Ketcham, K. (1991). *Witness for the defense: The accused, the eyewitness, and the expert who puts memory on trial.* New York: St. Martin's.

Marshall, E. (1992). Commentary. *Science, 258,* 880–882.

McEvoy, C. L., & Moon, J. R. (1988). Assessment and treatment of everyday memory problems in the elderly. In M. M. Gruneberg, P. E. Morris, & R. N. Sykes (Eds.), *Practical Aspects of memory: Current research and issues. Volume 2. Clinical and educational implications* (pp. 155–160). Chichester, England: Wiley.

Miller, K. (Ed.) (1995). Why should federal dollars be spent to support scientific research? *Sigma Xi Forum: 1995 Vannevar Bush II Science for the 21st Century.* Research Triangle Park, NC: Sigma Xi.

Mullin, P., Herrmann, D. J., & Searleman, A. (1993). Forgotten variables in memory research. *Memory, 15,* 43.

Munsterberg, H. (1914). *Psychology: General and applied.* New York: Appleton.

Neisser, U. (1976). *Cognitive Psychology.* New York: Appleton Century Crofts.

Neisser, U. (1978a). *Cognition and reality.* San Francisco: Freeman.

Neisser, U. (1978b). Memory: What are the important questions? In M. M. Gruneberg, P. Morris, & R. N. Sykes (Eds.), *Practical aspects of memory* (pp. 00–00). New York: Academic Press.

Parente, R., & Herrmann, D. (1996). *Retraining cognition: Techniques and applications.* Gaithersburg, MD: Aspen Publishers.

Payne, D. G., & Conrad, F. G. (Eds.). (1997). *Intersections in basic and applied memory research.* Mahwah, NJ: Lawrence Erlbaum Associates.

Payne, D. G., Conrad, F. G., & Hager, D. R. (1997). Basic and applied memory research: Empirical, theoretical, and metatheoretical issues. In D. G. Payne & F. G. Conrad (Eds.), *Intersections in basic and applied memory research* (pp. 45–68). Mahwah, NJ: Lawrence Erlbaum Associates.

Pedhazur, E. J., & Schmelkin, L. P. (1991). *Measurement, design, and analysis: An integrated approach.* Hillsdale, NJ: Lawrence Erlbaum Associates.

Schönflug, W. (1993a). Applied psychology: Newcomer with a long tradition. *Applied Psychology: An International Review, 42,* 5–30.

Schönflug, W. (1993b). Practical and theoretical psychology: Singles with wedding rings? *Applied Psychology: An International Review, 42,* 58–60.

Searleman, A., & Herrmann, D. (1994). *Memory from a broader perspective.* New York:

McGraw Hill.

Semmer, N. (1993). Differentiation between social groups: The case of basic and applied psychology. *Applied Psychology: An International Review, 42,* 40–46.

Sternberg, R. J. (Ed.). (1992). *Handbook of human intelligence.* New York: Cambridge University Press.

Tulving, E. (1983). *Elements of episodic memory.* Oxford,UK: Oxford University Press.

West, R. (1985). *Memory fitness over forty.* Gainesville, FL: Triad Publishing Company.

Wilson, B. (1987). *Rehabilitation of memory.* New York: Guilford.

Wilson, B. (1993). Coping with memory impairment. In G. M. Davies & R. H. Logie (Eds.), *Memory in everyday life* (pp. 461–481). Amsterdam: North-Holland.

Yesavage, J. A., Sheikh, J. I., & Lapp, D. (1989) Mnemonics as modified for use by the elderly. In L. Poon, D. Rubin, & B. Wilson (Eds.), *Everyday cognition in adult and late life.* New York: Cambridge University Press.

Yuille, J. C., & Cutshall, J. L. (1986). A case study of eyewitness memory of a crime. *Journal of Applied Psychology, 71,* 291–301.

3

The Bounty of Everyday Memory

Charles P. Thompson
Kansas State University

The title of this chapter is, of course, a deliberate reference to the paper by Banaji and Crowder (1989) titled "The bankruptcy of everyday memory." There was a vigorous rebuttal of that paper (e.g., Bruce, 1991; Roediger, 1991) and, therefore, I do not revisit that debate. Instead, the focus of this chapter is on the great riches that have sprung from the study of everyday memory. What follows is based on my presentation at the first meeting of the Society for Applied Research in Memory and Cognition (SARMAC) and, therefore, I present only a few of the important research findings based on memory for everyday events. In addition, some new data from our research program are presented. Specifically, two findings from our diary memory research are presented: One shows clear and convincing evidence for temporal schemata; the other result is preliminary but has, in our view, intriguing implications for the current repressed memory controversy.

SOME IMPORTANT CONTRIBUTIONS FROM EVERYDAY MEMORY RESEARCH

A short summary of the bounty of everyday memory begins with the very important work on the development of autobiographical memory in children. Fivush and Nelson have both been important players in that

29

research (e.g., Fivush & Fromhoff, 1988; Nelson, 1993). Much of their research is critically dependent on the observation of mothers interacting with their children and discussing events from their lives. Based on those observations, Fivush, Nelson, and their colleagues have developed a comprehensive theory defining the relation among autobiographical memory, episodic memory, and generic memory. Their theory proposes that children learn to tell their life story as a narrative. Most interestingly, their theory accounts for childhood amnesia, which has always been a major puzzle to researchers in memory. Nelson (and others) propose that as children develop their narrative skill, they forget those events that have not been incorporated into the narrative.

Another important line of research deals with the validity of eyewitness testimony from children (e.g., Ceci & Bruck, 1993; Ceci & Loftus, 1994). In modern research in eyewitness memory, it is relatively common to stage events outside the laboratory with participants believing they have witnessed some naturally occurring event. That kind of study is important for two reasons. First, we need not worry that the reactions of participants are somehow contaminated by the knowledge that they are taking part in an experiment. Second, I strongly suspect that studies using witnesses recalling naturally occurring events are much more convincing to attorneys and judges.

A third line of research in everyday memory is the studies examining the maintenance of knowledge over long retention intervals. Certainly one of the most important contributions to cognitive psychology over the last two decades has been the work of Bahrick on the maintenance and durability of knowledge. He has looked at memory for names and faces (Bahrick, Bahrick, & Wittlinger, 1975), Spanish (Bahrick, 1984), and mathematics (Bahrick & Hall, 1991)—all over retention intervals extending up to as much as 50 years. His work has shown us that initial forgetting continues over a 3- to 5-year period but that the information remaining after that period remains intact for as much as 50 years.

The study of memory for the *Challenger* explosion can be placed in the "maintenance of knowledge" category as well (Neisser & Harsch, 1992). Neisser and Harsch had their participants record the characteristics of the event the following day and then tested memory for the event 3 years later. The important finding was that their participants were extremely confident in their memories (virtually all confidence ratings for the details of the memory were 4 or 5 on a 5-point scale) but they were often wrong (only 15% of the participants were correct on all the details and 25% were wrong on all details). As experts in memory, we may forget how startling it is for most people to learn that clear and vivid memories can be absolutely wrong.

Bahrick's studies emphasize the *durability* of memory whereas Neisser's studies point out the *fallibility* of memory. Both are immensely important contributions to our understanding of memory—and both are extremely difficult, if not impossible, to duplicate in the laboratory.

Then there are a large number of diary studies—including our research using that procedure. As in Neisser's *Challenger* study, participants in these studies record events at the time, or shortly after, they occur. Some time later, they are tested to determine how well, and how accurately, they remember the events.

The seminal work here was the 1975 study by Linton in which she kept a diary of a personal event each day for 6 years—with memory tests of subsets of events at intervals during that period. Shortly after her study, other memory experts (Wagenaar, 1986; White, 1982) added to that database by keeping similar diaries. In an important study, Larsen (1992) made the distinction between memory for personal events and memory for news events in his year-long diary. He found that memory for personal events was much better than memory for news events. All of these diaries gave us an important look at memory for real events over retention intervals of as much as 6 years. That kind of information cannot be duplicated in the laboratory.

In 1982, I began adding to the diary memory database by reporting results from a group of nonexperts in memory—students at Kansas State who kept a diary for a semester (Thompson, 1982). If for no other reason, my series of studies were important because they confirmed that the results from Linton and other memory experts were not restricted to memory experts. They also greatly increased the N in the database—we now have collected over 425 diaries. A few of the specific contributions from our recent studies are presented later in this chapter.

Fairly recently, Brewer (1988) reported a clever study that spoke to a methodological concern that many researchers had about the diary procedure. Specifically, the concern was that the self-selection of the diary events might introduce significant error in the results. To avoid the self-selection problem, Brewer had his participants carry around a beeper programmed to sound at random intervals. When the beeper sounded, the participant recorded whatever he or she was doing at the time. The procedure did not work perfectly because the beeper would occasionally sound when the participant was too busy to record the event—or when the participant was engaged in some activity that he or she did not wish to record. Nonetheless, that procedure eliminated most of the concerns about selection of events.

Finally, there was a clever technique introduced very recently. Burt and his colleagues (Burt, Mitchell, Raggatt, Jones, & Cowan, 1995) gave students all the film they wanted for their summer holiday. The film was free but the students had to return it to the researchers to have it developed. The pictures were then used in a recognition procedure—with pictures taken by other students in the same or similar locations used as foils. One of the interesting findings was that embedded specific events were more quickly accessed from memory than were isolated specific events. As might be expected, decisions were made about remembered events more quickly than foils.

Their procedure is an absolutely delightful idea that should prove to be a excellent tool in the study of everyday memory. How useful to capture a snapshot of everyday memory!

RECENT CONTRIBUTIONS FROM DIARY MEMORY RESEARCH

Let me turn now to some new data from our diary research. We have been conducting research with memory diaries for the last 15 years, and most of that research is summarized in a book (Thompson, Skowronski, Larsen, & Betz, 1996). In our experiments, we have participants record one unique event per day for a period of time, and then we test their memories for those events at the end of the recording period. We have collected over 450 such diaries. Most of our diary studies have been for a semester, but we recently had the opportunity to collect diaries from six participants for periods ranging from 1.5 years to 2.5 years.

Two results from our research could not be duplicated in the laboratory. The first was an absolutely serendipitous finding that Skowronski discovered when we were working together on a paper (Thompson, Skowronski, & Betz, 1993). One of the things we do when testing our participants is ask them to estimate, using a calendar, the exact day on which the event occurred. We have looked at those data in all sorts of ways, and Skowronski decided to take a look at the distribution of dating errors. He found a fascinating pattern that we quickly found was duplicated in all of our diary studies. Figure 3.1 shows the distribution of absolute dating errors (i.e., ignoring direction of error) for a recent semester-long study. As can be seen, peaks in dating errors occur at regular 7-day intervals. Obviously, people are getting the correct day of the week although they cannot get the correct week.

It only takes a little reflection to realize that there are all sorts of ways for someone to hit the correct day of week for an event. As one example, consider a man remembering a conversation during a duplicate bridge game. He knows that he only plays duplicate bridge on Thursdays and his estimate will reflect that knowledge. His date estimate may be several weeks off, but the day of week will be correct.

Consider a second example of a woman remembering a golf game. She only has time for golf on the weekends, so she knows the event happened on

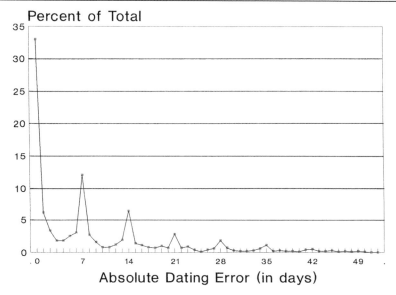

FIG. 3.1.   The distribution of absolute dating errors for a semester-long diary memory study.

Saturday or Sunday. If she guesses randomly, she will hit the correct day of the week 50% of the time. Of course, she will be a day short 25% of the time — and a day long 25% of the time. It is easy to show that, in all cases using multiple days (e.g., the 5-day work week, or a 3-day weekend), random guessing will create a symmetrical distribution with the maximum frequency at the correct day of the week.

As a result of the error distribution data shown in Fig. 3.1, we have focused on day of the week errors and ignored whether our participants picked the correct week or were several weeks in error. Figure 3.2 shows the data from Fig. 3.1 transformed to reflect day of the week error. An error of 0 means that the person picked the correct day of the week. An error of +1 or −1 means that they were either a day short or a day over in their estimate and so on. As can be seen, people often pick the correct day of the week (an error of 0). They are next most likely to be a day short or a day over and so on. The reader should note that the day of the week curve is normalized to add to 100%.

In Fig. 3.2, the data are presented in two ways. The correct day can be hit using either semantic or schematic information. As part of our semantic memory, we have the dates for holidays such as Christmas as well as many birthdays and anniversaries. Any event falling on those dates can be nailed exactly with the use of a calendar. We also have schematic information that allows us to determine the exact or approximate day of the week on which

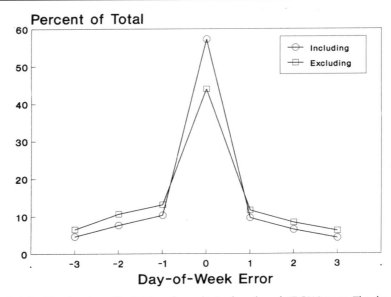

FIG. 3.2.   The data from Fig. 3.1 transformed into day-of-week (DOW) error. The data
are plotted separately for the total data (including the correct week) and the data
excluding errors in the correct week (i.e., within 3 days of the correct date).

an event occurs. I mentioned the bridge and golf examples earlier. We can
approximate the contribution of schematic information by excluding exact
dates. To avoid distorting the normalized day of the week curve, we exclude
the "correct week"—that is, the 3 days on either side of the exact date. Thus,
Fig. 3.2 shows all the data (including the correct week) as well as the data
excluding the correct week. To reiterate, the curve excluding the correct
week approximates the contribution of schematic knowledge. The difference between the two zero points approximates the contribution of semantic
information.

I want to talk about the durability of this day of the week information,
but let me first point out that we saw evidence for memory for other cyclic
temporal effects as well. In our six very long-term diaries, participants
could make errors of over a year in dating events. The distribution of dating
errors for those diaries showed the very interesting pattern of errors
depicted in Fig. 3.3.

As can be seen, participants sometimes get the correct day of the year but
place it in the wrong year. Obviously, every person has a memory store of
several well-known yearly events such as birthdays and public holidays.
These data also show that there is a marked day of the week effect even
when the individual misses the correct week by as much as 50 or 51 weeks.
There is an artifactual garbling of the effect when the interval is more than

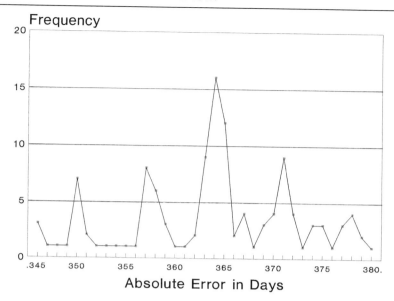

FIG. 3.3. The distribution of absolute dating errors (between 345–380 days in error) from the long-term study. Note the day-of-year peak at 365 days.

1 year because the day of the week for a specific date (e.g., January 5) changes from year to year.

Let me turn now to the durability of schematic information. We wondered whether day of the week information would be used by participants over extended periods of time. Day of the week information may be readily available over a period of 3 months but it may be forgotten over longer periods of time. Using the data from our six long-term participants, we began by looking at the day of the week error for events falling within the most recent year.

To focus on schematic reconstruction, we eliminated exact dates by removing responses that were within the correct week. Figure 3.4 shows the long-term data for both the most recent year and for events more than 1 year old. Even when events that have been dated exactly are removed it is evident that the participants are using day of week when making date estimates for events that occurred in the most recent year. In fact, the participants picked the correct day of the week on about a third of those events.

If we look at events that are more than a year old we still see a peak at the 0 error point. Once again, participants are selecting the correct day of the week when making their date estimates even when events that were dated exactly were removed. This peak is slightly lower than the peak on the previous graph. Nevertheless, the participants are still choosing the correct

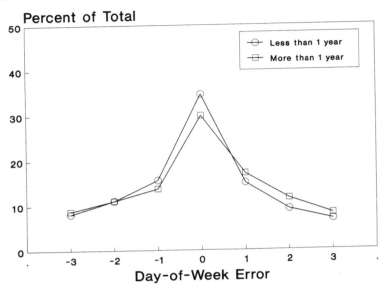

FIG. 3.4.   Day-of-week errors for the long-term study plotted separately for events with less than a 1-year retention interval and events with more than a 1-year retention interval.

day of the week about a third of the time. The evidence clearly shows that our participants are using day of week information to date events.

These data provide strong evidence for schema at work in locating events in time. These data represent a portion of the data that, together with reports from our participants, have led us to the conclusion that there is no temporal trace in autobiographical memory. In a relatively few instances, we store the date of an event as part of the memory. However, we believe that in the great majority of cases the location of a personal event in time is entirely reconstructed. Spend a little time thinking about how you locate events from your life in time — and I think you will agree with us.

The second major finding is from data that were collected too recently to be included in our book (Thompson et al., 1996). The highlights of the data are presented here, and the details will appear in a journal article (Walker, Vogl, & Thompson, 1995). Although our data must be regarded as preliminary because our N is small, we find them quite thought provoking. They raise the possibility that Freud may have focused on the wrong mechanism when he talked about the repression of unpleasant memories.

The starting point in considering these data is a set of virtually universal experiences. Most of us can probably remember our mother comforting us at bedtime when we were still hurting from some unpleasant experience during the day. She usually told us, "Go to sleep and you'll feel better in the morning." And we usually did.

Most of us also have had some very unpleasant experiences — such as the grief associated with the death of a loved one. The pain we feel at such times is real, intense, and prolonged; but it eventually fades away. In fact, both the pain and the pleasure associated with personal memories seem to fade with time.

Our experience suggests that the affective component of personal memory simply decays. We merely lose the emotional aspects of our memories over time, resulting in more neutral judgments of an event's pleasantness or unpleasantness as the retention interval increases. The loss of affect seems clear but the mechanism producing it is not. There are several possibilities; one is that the fading affect occurs because our memories are less clear and vivid.

In earlier research, Holmes (1970) looked at the drop in emotional intensity over time. Based on the findings of Cason (1932), Holmes hypothesized that negative affect would decline more than positive affect. In order to test his predictions, Holmes had participants record pleasant and unpleasant events for a week and tested their recall and current affect for the events after a 1-week retention interval. As predicted, negative events faded in emotional intensity more quickly than positive events.

We decided to use our memory diaries to replicate and extend Holmes' findings as well as to correct a potential flaw. Holmes' (1970) study has one retention interval and, thus, the results might be explained in terms of the pleasantness ratings showing regression toward the mean. That is, it is common for extreme ratings on a dimension to be reduced when the ratings are repeated. However, that flaw can be eliminated by using several retention intervals to show a systematic change over time (any artifactual regression toward the mean should be constant over time). We also thought it was important to show that the differential fading of pleasant and unpleasant events continues over longer, more realistic retention intervals.

We focused on three studies in which participants rated the pleasantness of the event both at the time that it was recorded and during the test period. The rating was on a 7-point scale ranging from − 3 (*unpleasant*) to + 3 (*very pleasant*). The data for the first study are from 43 participants keeping diaries for approximately 3 months.

In Fig. 3.5, we have plotted the mean intensity of pleasantness ratings for both pleasant and unpleasant events at the time of recording and at the time of test. For the intensity measure, negative scores (i.e., unpleasantness) have been reversed. As can be seen, pleasantness ratings become less extreme as we move from the initial rating to the rating given at test. Most importantly, notice that this drop is reliably larger for unpleasant events than for pleasant events.

The second set of data is from our long-term study with six participants.

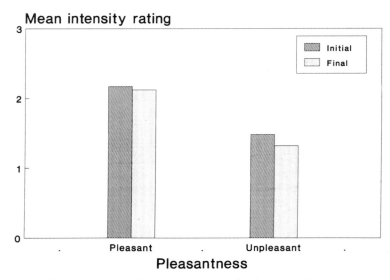

FIG. 3.5.   The mean initial and final intensity ratings for pleasant and unpleasant events in the semester-long study. The sign of the ratings is reversed for unpleasant events.

Six undergraduates kept diaries for periods ranging from 1.5 to 2.5 years. These data are presented in Fig. 3.6.

Because the diaries were kept for different lengths of time, we included only the most recent year so that the findings can be generalized across all six participants. As can be seen, the change in pleasantness ratings is much sharper after a 1-year retention interval than a 3-month retention interval. Again, notice that this change was larger for unpleasant events than for pleasant events.

The third set of data is from a single participant tested last fall. A graduate student kept a 9-month diary in an effort to keep pace with our six long-term diary participants. Because of a misunderstanding, he was not tested with the other participants. This oversight was not discovered for almost 4.5 years, at which time he was tested.

Figure 3.7 shows the mean intensity of pleasantness ratings for the time of recording and time of test. After a 4.5-year retention interval, judgments of intensity dropped even further. As before, pleasantness ratings become less extreme as we move from the initial rating to the rating given at test. Once again, this change is more substantial for unpleasant events than for pleasant events.

Figure 3.8 summarizes the mean change in emotional intensity for pleasant and unpleasant events for the 3-month, 1-year, and 4.5-year retention intervals. As can be seen, increased retention interval led to

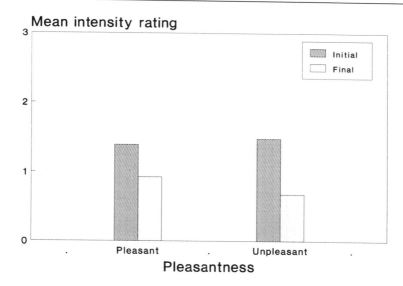

FIG. 3.6.   The mean initial and final intensity ratings for pleasant and unpleasant events in the long-term study. Only the events during the most recent year were used for these data. The sign of the ratings is reversed for unpleasant events.

increased change in intensity ratings. More importantly, the change for unpleasant events is reliably greater than the change for pleasant events at each retention interval.

It is not surprising that these data support our everyday knowledge that pleasantness and unpleasantness fade with time. What is interesting is that the emotion connected with negative events fades more rapidly than the emotion connected with positive events.

If the change in intensity of pleasantness just reflects memory for the events, then pleasant events should be remembered better than unpleasant events. Indeed, much research in autobiographical memory suggests that people recall pleasant events better than unpleasant events (e.g., Bower & Gilligan, 1979; Holmes, 1970; Linton, 1975; Matlin & Stang, 1978; Thompson et al., 1996; Wagenaar, 1986).

We were able to investigate that possibility because, at the time of test in all three studies, participants made judgments of how well they remembered each event on a 7-point scale ranging from 1 (*did not remember the event at all*) to 7 (*remembered the event perfectly*). We entered the memory rating data into a regression analysis with four relevant predictors: linear event age, quadratic event age, event emotional intensity, and event pleasantness. As a reminder, emotional intensity refers to the absolute value of the initial pleasantness rating. One would expect more emotionally intense events to

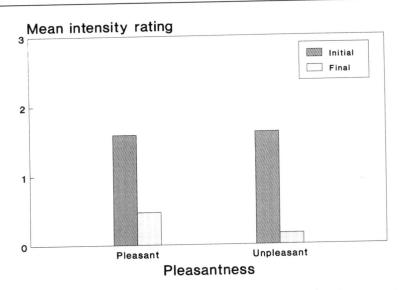

FIG. 3.7.   The mean initial and final intensity ratings for pleasant and unpleasant events
in the study with the 4.5-year retention interval. The sign of the ratings is reversed for
unpleasant events.

be better remembered than less emotionally intense events. Pleasantness
refers to whether the event was initially positive or negative ([events initially
rated as neutral, at 0, were excluded).

The results of our memory analyses can be briefly summarized as
follows: Events initially rated as extremely positive or negative were better
remembered than events that were less extreme. In addition, there is a very
small (but reliable) effect of pleasantness such that positive events were
remembered slightly better than negative events. Finally, as would be
expected, memory ratings dropped as the retention interval increased. Most
importantly, the regression analyses suggest that we cannot account for the
rather large difference in reduction of emotional content by differences in
memory for pleasant and unpleasant events.

The two important points bear repeating: Unpleasant events are remembered almost as well as pleasant events, but the emotion associated with
them drops relatively rapidly over time. In effect, the memory for unpleasant events remains but the emotion is forgotten.

Freud's theoretical mechanism of unconscious repression has it just the
other way around. According to Freud, the memories of unpleasant events
are repressed into the unconscious and the emotion remains (although
sometimes transformed to anxiety) to bother the conscious mind. Put more
simply, unpleasant memories are forgotten but the unpleasant emotions

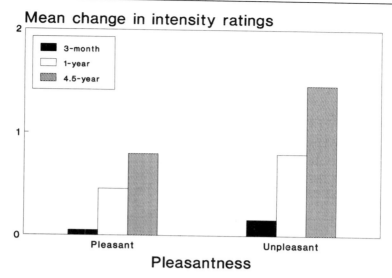

FIG. 3.8. The mean change in intensity ratings (from initial to final rating) for pleasant and unpleasant events in the three studies. The sign of the ratings is reversed for unpleasant events.

associated with them are not. Here we need to emphasize that we have attempted to capture Freud's complex (and often inconsistent) descriptions of repression in a few sentences. Perhaps the best modern source discussing Freud's theory of memory (including repression and screen memories) is Ross (1991).

It is important to note that Freud clearly specified that he was talking about repression resulting from ego-threatening events. Although our current procedure does not allow us to distinguish between ego-threatening and other unpleasant events, we are certain that our diaries contain many ego-threatening events (often having to do with the breakup of a relationship).

Those events should be likely candidates for repression, but our data show no evidence of any such effect. It is true that pleasant events were remembered slightly better than unpleasant events, but this effect was very small. On the other hand, unpleasant emotions faded much more rapidly than pleasant emotions across all three retention intervals. That change in emotional intensity is obviously very helpful for maintaining a sense of well-being in an individual. Given that positive and healthy mechanism, it is not clear why anyone would need the mechanism of repression, which is obviously not helpful in the long run.

Our data are consistent with the short-term mobilization and long-term minimization hypothesis proposed by Taylor (1991). As can be inferred from the name, this hypothesis has two components. According to this hypothesis, negative events initially evoke strong physiological, cognitive, emotional, and social responses. These responses are the mobilization the person experiences at the time of the negative event. Some time after the event, the person tries to minimize the impact of the negative event. This pattern of mobilization and minimization appears to be greater for negative events than for neutral or positive events.

The mobilization–minimization strategy is beneficial in many respects. First, the strategy serves to cushion the self from the impact of negative events. Experiences of failure and rejection are some of the most powerful events that people encounter. In order to maintain a generally positive self-concept in light of such events, people need to discount or reevaluate many of these events. Second, this type of strategy can be employed to undo the social impact that negative events often have. These strategies may be directed at improving one's image in the eyes of others. Our participant tested after 4.5 years pointed out that there are strong social pressures to deemphasize the negative events and focus on the positive.

Our data suggest that when people minimize negative events, the minimization process focuses on the emotion of the event, rather than the memory of the event itself. Experience tells us this is true. We do not forget the negative events in our lives, we forget the emotion. We do not repress the memories of negative events into our unconscious, we cope with them. It seems as if we cope very well most of the time.

ACKNOWLEDGMENTS

I wish to extend my thanks to Dan Aeschliman, Minida Dowdy, Will Eckels, Charlie Galvin, Cosima Hadidi, Tricia Hoard, Traci Jackson, Grant Nurnberg, and David Welch, who served as participants and testers for long-term diary studies. Thanks also to Rod Vogl and Rich Walker who were the participant and tester, respectively, for the 4.5-year diary study. The research for the long-term diaries was supported by National Institute of Mental Health Grant MH44090 with the author as the principal investigator.

REFERENCES

Bahrick, H. P. (1984). Semantic memory content in permastore: Fifty years of memory for Spanish learned in school. *Journal of Experimental Psychology: General, 113,* 1–29.
Bahrick, H. P., Bahrick, P. C., & Wittlinger, R. P. (1975). Fifty years of memories for names and faces: A cross-sectional approach. *Journal of Experimental Psychology: General, 104,* 54–75.
Bahrick, H. P., & Hall, L. K. (1991). Lifetime maintenance of high school mathematics

content. *Journal of Experimental Psychology: General, 120,* 20–33.

Banaji, M. R., & Crowder, R. G. (1989). The bankruptcy of everyday memory. *American Psychologist, 44,* 1185–1193.

Bower, G. H., & Gilligan, S. G. (1979). Remembering information related to one's self. *Journal of Research in Personality, 13,* 420–432.

Brewer, W. F. (1988). Memory for randomly sampled autobiographical events. In U. Neisser & E. Winograd (Eds.), *Remembering reconsidered: Ecological and traditional approaches to the study of memory* (pp. 21–90). New York: Cambridge University Press.

Bruce, D. (1991). Mechanistic and functional explanations of memory. *American Psychologist, 46,* 46–48.

Burt, C. D. B., Mitchell, D. A., Raggatt, P. T. F., Jones, C. A., & Cowan, T. M. (1995). A snapshot of autobiographical memory retrieval characteristics. *Applied Cognitive Psychology, 9,* 61–74.

Cason, H. (1932). The learning and retention of pleasant and unpleasant activities. *Archives of Psychology, 21*(134), 5–96.

Ceci, S. J., & Bruck, M. (1993). The suggestibility of the child witness: A historical review and synthesis. *Psychological Bulletin, 113,* 403–439.

Ceci, S. J., & Loftus, E. F. (1994). "Memory work": A royal road to false memories? *Applied Cognitive Psychology, 8,* 351–364.

Fivush, R., & Fromhoff, F. A. (1988). Style and structure in mother–child conversations about the past. *Discourse Processes, 11,* 337–355.

Holmes, D. S. (1970). Differential change in affective intensity and the forgetting of unpleasant personal experiences. *Journal of Personality and Social Psychology, 3,* 234–239.

Larsen, S. F. (1992). Potential flashbulbs: Memories of ordinary news as the baseline. In E. Winograd & U. Neisser (Eds.), *Affect and accuracy in recall: Studies of flashbulb memories* (pp. 32–64). New York: Cambridge University Press.

Linton, M. (1975). Memory for real-world events. In D. A. Norman & D. E. Rumelhart (Eds.), *Explorations in cognition* (pp. 376–404). San Francisco: Freeman.

Matlin, M. W., & Stang, D. J. (1978). *The Pollyanna principle.* Cambridge, MA: Schenkman.

Neisser, U., & Harsch, N. (1992). Phantom flashbulbs: False recollections of hearing the news about Challenger. In E. Winograd & U. Neisser (Eds.), *Affect and accuracy in recall: Studies of flashbulb memories* (pp. 9–31), New York: Cambridge University Press.

Nelson, K. (1993). The psychological and social origins of autobiographical memory. *Psychological Science, 4,* 7–14.

Roediger, H. L. (1991). They read an article? A commentary on the everyday memory controversy. *American Psychologist, 46,* 37–40.

Ross, B. M. (1991). *Remembering the personal past: Descriptions of autobiographical memory.* New York: Oxford University Press.

Taylor, S. E. (1991). Asymmetrical effects of positive and negative events: The mobilization- -minimization hypothesis. *Psychological Bulletin, 110,* 67–85.

Thompson, C. P. (1982). Memory for unique personal events: The roommate study. *Memory & Cognition, 10,* 324–332.

Thompson, C. P., Skowronski, J. J., & Betz, A. L. (1993). The use of partial temporal information in dating personal events. *Memory & Cognition, 21,* 352–360.

Thompson, C. P., Skowronski, J. J., Larsen, S. F., & Betz, A. L. (1996). *Autobiographical memory: Remembering what and remembering when.* Mahwah, NJ: Lawrence Erlbaum Associates.

Wagenaar, W. A. (1986). My memory: A study of autobiographical memory over six years. *Cognitive Psychology, 18,* 225–252.

Walker, W. R., Vogl, R. J., & Thompson, C. P. (1995). *Autobiographical memory: Pleasantness and unpleasantness fade with time.* Unpublished manuscript, Kansas State University, Manhattan, KS.

White, R. T. (1982). Memory for personal events. *Human Learning, 1,* 171–183.

II

Autobiographical Memory

4

Beginnings of a Theory of Autobiographical Remembering

David C. Rubin
Duke University

This chapter is not a summary of past work, but an expansion of earlier thoughts (Rubin, 1995b, 1996) into the outline of a project for the future. It is a reaction to what has been the dominant metaphor in the study of human memory for the last few decades: the human mind as a computer. A better metaphor might be a mind modeled on what we know about the brain. I want to reconceptualize the phrase "having a memory" from a computer retrieval, where it is well understood, to a biological act where it is not. To do this I outline the minimum model that could provide autobiographical memories of the full-blown kind you might have when you remember what happened to you at the time of a nationally or internationally important event (Brown & Kulik, 1977; Conway, 1995; Winograd & Neisser, 1992), or remember experiencing a personally important event (Rubin & Kozin, 1984), or even the details from this morning's breakfast (Galton, 1879).

For the last few decades psychologists have viewed human memory as an analog of computer memory with its encoding, storage, and retrieval of information. We have concentrated on data structures and retrieval schemes, neglecting the different natures of the informational, sensory, emotional, and phenomenological qualities of memory (see Tulving, 1983, for a similar observation). After all, computers are highly flexible, general-purpose information processors. One of their strengths is that the exact nature of the information they process is not important: It is all just bits and bytes.

In contrast to this general data processing of the computer, the brain processes different kinds of information in different systems, integrating these processes into a unitary consciousness. Unlike the computer, the individual neural systems are not viewed as the result of efficient engineering. The brain is most often viewed as a collection of spare parts that at each point in a long evolutionary history were patched together in a way that increased genetic fitness at each point in each existing niche. Parts that evolved for one purpose were modified for a new purpose. Under this view, complex cognitive behavior can be seen either as relying on recently expanded modules or as a novel integration of existing parts that underwent more modest changes. Autobiographical memory appears to follow the latter pattern. All brain systems that can benefit from experience, by definition, have a form of memory. Autobiographical memory requires the integration of many such systems.

For instance, autobiographical memory makes use of a well-developed spatial ability and the spatial memory that comes with it, an ability and memory that exists in various forms in various species. Spatial ability may have been modified for use in autobiographical memory, but it did not have to be invented. But even if I were to claim that autobiographical memory is a purely human, highly specialized faculty, I would not have to claim that it or the individual memories that are its products are localized in a single brain system. Language is the prototypical rapidly developed, species-specific, highly specialized human ability, and language is spread over a large part of the cortex, with damage in various locations causing different changes in behavior.

In pursuing this view, the first question becomes: What are the systems of the mind and brain that must be involved in having an autobiographical memory and how are they related? Put this way, the initial answer, and that is all I have to offer here, is the beginnings of a boxes-and-arrows flowchart of the type psychologists, inspired by computer models of the mind, are fond of producing. This is my first attempt at one. I try it now 20 years after it would have been stylish because each box and arrow is no longer just a promissory note for a to-be-filled-in mechanism, process, or mathematical equation. The boxes and arrows are not as free as they once were to change as needed to account for changes in the behaviors they were explaining. They have additional constraints because the boxes are linked to claims about neural systems. Claims about the boxes and arrows used to describe autobiographical memory in the mind must be consistent with neuropsychological studies of amnesia and ongoing work in brain imaging as well as with behavioral data. Instead of treating the mind as one large black box, we treat it as a set of somewhat smaller black boxes. Not a major advance, but a step in what might be a useful direction.

To begin the search, I return to the behavior to be described, autobiographical memory. Philosophers (see Brewer, 1996, for a review) and psychologists (Tulving, 1983) have wondered whether autobiographical memory is something worth studying as a separate entity. I just assume that it is and begin by discussing its properties. For a working definition of autobiographical memory, I simply use the word *recollection* (Baddeley, 1992; Brewer, 1996). Autobiographical memory is conscious recall; it is episodic memory (Tulving, 1972, 1983). It is accompanied by a sense of reliving, a sense that the remembered event actually occurred to you at a specific place and time. A clear abstract, scholarly description comes from Brewer (1986), a description that he later expanded under the term *recollective memory* (Brewer, 1996):

> Recollective memory is memory for a specific episode from an individual's past. It typically appears to be a "reliving" of the individual's phenomenal experience during the earlier moment. Thus these memories typically contain information about place, actions, persons, objects, thoughts, and affect. . . . The information in this form of memory is expressed as a mental image. . . . They are accompanied by a belief that the remembered episode was personally experienced. . . . Recollective memories give rise to high confidence in the accuracy of their content. (pp. 60–61)

To complement Brewer's philosophical review of the properties of autobiographical memory, a clear example of the phenomenon of autobiographical memory comes from the classic passage from Proust (1928/1956) in which the smell and taste of a "petite madeleine" first produces "an exquisite pleasure . . . detached, with no suggestion of its origin" (p. 62) and then after a time "the memory returns . . . immediately the old grey house upon the street . . . rose up like the scenery of a theatre . . . and with the house the town" (pp. 65, 66). The sensory cues work quickly to change mood, but the memory comes more slowly, and when it does come it consists in large part of a visual image. Olfactory stimulation in a laboratory setting can be used reliably to produce similar effects, although the students' descriptions do not rival Proust's (Rubin, Groth, & Goldsmith, 1984).

Several observations are worth noting. First, the sequence of remembering was a rapid change in affect followed by a pause and then a linguistic label of the original occurrence of the cue, followed immediately by a visual image. Second, in addition to the linguistic description at which Proust excels, were large affective and visual imagery components. Third, Proust was distracted by daily activities when he "mechanically" tasted the petite madeleine soaked in tea. The taste came as a surprise to him. It was out of the context in which he initially experienced it in his childhood. Such surprising, or initially unconscious activation, may often enhance the effect. The smell of coffee from a cup that is in view is more likely to be attributed to coffee present than coffee past. Unlabeled odors from unmarked or unseen containers provide similar out-of-context surprising stimuli in the laboratory.

Fourth, it takes a long time to produce a recollection even though olfaction can produce virtually instantaneous warnings of unpleasant or dangerous stimuli. In the written form, it takes Proust about two pages, which is relatively brief for Proust. In the laboratory it takes about 15 seconds in our current work. This is not out of line for autobiographical memory retrieval. In other work with word cues it takes undergraduates about 10 seconds to begin writing a memory (Rubin & Schulkind, in press a, in press b). There must be a great deal of conscious or unconscious cognition (i.e., brain activity) between the initial sensation and the recollection. As Proust (1928/1956) put it, "What is thus palpitating in the depths of my being must be the image, the visual memory, which, being linked to that taste, has tried to follow it into my conscious mind" (p. 64). This "palpitating" needs to be measured and understood. Fifth, no one would claim that petites madeleines soaked in tea are extremely positive universal stimuli for all people in all cultures. It must have helped that the taste was associated in life with an aunt and her room in Combray on Sunday mornings. Proust was describing long-term, episodic memory, and in particular how cues evoke past affect and life experiences.

Proust's anecdote is a unique case and needs to be treated that way. It is a stimulus for further analysis, not a final answer. For instance, we know that a change in affect need not be reported for all vivid memories (Rubin & Kozin, 1984). It is not clear whether the change in affect that occurs in olfactory cuing of vivid memories is all rapid. It is even less clear whether any change in affect that occurs from cuing by other senses, such as vision and audition, is rapid or whether any change in affect waits until the memory can been "seen" and described. With luck, future research will decide.

Psychologists have been slow to study autobiographical memory as a brain phenomenon that integrates many components. One reason to invoke the brain as a metaphor is to foster this integrative approach. Although the verbal reports of the memory-eliciting effects of tastes, smells, and other stimuli are frequent and consistent, they are anecdotal, introspective, subjective, complex, and thought to be difficult to bring under laboratory control. In fact, Miller (1962) began his chapter on "Memory" in his book *Psychology: The Science of Mental Life* with a quote from the same passage of Proust I just used. Miller noted, "A prudent psychologist might well decide to leave such fragile flowers to Proust and his fellow artists" (p. 161). However, recent advances in autobiographical memory provide a solid new cognitive framework in which to study this phenomenon, and recent advances in brain imaging provide a new means to corroborate verbal reports with changes in neural activity.

It is clear from Brewer's and Proust's descriptions that autobiographical memory must have a minimum of five components. There must be some cuing that leads to a search process or processes that retrieves (and, to the extent needed, integrates) narrative, visual imagery, and affect components. In traditional accounts of cognitive psychology, the brain, and neuropsychology, these five components are usually viewed as five separate entities or processes. They are therefore easy to view as good candidates for subsystems of a larger integrated process. The five components—cuing, retrieval, language, imagery, and affect—are a first approximation. The five are a rough minimal set for recall; encoding is left out for now as the act of encoding is harder to study than the act of recall. Each component could and may need to be subdivided; certainly language and imagery do. No claims are made about the neural substrate of the components and their connection, except for the retrieval component, although many could be. Few claims are made about the arrows connecting these five boxes. The five components may not even be of the same kind. All are viewed here as processes operating on structures, but language, imagery, and perhaps affect can be seen as having storage functions that cuing and retrieval do not. Cuing, as separate from retrieval, is used as a combination of the classic role of perception and the need to allow for cuing by internal thoughts or states. With refinement, it is hoped that these a priori divisions will alter to fit the data better and to provide a more coherent theory, but for now this is my best attempt.

CUING

Although the example Proust used is of smell and taste, the more general case needs to be considered. Cues can be classified into three loose categories for purposes of exposition. First are internal cues such as known thoughts, emotions, and states of mind. Second are external cues that come from known, observable stimuli external to the person. Third are the memories that come unbidden (Berntsen, in press), which could be from either one of the first two categories but that have no likely known referent. The most is known about external cuing. Words rated as high in imagery and meaningfulness cue the oldest memories in undergraduates. Words rated as high in imagery, meaningfulness, familiarity, and age of acquisition produce more memories and presumably produce memories more quickly. Correlations for these effects are around .5 (Rubin, 1980). Odors, contrary to expectation, do not cue older memories than words with the same referent, but do cue memories that were not thought about as often. As words that have the same referent as odors are all easy to image, the overall observation that odors cue old memories is not challenged, but refined (Rubin et al., 1984).

RETRIEVAL PROCESSES

Retrieval is the most mysterious aspect of the whole process. We as psychologists are always poorer at process than structure (Rubin, 1988), but here we are in even poorer shape than usual because most memory processes that we use come directly from the computer metaphor. Note that the title of this section, "Retrieval Processes," is straight from that metaphor. If we maintain the computer metaphor, reasonable understandings of the retrieval of autobiographical memories are certainly possible (Conway, 1996; Conway & Rubin, 1993; Reiser, Black, & Kalamarides, 1986; Tulving, 1983). In contrast, the mechanisms of retrieval in the brain are not as clear as those in the computer, which is one reason that we have kept the computer model.

However we view retrieval, we need to include integration with it. Either the multimodal narrative–imagery–affect autobiographical memories are integrated on retrieval, or they are stored as an integrated or connected unit, or they slowly become more integrated over time (Squire, 1992; Squire & Zola-Morgan, 1991) or repeated retrieval.

One observation about retrieval is especially noteworthy: It takes a very long time. In a sample of 20 undergraduates who were each cued individually with 124 words, the mean time to produce a memory was 10 seconds (Rubin & Schulkind, in press a, in press b), or in the more usual cognitive psychological measure, 10,000 milliseconds. Seventy-year-old volunteers took about 17,000 milliseconds. Elsewhere in the literature, in one of the earliest studies Robinson (1976) found his undergraduates also took about 10 seconds to retrieve memories for object and activity words, but 14 seconds for affect words. Fitzgerald and Lawrence's (1984) undergraduates were a bit faster, taking 7 seconds for nouns and 11 seconds for affect words. His older adults were slower (taking 8 and 14 seconds, respectively) and his junior high students faster (taking 4 and 6 seconds, respectively). As the stimuli used in autobiographical memory studies are perceived and responded to in a few hundred milliseconds in other tasks, there is a lot of time being spent on retrieval; so much, that if I did not now take twice as long to think of the names of people I know and if I did not try to think of similar memories from similar cues in everyday life, I might consider the task too artificial. One cognitive mechanism that might produce such a delay is cyclical retrieval (Conway, 1996). Each successive retrieval serves as the cue for the next search. Such mechanisms are common in computer models and are consistent with a nervous system that has closed-loop pathways and well-developed efferent as well as afferent communication.

LANGUAGE AND NARRATIVE STRUCTURE

Language and especially narrative structure are necessary components of autobiographical memory. Autobiographical memories are usually recalled as narrative. They are told to another person and to oneself. What is included and excluded depends in part on the language available and the narrative structures used. If no words exist to describe something or if the narrative structure omits something, it is less likely to be remembered. Three examples illustrate this point. First, Brown and Kulik (1977) observed that reports of especially vivid, or flashbulb, memories tend to have canonical categories such as the place, ongoing event, informant, affect in others, own affect, and aftermath. Neisser (1982) countered that these may not be properties of flashbulb memories at all, but rather properties of the narrative genre used to report any news. Thus, Neisser claimed that these autobiographical memories are shaped by narrative conventions of the culture. Second, in trying to account for the vividness of such memories, Rubin and Kozin (1984) made the claim that all memories start out as clear vivid memories, but then most fade. The ones that remain are the ones that are rehearsed, or otherwise practiced, often by being told to others. Verbal rehearsal thus shapes the memories. Routine autobiographical memories follow the same pattern. Third, Barsalou (1988) asked people to recall events from their previous summer in the order in which they came to mind. The structures Barsalou formulated to describe and explain these data can be considered either as properties of a memory system or as properties of the narrative structure used to describe memories.

In fact, most researchers who have examined the form and content of autobiographical memory have focused on narrative structure, as the following list shows. Robinson (1981) integrated theories of narrative from linguistics and folklore into cognitive psychology. His chapter in this volume (Robinson & Taylor, chap. 8) carries this early work forward. Barclay (1986, 1996; Barclay & Smith, 1992) examined the schematic nature of autobiographical memory and how it relates to the local and general culture in which the individual is located. This produces the "conversational nature of autobiographical remembering" (Barclay & Smith, 1992, p. 82). Fitzgerald (1986, 1988, 1992) used concepts like *narrative thought* and *self-narratives* to account for autobiographical memory and how it changes over the life span and with mood shifts. Schank and Abelson (1995) claimed that "the content of story memories depends on whether and how they are told to others, and these reconstituted memories form the basis of the individual's *remembered self*" (p. 1). Using a psychoanalytic framework, Schafer (1981) and Spence (1982) noted the importance of narrative. Freeman (1993) tied narrative to autobiographical memory in a more humanistic approach, and Gergen and Gergen (1988) used narrative structure and communication to stress the social nature of remembering and of the self. On the more applied side Wagenaar, van Koppen, and Crombag (1993) documented the all-too-important role of a good story in the legal system. They found that observations that fit the narrative summary being prepared by the court were more likely to be summarized and thus "remembered" by the court, whereas observations that did not fit the narrative were more likely to be omitted and therefore "forgotten."

There has also been detailed analysis of the narrative structure of autobiographical memory in social situations. The narrative structure of autobiographical memory appears indistinguishable from the narrative structure of other social communication, and the recall of autobiographical memories is usually a social act (Hirst & Manier, 1996) that can define the social group (Bruner & Feldman, 1996). An especially interesting social situation is that of parents teaching their children the narrative conventions used in telling, and therefore in having autobiographical memories (Fivush, chap. 6, this volume; Fivush, Haden, & Reese, 1996; Fivush & Reese, 1992; Miller, Potts, Fung, Hoogstra, & Mintz, 1990; Miller & Sperry, 1988; Nelson, 1993). For example, Fivush et al. (1996) observed longitudinal changes in parent–child recall of unique family events such as trips taken during vacations. The style the parents used to draw out the children's autobiographical memories when the children were 3½ years old predicted the children's style at age 6.

IMAGERY

Imagery is another major component of autobiographical memory. Following Brewer's analyses, I concentrate on visual imagery. In general terms, visual imagery is an analog system that shares many properties with visual perception. It can be broken down behaviorally and neurally into spatial and object components (see Rubin, 1995a, for a review) and in its role in autobiographical memory may need further division (Cornoldi, De Beni, & Pra Baldi, 1989). As Brewer (1986, 1996) noted, autobiographical memories consist in part of images, and this is one way to separate them from facts about one's life that are not autobiographical memories.

Imagery is a part of the metaphor of taking a picture that was used to name the *flashbulb memory* phenomenon (Brown & Kulik, 1977) and an attempt to rename it *vivid memory* (Rubin & Kozin, 1984). Imagery is found throughout the flashbulb memory literature as an important component of what makes vivid memories vivid (see Conway, 1995, and Winograd & Neisser, 1992, for recent reviews). In addition there is a literature on field versus observer point of view in autobiographical memory (i.e., on whether one sees oneself in the memory or sees it from the original observer's viewpoint) going back at least to Freud (see Robinson & Swanson, 1993, for a recent review). Thus, we have at least two metaphors of imagery: one as a static, accurate picture and another as a fluid mental-model image that can be seen from different points of view (both literally and figuratively). The contrast between the two metaphors is one reason that the classic conflict between the view of memories as fixed and memories as constructions (e.g., Neisser, 1967) becomes so heated when applied to autobiographical memory.

Imagery has a central role in autobiographical memory for several reasons. The first is that it provides a powerful memory aid (Paivio, 1971, 1986, 1991), an observation that predates experimental work on imagery by a millennium or two. Almost all the mnemonic systems developed from the time of the ancient Greeks and Romans through the Middle Ages to the present generation of stage mnemonists and authors of books on how to improve memory are based on visual imagery (Paivio, 1971; Yates, 1966). Most of the evidence for imagery's mnemonic role comes from long-term memory effects, but imagery is also important in short-term or working memory (Baddeley, 1986) and can even be seen as having most of its effects there rather than in long-term representation (Marschark, Richman, Yuille, & Hunt, 1987).

Imagery is also important in autobiographical memory because of its role in increasing the specific, relived, personally experienced aspect of autobiographical memory. Specific, concrete details do more than improve memory. Concrete details make stories seem more accurate, thoughtful, and believable (Pillemer, 1992; Pillemer, Desrochers, & Ebanks, chap. 9, this volume; Pillemer, Picariello, Law, & Reichman, 1996). Although vivid images do not guarantee accuracy (Winograd & Neisser, 1992), people act as if memory for details implies that the central points are remembered correctly. For instance, eyewitness testimony is more effective if details are included, even if they are irrelevant to the case (Bell & Loftus, 1989), and sensory details make people likely to judge that they did an action rather than just thought about it (Johnson, Hashtroudi, & Lindsay, 1993; Johnson & Raye, 1981). You are more likely to decide that you really did lock the door as opposed to just thinking you did if you can image yourself doing it. Chafe (1982, 1990) noted that language varies along the dimension of *involvement*. Involvement is marked by the use of first person and of dialogue, the same traits that are present when one seems to others to be reliving an experience or seeing it in one's mind's eye. Thus evidence that the rememberer has an image is routinely taken as evidence for a relived, personally experienced, accurate autobiographical memory.

In this role of increasing the specific, imagery and narrative interact. The language of a journal article, which I have lapsed from at times here, is abstract, general, and low in imagery; a good story is not. Bruner (1986) made this distinction in isolating two kinds of thought. The narrative mode of thought "strives to put its timeless miracles into the particulars of experience, and to locate the experience in time and place. The paradigmatic mode, by contrast seeks to transcend the particular by higher and higher reaching for abstraction" (p. 13). It is no accident that *Time, Newsweek,* and other magazines begin articles on general topics with specific, concrete case studies.

Imagery integrates with affect as well as narrative structure. Specific details aid in maintaining emotional balance (Williams & Dritschel, 1988), and increase affect, intimacy, and immediacy when compared to abstract statements that remove the events described from particular situations (Pillemer, 1992), and foster involvement (Chafe, 1982, 1990). Concrete details that increased affect, intimacy, immediacy, and involvement should lead to more frequent tellings and through this rehearsal mechanism to easier future recall.

Specific details are more likely to be mentioned if a speaker has an image, and thus a listener is likely to take specific details as a sign the speaker has an image. However, specific details are also part of the narrative and affective component as well as imagery. For some of the added functions of the specific, it is still reasonable to argue that the image is the driving force. Imagery is a process, of which we are sometimes aware, that aids memory. In the everyday sense of memory as reliving an experience, however, an image of which one is aware may be the memory, whereas the words may not be the memory at all but just a way of describing it.

The intimate relation of having an image and having an autobiographical memory, however, does cause problems. The two metaphors of imagery as a picture and imagery as a mental model are in conflict. Having an image makes a memory more believable. However, from both the literature on field versus observer perspective as well as the more general view of imagery as an analog system that allows actions and events to be simulated, imagery allows memory to be malleable (Rumelhart & Norman, 1986; Shepard,

1978). Thus imagery both increases the belief that memories are accurate and facilitates changes from initial perception. In the quote defining autobiographical memory earlier in the chapter, Brewer (1996) noted that an autobiographical memory includes both a belief of being a veridical record and a report of visual imagery. The conflict that can arise due to discrepancies between the belief that autobiographical memories are veridical and their accuracy is one of the most interesting and heated debates in all of memory research, as the chapters on eyewitness testimony in the companion volume show. The visual imagery component of autobiographical memory is a central contributor to this conflict.

AFFECT

Affect is another main component of autobiographical memory, but unlike narrative and imagery, affect is traditionally seen as outside cognition rather than as an aspect of it. As seen in the work of Christianson and Safer (1996) and of Williams (1996; Williams et al., 1996), affect has profound effects on autobiographical memory. It can focus attention on one aspect of a scene and it can reduce the ability to retrieve specific, as opposed to generic autobiographical memories of generalized categories of events. Recent work on the psychological and neural basis of affect and its relation to memory is growing (e.g., Christianson, 1992; the journal *Cognition and Emotion*) and should provide a too often ignored way of understanding autobiographical memory.

The effects of affect can often be seen as interactions with the imagery component. Christianson and Safer (1996) compared the focusing of memory on emotionally salient objects in an event to the focusing of attention in vision, allowing the focusing to be mediated by imagery. The inability of depressed individuals to retrieve specific, single-occurrence autobiographical memories documented by Williams may be related to the inability of abstract versus concrete, imageable memories to produce specific details (Chase & Ericsson, 1981; Schwanenflugel, Akin, & Luh, 1992). In addition, Robinson (1996) and Pillemer et al. (chap. 9, this volume) observed that changes in the viewer's perspective of an image affects the intensity of affect.

THE NEURAL BASIS OF RECOLLECTION

Existing neuropsychology, along with recent work using imaging techniques, is beginning to show what areas of the cortex are activated when retrieval occurs. A much greater neuropsychology and brain-imaging effort is devoted to the visual imagery and language components that can help support theoretical claims for these processes. Whatever the ultimate definition and localization of language, visual imagery, affect, and retrieval, it is clear that they are subsystems of the mind and brain (e.g., Damasio, 1989, 1994). Each component can be seen as an aspect of a system that evolved for purposes other than having autobiographical memories and each has been adapted and integrated for that purpose.

In addition, there is considerable evidence on the neural basis of autobiographical memory itself from the neuropsychological study of specific types of amnesias that can help localize various memory functions. For instance, some frontal lobe patients confabulate wildly, showing an intact ability to create autobiographical "memories," but they have severe problems finding and integrating facts and monitoring their recall against reality (Baddeley & Wilson, 1986). Other observations about the nature of autobiographical memory could continue with particular lesions or diseases, each with its own particular damage site or neurotransmitter deficit that in combination with other cases can help triangulate on the neural underpinnings of autobiographical memory. Unfortunately, what we know here is not always easy to apply. In most neuropsychological cases, the syndrome does not fit neatly into existing cognitive theories, every case is different from all other cases in both behavior and neurology, and different investigators report different things, especially if one includes historical cases. This variety, however, does broaden the range of observations.

Although brain imaging and neuropsychology provide considerable evidence and analysis, there is no comprehensive neurally based model of how autobiographical memory works and so the task of integrating these findings remains. From our behavioral analysis the model will have at least language, imagery (both spatial and object), affect, and memory retrieval, and, if Proust's experience is to be modeled, olfactory cuing. The most is known about the language and imagery components, but even here the effect of studies of acquired cortical blindness or particular types of language loss on autobiographical memory are generally missing (but see Ogden, 1993, for a fascinating exception). Even the extent to which the basic data for a memory are stored together in one location or separately in these and other components is open, but retrieval or integration over the 10-second process of a cue evoking a memory is needed and provides a unique window on the nature of the integration process. We know the perceptual portion of the cuing process must be rapid. Next, if Proust's example is general, at least for olfaction, comes the affect component. Retrieval ends with activation in the visual and language areas. The exact time course and localization within general neural systems remains to be discovered.

We have less certain expectations of where and in what sequence brain activity will occur during the long time that occurs between the initial perceptual effect of the cue and the retrieval of a memory. Although there is a growing body of knowledge on the neural basis of episodic memory in general (e.g., Aggleton, 1991; Buckner, 1996; Kapur, 1993; Mishkin, Malamut, & Bachevalier, 1984; Nyberg, Cabeza, & Tulving, 1996; Petri & Mishkin, 1994; Squire, 1987, 1992; Tulving, 1989), in the context of the framework and task used here, the least is known about the process of retrieval. Having the less well localized retrieval portion of the process bounded by the more well localized processes of sensation and visual imagery is an ideal preparation for exploration.

Admitting our large degree of ignorance, there is considerable evidence about the most likely source of the "retrieval" or integration component(s) that is active when we have a full-blown autobiographical memory. There are two sources of evidence that both point to the same locations. The first line of evidence comes from neuropsychological and animal studies of amnesia (for reviews see Petri & Mishkin, 1994, and Squire, 1987). From such studies, it is known that damage either to the hippocampus and surrounding areas in the medial temporal lobe or damage to the medio-dorsal thalamic and mammillary nuclei can both cause dense amnesias (e.g., Kapur, Thompson, Cook, Lang, & Brice, 1996). As these two areas can be considered as parts of a common circuit (Petri & Mishkin, 1994), this circuit could be (or could contain) the retrieval component.

The second line of evidence supports the idea that the limbic structures in the medial temporal lobe are the main source of the retrieval component, although this localization within a circuit may be an accident of the way the data were collected. Penfield, in his classic studies, was able to produce a dreamlike sense of reliving in his patients by stimulating the surface of their brains while probing for localization of function during surgery (see Squire, 1987, for a review and critique of this work). Whether these experiential responses were memories or new constructions is not at issue here; the often vivid sense of reliving is the relevant point. Whether these experiential responses were a dream or a memory is only important here if the sense of reliving in dreams and in recollections have different neural substrates. As Squire (1987) noted in his review of Penfield's work and studies that follow it, cases of experiential responses were rare, occurring in only about 8% of the stimulations of the temporal lobes. However, they were highly localized, occurring only with stimulation of the temporal lobes. Moreover, in later studies medial temporal lobe limbic structures were always involved in the complex experiential responses that most closely match what we would call a sense of reliving. Squire (1987) hypothesized that "limbic structures may possess such a capacity to evoke experiential phenomena because they have afferent and efferent connections to widespread areas of neocortex, including temporal neocortex" (p. 82). Thus, for now our best guess at the localization of the retrieval or integration component is the medial-temporal/medial-thalamic circuit.

A third line of evidence could come from neuroimaging studies of people having autobiographical memories, preferably vivid autobiographical memories. Such evidence is possible. One general technical problem is that at the current time it is not clear how the magnitude of change in metabolic measures associated with neuronal activity relates to the processes of interest. Small increases in firing above a baseline (or moderate increases above a noisy baseline) may be undetected but important. For instance, the hippocampus has been shown to be important for memory from damage studies but does not appear to be as noticeable in activation measures in tasks where it might be expected (McCarthy, 1995). With more experience, the strengths and limits of the various sources of evidence should become clearer.

Although there is little work testing autobiographical memory directly, there has been considerable study of episodic memory in laboratory tasks. Encoding and retrieval of episodic memories are mediated by separate locations in the prefrontal cortex, encoding being mediated by the left hemisphere and retrieval by the right (Nyberg et al., 1996). More specifically, during retrieval the right anterior prefrontal area at or near Brodmann area 10 is active (Buckner, 1996). The relation of these frontal lobe centers to the more traditional medial-temporal/medial-thalamic circuit remains a challenge that may be clarified by neuroimaging studies of autobiographical memory or reexamination of neuropsychological cases. It is possible that the retrieval component postulated here may have to be further divided, for example possibly into one involved in determining specific temporal periods and one involving integration. Alternatively, the sense of reliving that has been attributed to the retrieval component may not really be a part of the retrieval component or even have a location in any component. Rather it might occur when several of the components, isolated here as being necessary for autobiographical memory, work in unison. Thus activity in the medial-temporal/medial-thalamic circuit, an area that in Squire's (1987) words has "afferent and efferent connections to widespread areas of neocortex" (p. 82), would be a symptom rather than a cause of the sense of reliving.

There remains one problem with the view that the medial-temporal/medial-thalamic circuit is the source of retrieval. Damage to this circuit appears to produce mainly anterograde amnesia; memories prior to the onset of the amnesia can often be recalled, whereas memories after the onset cannot. Therefore, from the damage studies, it appears that this circuit may be an encoding more than a retrieval area. In contrast, from the stimulation studies, the circuit appears to be a retrieval center.

There are at least three resolutions to this problem. The first is to accept

Squires' view that the medial-temporal/medial-thalamic circuit is needed for encoding and only initially for retrieval, with very long-term memory occurring without the need for the medial-temporal/medial-thalamic circuit. Under this view, the various aspects of older autobiographical memories connect to each other directly without the need of a retrieval component as hypothesized here. If one aspect of the memory is activated, that aspect could activate the other aspects directly as in most distributed models of long-term memory. From the evidence available, very long-term memory could still use the medial-temporal/medial-thalamic circuit for difficult retrievals like the one Proust described, but it would not be needed for all memories.

The second resolution is to ask what damage produces severe retrograde as well as anterograde amnesia; that is what damage affects all recollection, both of events prior and after the onset of the amnesia. Damage that produces such amnesias could provide evidence to help localize the retrieval or integration mechanism. There are two general causes of such retrograde amnesia (Hodges & McCarthy, 1993). One is herpes simplex encephalitis with medial temporal lobe damage. Another case of localized damage is in alcoholic Korsakoff's amnesia (e.g., Butters & Cermak, 1986), in which the mediodorsal thalamic and mammillary nuclei are affected. Although the retrograde amnesia is not complete, it usually extends back several decades, and even for the older memories it is difficult to get detailed autobiographical memories (Zola-Morgan, Cohen, & Squire, 1983). Depression also produces a general loss of specific recollections (Williams, 1996; Williams et al., 1996).

Alternatively, one could look at cases that had only retrograde amnesia. These are rarer, but do exist. Some retrograde amnesias have no clearly associated anatomical damage and are called *functional retrograde amnesia* (e.g., Schacter, Wang, Tulving, & Freedman, 1982) even if their onset was caused by a physical insult (e.g., Treadway, McCloskey, Gordon, & Cohen, 1992). Other retrograde amnesias have known neural bases and are called *focal retrograde amnesia* (Kapur, 1993). Several of these amnesias are accompanied by left temporal lobe abnormalities in electroencephalograms, positron emission tomography, or magnetic resonance imaging. Often these cases begin with both anterograde and retrograde amnesia, but after a period of time only the retrograde amnesia remains. From evidence such as this as well as other cases (Kapur et al., 1996), one might suspect that cortical damage is necessary for retrograde amnesia, but as in all of neuropsychology, nothing is simple and other cases lead to different conclusions (Hodges & McCarthy, 1993). Teasing apart necessary from sufficient in complex interconnected systems is not easy, but it still could be that damage to the left temporal lobe produces (or even is necessary for) retrograde amnesia in the absence of anterograde amnesia.

A third resolution is to examine the retrograde memory of patients in

more detail, especially the retrograde memories patients that have anterograde amnesia but are claimed to have no retrograde amnesia. To what
extent are their retrograde memories really complete? How would they be
rated on the scales we normally use to assess autobiographical memories
such as scales of vividness and emotionality? Can examination of such
memories show the degree to which anterograde amnesia patients have a
sense of reliving, or vivid autobiographical memories, or recollection in
general? Is there any relation between the type and severity of damage and
the type and severity of retrograde memory loss?

In this regard the case description by Hodges and McCarthy (1993) is
especially interesting. A 67-year-old man suffered bilateral lesions to the
mediodorsal thalamic nuclei and the pathway connecting them to the
mammillary nuclei. He had both dense anterograde and retrograde amnesias, demonstrating that damage to just the medial-thalamic circuit can
cause severe retrograde amnesia. In studying the retrograde amnesia in
detail it was found to be for autobiographical memories and public events,
but his ability to identify famous people and order when in time they were
famous was spared. Hodges and McCarthy suggested that the deficit might
be in a thematic retrieval framework. Their patient was unable to index,
retrieve, and integrate autobiographical memories but well may have had
the component information for such memories.

Thus, a review of the neuropsychological and animal memory literature
leaves several important questions about the long-term role of the retrieval
or integration component. However, posing the question suggests the kinds
of evidence that would be needed to address these questions. Much of this
evidence exists, but like an autobiographical memory it needs to be retrieved
and integrated.

Two other observations remain. First, when there is a long period of
retrograde amnesia, it often stops in early adulthood. Other evidence
suggests that this is a special period for encoding memories (Rubin, Rahhal,
& Poon, 1996; Rubin & Schulkind, in press a, in press b; Rubin, Wetzler,
& Nebes, 1986). Ways of integrating this observation and contrasting it with
the more continuous time line view held in the consolidation views of
neuropsychology remain open. Second, following Brewer's (1996) review of
the literature, the time at which an event occurred has not been considered
here as an intrinsic aspect of an autobiographical memory. However, there
is evidence for time as an organizing factor that can describe the nature of
memory loss in functional retrograde amnesia (e.g., Treadway et al., 1992)
and in focal retrograde amnesia (e.g., Butters & Cermak, 1986).

SUMMARY

The goal of this chapter has been to explore what it would mean to begin
developing a comprehensive theory of retrieval from autobiographical

memory within an individual, a theory that could benefit from what we know about the brain, behavior, and phenomenology (Larsen, chap. 10, this volume) during the act of having an autobiographical memory. Given the observations and theories reviewed here, converging evidence from these three domains should be of both theoretical and applied value.

ACKNOWLEDGMENTS

I wish to thank Darryl Bruce for his patience and encouragement, Herb Crovitz and Greg Kimble for trying to keep me honest, and the Olfactory Research Fund for their support.

REFERENCES

Aggleton, J. P. (1991). Anatomy of memory. In T. Yanagihara & R. C. Peterson (Eds.), *Memory disorders: Research and clinical practice* (pp. 23–61). New York: Marcel Dekker.

Baddeley, A. D. (1986). *Working memory.* Oxford, UK: Oxford University Press.

Baddeley, A. D. (1992). What is autobiographical memory? In M. A. Conway, D. C. Rubin, H. Spinnler, & W. A. Wagenaar (Eds.), *Theoretical perspectives on autobiographical memory* (pp. 13–29). Dordrecht, The Netherlands: Kluwer Academic.

Baddeley, A., & Wilson, B. (1986). Amnesia, autobiographical memory, and confabulation. In D. C. Rubin (Ed.), *Autobiographical memory* (pp. 225–252). Cambridge, UK: Cambridge University Press.

Barclay, C. R. (1986). Schematization of autobiographical memory. In D. C. Rubin (Ed.), *Autobiographical memory* (pp. 82–99). Cambridge, UK: Cambridge University Press.

Barclay, C. R. (1996). Autobiographical remembering: Narrative constraints on objectified selves. In D. C. Rubin (Ed.), *Remembering our past: Studies in autobiographical memory* (pp. 94–125). Cambridge, UK: Cambridge University Press.

Barclay, C. R., & Smith, T. S. (1992). Autobiographical remembering: Creating personal culture. In M. A. Conway, D. C. Rubin, H. Spinnler, & W. A. Wagenaar (Eds.), *Theoretical perspectives on autobiographical memory* (pp. 75–97). Dordrecht, The Netherlands: Kluwer Academic.

Barsalou, L. W. (1988). The content and organization of autobiographical memories. In U. Neisser & E. Winograd (Eds.), *Remembering reconsidered: Ecological and traditional approaches to the study of memory* (pp. 193–243). Cambridge, UK: Cambridge University Press.

Bell, B. E., & Loftus, E. F. (1989). Trivial persuasion in the courtroom: The power of (a few) minor details. *Journal of Personality and Social Psychology, 56,* 669–679.

Berntsen, D. (in press). Voluntary and involuntary access to autobiographical memory. *Memory.*

Brewer, W. F. (1986). What is autobiographical memory? In D. C. Rubin (Ed.), *Autobiographical memory* (pp. 25–49). Cambridge, UK: Cambridge University Press.

Brewer, W. F. (1996). What is recollective memory? In D. C. Rubin (Ed.). *Remembering our past: Studies in autobiographical memory* (pp. 19–66). Cambridge, UK: Cambridge University Press.

Brown, R., & Kulik, J. (1977). Flashbulb memories. *Cognition, 5,* 73–99.

Bruner, J. (1986). *Actual minds, possible worlds.* Cambridge, MA: Harvard University Press.

Bruner, J., & Feldman, C. F. (1996). Group narrative as a cultural context of autobiography. In D. C. Rubin (Ed.), *Remembering our past: Studies in autobiographical memory* (pp.

291–317). Cambridge, UK: Cambridge University Press.

Buckner, R. L. (1996). Beyond HERA: Contributions of specific prefrontal brain areas to long-term memory retrieval. *Psychonomic Bulletin & Review, 3,* 149–158.

Butters, N., & Cermak, L. S. (1986). A case study of forgetting of autobiographical knowledge: Implications for the study of retrograde amnesia. In D. C. Rubin (Ed.), *Autobiographical memory* (pp. 253–272). Cambridge, UK: Cambridge University Press.

Chafe, W. (1982). Integration and involvement in speaking, writing and oral literature. In D. Tannen (Ed.), *Spoken and written language: Exploring orality and literacy* (pp. 35–53). Norwood, NJ: Ablex.

Chafe, W. (1990). Some things that narratives tell us about the mind. In B. K. Britton & A. D. Pellegrini (Eds.), *Narrative thought and narrative language* (pp. 79–98). Hillsdale, NJ: Lawrence Erlbaum Associates.

Chase, W. G., & Ericsson, K. A. (1981). Skilled memory. In J. R. Anderson (Ed.), *Cognitive skills and their acquisition* (pp. 141–189). Hillsdale, NJ: Lawrence Erlbaum Associates.

Christianson, S.-A. (Ed.). (1992). *The handbook of emotion and memory: Research and theory.* Hillsdale, NJ: Lawrence Erlbaum Associates.

Christianson, S.-A., & Safer, M. A. (1996). Emotional events and emotions in autobiographical memories. In D. C. Rubin (Ed.), *Remembering our past: Studies in autobiographical memory* (pp. 218–243). Cambridge, UK: Cambridge University Press.

Conway, M. A. (1995). *Flashbulb memories.* Hillsdale, NJ: Lawrence Erlbaum Associates.

Conway, M. A. (1996). Autobiographical knowledge and autobiographical memories. In D. C. Rubin (Ed.), *Remembering our past: Studies in autobiographical memory* (pp. 67–93). Cambridge, UK: Cambridge University Press.

Conway, M. A., & Rubin, D. C. (1993). The structure of autobiographical memory. In A. E. Collins, S. E. Gathercole, M. A. Conway, & P. E. Morris (Eds.), *Theories of memory* (pp. 103–137). Hove, UK: Lawrence Erlbaum Associates.

Cornoldi, C., De Beni, R., & Pra Baldi, A. (1989). Generation and retrieval of general, specific and autobiographic images representing concrete nouns. *Acta Psychologica, 72,* 25–39.

Damasio, A. R. (1989). Time-locked multiregional retroactivation: A systems-levels proposal for the neural substrates of recall and recognition. *Cognition, 33,* 25–62.

Damasio, A. R. (1994). *Descartes' error: Emotion, reason, and the human brain.* New York: Putnam.

Fitzgerald, J. M. (1986). Autobiographical memory: A developmental perspective. In D. C. Rubin (Ed.), *Autobiographical memory* (pp. 122–133). Cambridge, UK: Cambridge University Press.

Fitzgerald, J. M. (1988). Vivid memories and the reminiscence phenomenon: The role of a self narrative. *Human Development, 31,* 261–273.

Fitzgerald, J. M. (1992). Autobiographical memory and conceptualizations of the self. In M. A. Conway, D. C. Rubin, H. Spinnler, & W. A. Wagenaar (Eds.), *Theoretical perspectives on autobiographical memory* (pp. 99–114). Dordrecht, The Netherlands: Kluwer Academic.

Fitzgerald, J. M., & Lawrence, R. (1984). Autobiographical memory across the life-span. *Journal of Gerontology, 39,* 692–699.

Fivush, R., Haden, C., & Reese, E. (1996). Remembering, recounting, and reminiscing: The development of autobiographical memory in social context. In D. C. Rubin (Ed.), *Remembering our past: Studies in autobiographical memory* (pp. 341–359). Cambridge, UK: Cambridge University Press.

Fivush, R., & Reese, E. (1992). The social construction of autobiographical memory. In M. A. Conway, D. C. Rubin, H. Spinnler, & W. A. Wagenaar (Eds.), *Theoretical perspectives on autobiographical memory* (pp. 115–132). Dordrecht, The Netherlands: Kluwer Academic.

Freeman, M. (1993). *Rewriting the self: History, memory, narrative.* London: Routledge.

Galton, F. (1879). Psychometric experiments. *Brain, 2,* 149–162.

Gergen, K. J., & Gergen, M. M. (1988). Narrative and the self as relationship. *Advances in Experimental Social Psychology, 21,* 17–56.

Hirst, W., & Manier, D. (1996). Remembering as communication: A family recounts its past. In D. C. Rubin (Ed.), *Remembering our past: Studies in autobiographical memory* (pp. 271–290). Cambridge, UK: Cambridge University Press.

Hodges, J. R., & McCarthy, R. A. (1993). Autobiographical amnesia resulting from bilateral paramedian thalamic infarction. *Brain, 116,* 921–940.

Johnson, M. K., Hashtroudi, S., & Lindsay, D. S. (1993). Source monitoring. *Psychological Bulletin, 114,* 3–28.

Johnson, M. K., & Raye, C. L. (1981). Reality monitoring. *Psychological Review, 88,* 67–85.

Kapur, N. (1993). Focal retrograde amnesia in neurological disease: A critical review. *Cortex, 29,* 217–234.

Kapur, N., Thompson, S., Cook, P., Lang, D., & Brice, J. (1996). Anterograde but not retrograde memory loss following combined mammillary body and medial thalamic lesions. *Neuropsychologia, 34,* 1–8.

Marschark, M., Richman, C. L., Yuille, J. C., & Hunt, R. R. (1987). The role of imagery in memory: On shared and distinctive information. *Psychological Bulletin, 102,* 28–41.

McCarthy, G. (1995). Functional neuroimaging of memory. *The Neuroscientist, 1,* 155–163.

Miller, G. (1962). *Psychology: The science of mental life.* New York: Harper & Row.

Miller, P. J., Potts, R., Fung, H., Hoogstra, L., & Mintz, J. (1990). Narrative practices and the social construction of self in childhood. *American Ethnologist, 17,* 292–311.

Miller, P. J., & Sperry, L. L. (1988). Early talk about the past: The origins of conversational stories of personal experiences. *Journal of Child Language, 15,* 293–315.

Mishkin, M., Malamut, B., & Bachevalier, J. (1984). Memories and habits: Two neural systems. In G. Lynch, J. L. McGaugh, & N. M. Weinberger (Eds.), *Neuropsychology of memory* (pp. 65–77). New York: Guilford.

Neisser, U. (1967). *Cognitive psychology.* New York: Appleton-Century-Crofts.

Neisser, U. (1982). Snapshots or benchmarks? In U. Neisser (Ed.), *Memory observed* (pp. 43–48). San Francisco, CA: Freeman.

Nelson, K. (1993). The psychological and social origins of autobiographical memory. *Psychological Science, 4,* 7–14.

Nyberg, L., Cabeza, R., & Tulving, E. (1996). PET studies of encoding and retrieval: The HERA model. *Psychonomic Bulletin & Review, 3,* 135–148.

Ogden, J. A. (1993). Visual object agnosia, prosopagnosia, achromatopsia, loss of visual imagery, and autobiographical amnesia following recovery from cortical blindness: Case M. H. *Neuropsychologia, 31,* 571–589.

Paivio, A. (1971). *Imagery and verbal processes.* New York: Holt, Rinehart & Winston.

Paivio, A. (1986). *Mental representations: A dual coding approach.* New York: Oxford University Press.

Paivio, A. (1991). Dual coding theory: Retrospect and current status. *Canadian Journal of Psychology, 45,* 255–287.

Petri, H. L., & Mishkin, M. (1994). Behaviorism, cognitivism and the neuropsychology of memory. *American Scientist, 82,* 30–37.

Pillemer, D. B. (1992). Remembering personal circumstances: A functional analysis. In E. Winograd & U. Neisser (Eds.), *Affect and accuracy in recall: Studies of "flashbulb" memories* (pp. 236–264). Cambridge, UK: Cambridge University Press.

Pillemer, D. B., Picariello, M. L., Law, A. B., & Reichman, J. S. (1996). Memories of college: The importance of specific educational episodes. In D. C. Rubin (Ed.), *Remembering our past: Studies in autobiographical memory* (pp. 318–337). Cambridge, UK: Cambridge University Press.

Proust, M. (1956). *Swann's way.* New York: Random House. (Original work published 1928)

Reiser, B. J., Black, J. B., & Kalamarides, P. (1986). Strategic memory search processes. In

D. C. Rubin (Ed.), *Autobiographical memory* (pp. 100–121). Cambridge, UK: Cambridge University Press.

Robinson, J. A. (1976). Sampling autobiographical memory. *Cognitive Psychology, 8,* 578–595.

Robinson, J. A. (1981). Personal narratives reconsidered. *Journal of American Folklore, 94,* 58–85.

Robinson, J. A. (1996). Perspective, meaning, and remembering. In D. C. Rubin (Ed.), *Remembering our past: Studies in autobiographical memory* (pp. 199–217). Cambridge, UK: Cambridge University Press.

Robinson, J. A., & Swanson, K. L. (1993). Field and observer modes of remembering. *Memory, 1,* 169–184.

Rubin, D. C. (1980). 51 properties of 125 words: A unit analysis of verbal behavior. *Journal of Verbal Learning and Verbal Behavior, 19,* 736–755.

Rubin, D. C. (1988). Go for the skill. In U. Neisser & E. Winograd (Eds.), *Remembering reconsidered: Ecological and traditional approaches to the study of memory* (pp. 374–382). Cambridge, UK: Cambridge University Press.

Rubin, D. C. (1995a). *Memory in oral traditions: The cognitive psychology of epic, ballads, and counting-out rhymes.* New York: Oxford University Press.

Rubin, D. C. (1995b). Stories about stories. In R. S. Wyer, Jr. (Ed.), *Knowledge and memory: The real story* (pp. 153–164). Hillsdale, NJ: Lawrence Erlbaum Associates.

Rubin, D. C. (1996). Introduction. In D. C. Rubin (Ed.), *Remembering our past: Studies in autobiographical memory* (pp. 1–15). Cambridge, UK: Cambridge University Press.

Rubin, D. C., Groth, L., & Goldsmith, D. (1984). Olfactory cuing of autobiographical memory. *American Journal of Psychology, 97,* 493–507.

Rubin, D. C., & Kozin, M. (1984). Vivid memories. *Cognition, 16,* 81–95.

Rubin, D. C., Rahhal, T. A., & Poon, L. W. (1996). Things learned in early adulthood are remembered best: Effects of a major transition on memory. Unpublished manuscript, Duke University, Durham, NC.

Rubin, D. C., & Schulkind, M. D. (in press a). The distribution of autobiographical memories across the lifespan. *Memory & Cognition.*

Rubin, D. C., & Schulkind, M. D. (in press b). The distribution of important and word-cued autobiographical memories in 20, 35, and 70 year-old adults. *Psychology and Aging.*

Rubin, D. C., Wetzler, S. E., & Nebes, R. D. (1986). Autobiographical memory across the adult lifespan. In D. C. Rubin (Ed.), *Autobiographical memory* (pp. 202–221). Cambridge, UK: Cambridge University Press.

Rumelhart, D. E., & Norman, D. A. (1986). Representation in memory. In R. C. Atkinson, R. J. Herrnstein, G. Lindzey, & R. D. Luce (Eds.), *Steven's handbook of experimental psychology: Vol. 2. Learning and cognition* (2nd ed., pp. 511–587). New York: Wiley.

Schacter, D. L., Wang, P. L., Tulving, E., & Freedman, M. (1982). Functional retrograde amnesia: A quantitative case study. *Neuropsychologia, 20,* 523–532.

Schafer, R. (1981). Narration in the psychoanalytic dialogue. In W. J. T. Mitchell (Ed.), *On narrative* (pp. 25–49). Chicago: University of Chicago Press.

Schank, R. C., & Abelson, R. P. (1995). Knowledge and memory: The real story. In R. S. Wyer, Jr. (Ed.), *Knowledge and memory: The real story* (pp. 1–85). Hillsdale, NJ: Lawrence Erlbaum Associates.

Schwanenflugel, P. J., Akin, C., & Luh, W. M. (1992). Context availability and the recall of abstract and concrete words. *Memory & Cognition, 20,* 96–104.

Shepard, R. N. (1978). The mental image. *American Psychologist, 33,* 125–137.

Spence, D. P. (1982). *Narrative truth and historical truth: Meaning and interpretation in psychoanalysis.* New York: Norton.

Squire, L. R. (1987). *Memory and brain.* New York: Oxford University Press.

Squire, L. R. (1992). Memory and the hippocampus: A synthesis from findings with rats, monkeys, and humans. *Psychological Review, 99,* 195–231.

Squire, L. R., & Zola-Morgan, S. (1991). The medial temporal lobe memory system. *Science, 253,* 1380–1386.

Treadway, M., McCloskey, M., Gordon, B., & Cohen, N. J. (1992). Landmark life events and the organization of memory: Evidence from functional retrograde amnesia. In S.-A. Christianson (Ed.), *The handbook of emotion and memory: Research and theory* (pp. 389–410). Hillsdale, NJ: Lawrence Erlbaum Associates.

Tulving, E. (1972). Episodic and semantic memory. In E. Tulving & W. Donaldson (Eds.), *Organization of memory* (pp. 381–403). New York: Academic Press.

Tulving, E. (1983). *Elements of episodic memory.* Oxford, UK: Oxford University Press.

Tulving, E. (1989). Remembering and knowing the past. *The American Scientist, 77,* 361–367.

Wagenaar, W. A., van Koppen, P. J., & Crombag, H. F. M. (1993). *Anchored narratives: The psychology of criminal evidence.* Hemel Hempstead, UK: Harvester Wheatsheaf.

Williams, J. M. G. (1996). Depression and the specificity of autobiographical memory. In D. C. Rubin (Ed.), *Remembering our past: Studies in autobiographical memory (pp. 244–267). Cambridge, UK: Cambridge University Press.*

Williams, J. M. G., & Dritschel, B. H. (1988). Emotional disturbance and the specificity of autobiographical memory. *Cognition and Emotion, 2,* 221–234.

Williams, J. M. G., Ellis, N. C., Tyers, C., Healy, H., Rose, G., & MacLeod, A. K. (1996). The specificity of autobiographical memory and imageability of the future. *Memory & Cognition, 24,* 116–125.

Winograd, E., & Neisser, U. (Eds.). (1992). *Affect and accuracy in recall: Studies of "flashbulb" memories.* New York: Cambridge University Press.

Yates, F. A. (1966). *The art of memory.* Chicago: University of Chicago Press.

Zola-Morgan, S., Cohen, N. J., & Squire, L. R. (1983). Recall of remote episodic memory in amnesia. *Neuropsychologia, 21,* 487–500.

5

Loss and Distortion of Autobiographical Memory Content

Harry P. Bahrick
Ohio Wesleyan University

Forgetting entails loss of content as well as systematic changes or distortions of content. Research on the loss of content has generally been conducted in the Ebbinghaus tradition, guided by associative-replicative[1] conceptualizations of memory, whereas inferential-reconstructive views of memory stimulated research on distortion of content (Bahrick, 1984b).

There is ample evidence that both replicative and reconstructive processing are involved in most naturalistic memory tasks (Hall, 1990). Memory for prose, for example, shows evidence of reconstructive processing when gist is recalled, and of replicative processing when verbatim quotes are recalled (Dooling & Christiaansen, 1977; Hasher & Griffin, 1978). In a test for retention of a foreign language (Bahrick, 1984a), recall of individual foreign words prompted by the equivalent English word suggests associative-replicative processing; the comprehension of paragraphs not previously encountered demonstrates inferential-reconstructive processing. Although both types of processing are plausibly involved in the retrieval of most autobiographical memory content, the interrelations between these two types of processing are rarely examined and are not well understood. As a corollary, the interrelations between the loss of content and the distortion of content are rarely examined and not well understood.

---

[1] I use the term *replicative processing* here and in previous papers (Bahrick, 1984, 1985) to refer to what is often labeled *reproductive processing*.

There are methodological reasons for this paucity of information. Distinct paradigms have guided research on loss versus distortion of content and these paradigms are not easily accommodated in a single investigation. As Koriat and Goldsmith (1994) pointed out, research dealing with the quantity of retention is commonly performed with content acquired in the laboratory, whereas research dealing with fidelity of content is usually performed with naturalistically acquired content.

This chapter discusses several aspects of the relation between loss and distortion of autobiographical memory content, and the implications for the relation between replicative and reconstructive processing. Data we presented (Bahrick, Hall, & Berger, 1996) suggest that reconstructive and replicative processing are supplementary and that reconstructive processing is invoked when attempts at replicative processing fail. Further, our data suggest that the role of positive affect differs in regard to replicative and reconstructive processing. Content that generates positive affect leads to replicative rehearsals, prolonging the life span of this material. In contrast, reconstructive processing often distorts in such a way that the reconstructed content generates more positive affect than would the veridical content.

The preceding inferences derive from an investigation in which 99 college students recalled 3,220 high school grades that we subsequently verified from high school transcripts. I first address the hypothesis that reconstructive processing is invoked when replicative processing fails. The hypothesis predicts that these two types of retrieval strategies are supplementary, so that inferential processing takes over when specific, episodic content is not accessible. The strategy of supplementing episodic content with inferentially retrieved generic content has also been suggested by Bruce and Van Pelt (1989), Dooling and Christiaansen (1977), and Murphy and Balzer (1986), and others.

An alternative displacement hypothesis asserts that reconstructive processing actively interferes with or blocks access to the veridical memory content. Gestalt psychologists advanced such a view. They stipulated processes of sharpening, leveling, and assimilation (Wulf, 1922) that systematically distort memory content so as to bring the content into better accord with familiar forms or schema (Bartlett, 1932). Psychoanalytic theory also stipulates dynamic changes that affect primarily traumatic or emotionally disturbing content. Screen memories actively displace anxiety-producing, veridical memories (Freud, 1899/1962). As Edwards (1942) described it, "Events are forcefully obliterated from consciousness because they are not in harmony with the ego's ideals, wishes and values" (p. 43).

Support for the replacement hypothesis also comes from retention tests based on clinical materials obtained from case records of individuals in therapy (Sharp, 1938). These findings indicate that acceptable content is remembered better than unacceptable content. However, case histories are not definitive in regard to the dynamics of the process. Substitution could take the form of active displacement, as psychoanalytic theory alleges, or the traumatic content could be lost as a result of such unrelated factors as retroactive inhibition or decay, and the screen memory content reconstructed after the fact. Case histories rarely include archival records documenting details of traumatic events, nor do they permit controlled comparisons of the rate of forgetting of traumatic versus nontraumatic content.

It is of course, also possible that the replacement hypothesis and the supplementing hypothesis are both valid under different circumstances, depending on the intensity of affect associated with a given content, or on individual differences in personality. One way to determine whether the forgetting of veridical content and the distortion of reconstructed content are sequential or interactive is to obtain separate indicants of the two processes from the same individuals. This is feasible for segmented content that permits scoring of the number of accurately remembered segments and of the degree of distortion of reconstructed segments. The absence of correlation between the amount of accurately retained content and the degree of distortion of reconstructed content would signal independence; that is, no interaction. A negative correlation between the amount of accurately retained content and the degree of distortion of reconstructed content would indicate that distortion occurs at the expense of accuracy, supporting the displacement hypothesis.

Examples of memory content that lend themselves to this type of analysis might include scores earned in successive athletic encounters, amounts contributed to a charity in successive years, traffic fines paid, or grades received in high school or college. Archival records are needed to determine the number of accurately retained targets and the degree of bias or distortion for targets that are not correctly recalled. If individuals who show the greatest degree of distortion tend to have the lowest number of correctly recalled targets, distorting may be the cause of forgetting. If, however, the number of correctly recalled targets is uncorrelated with the degree of distortion, one may infer that the processes of forgetting and distorting are sequential rather than interactive.

In the Bahrick et al. (1996) investigation, we verified the grades each participant recalled, and calculated an accuracy and a distortion score for each individual. The accuracy score was the percentage of recalled grades that corresponded to the verified grades. The distortion score reflected the degree of asymmetry of the error distribution, and was calculated as the proportion of incorrectly recalled grades that were inflations of the verified grade. We found no significant correlation between the degree of distortion of forgotten grades and the number of correctly recalled grades. From this, we concluded that the processes of forgetting and of distorting were sequential rather than interactive.

The circumstances that yield distortion of recall have been explored in a variety of research paradigms. Distortions may be induced by experimental interventions, for example, misinformation leading to distorted eyewitness testimony (Loftus, 1975) or the hindsight phenomenon (Fischoff, 1975). Findings appear to support the displacement hypothesis, although it is also possible that individuals have lost the relevant episodic memory content before the experimental intervention, so that the interventions bias the reconstruction, rather than distorting episodic memory. Interventions may also lead to failures of source memory that are difficult to distinguish from distortion of the episodic content (McCloskey & Zaragoza, 1985).

Distortions that are internally generated (not triggered by an experimental intervention) are most germane to the present discussion. They can yield the necessary correlational data, and they are more likely to reveal the affective and motivational dynamics underlying distortions.

In his seminal work, Ross (1989) explained distortions of the autobiographical past as reconstructions that bring the past into accord with current self-perceptions. He showed that this process may yield inflated or deflated recollections of past performance, depending on which modifications are most consistent with current beliefs about the self.

It is also true, however, that most distortions enhance rather than diminish past performance. Loftus (1982) described this effect: "Memory naturally shifts in a positive or prestige-enhancing direction, perhaps for the purpose of allowing us to have a more comfortable recollection of the past" (p. 146). We found (Bahrick et al., 1996) that 79 of 99 participants inflated their high school grades, 6 deflated their grades, 13 correctly recalled their grades, and 1 had a symmetrical error distribution. Our findings support Loftus' generalization; they show that distorting in a positive or prestige-enhancing direction applies to most but not all of our participants. Those who distort in a negative direction may have negative self-perceptions in regard to the targeted memory content and their distortion, according to Ross (1989), would bring the reconstructed memory content into better accord with their self-concept. To verify this prediction, appropriate indicants of self-perception need to be related to the direction of distortion.

THE ROLE OF AFFECT IN REPLICATIVE AND RECONSTRUCTIVE MEMORY

As previously stated, our findings suggest that positive affect plays a different role in replicative and reconstructive processing. It is associated with rehearsals that prolong the life span of replicatively retrieved content. It is also associated with systematic errors of memory that occur because reconstructed content tends to yield more positive affect than veridical content.

The inference regarding replicative processing is based on our finding that high grades are recalled with far greater accuracy than low grades (89% for grades of A vs. 29% for grades of D). The inference regarding reconstructive processing is based on the finding that 81% of errors in recall are inflations of the actual grade. Both inferences rest on assumptions. We assume that higher grades generate more positive affect than lower grades and that greater accuracy of recall reflects more frequent rehearsals. We assume further that systematic errors in recall reflect faulty reconstructive processing. Once episodic aspects of memory for a specific grade have been lost, bias is introduced through reconstructive inference.

It may seem contradictory that positive affect is associated with greater accuracy as well as with systematic error. However, the contradiction is resolved by distinguishing between the total number of errors and the variable and constant error components. This distinction is standard in the psychophysical method of average error (Woodworth, 1938). The number of correctly recalled targets and the total number of errors of recall (omission and commission) are logically complementary. However, the constant, directional component of error can increase even though the total number of errors declines. Variable (unsystematic) errors simply indicate the loss of information, and we found that content generating more positive affect is lost at a diminished rate. In contrast, systematic errors reflect the effect of additional, distorting variables. We infer that the process of reconstruction introduces systematic errors because we found that 81% of errors are inflations of the verified grade. For the great majority of individuals (over 90% of those exhibiting errors of recall) the mean of recalled grades is higher than the mean of actual grades. Assuming again that higher grades generate more positive affect than lower grades, the reconstructed content overall generates more positive affect than the veridical content.

The literature dealing with the relation between affect and memory is voluminous, and dates back to the early part of the century (Gordon, 1905). However, this research domain has been plagued by conceptual and methodological problems that have yielded conflicting findings (Christianson, 1992).

Conceptual problems relate to the use of inadequately defined, overlapping terms that include affect, mood, emotion, and arousal. The term *affect* has been used most frequently to denote positive or negative feelings associated with a particular memory content. *Mood* most commonly refers to the positive or negative affective state of the individual, independent of the particular memory content to be examined. *Arousal* usually refers to physiological correlates of emotion, with unspecified positive or negative affect, and *emotion* refers to various composites of physiological and affective states. Results of investigations that use one or the other of these concepts are often difficult to reconcile because of unspecifiable degrees of overlap among the phenomena examined (Isen, 1984; Mandler, 1992).

Investigators have used both naturalistic and experimental methods of investigation. The experimental approach has been most common in examining the effects of mood on memory. Constraints on the degree or intensity of inducing or manipulating mood in the laboratory have been a significant problem in this research (Kihlstrom, 1989) and explain in part why results regarding state-dependent retrieval or mood congruency effects have been inconsistent.

The naturalistic approach compares the retention of autobiographical memory content varying in affective intensity and polarity (positive, neutral, negative). The affective characteristics of the content are usually self-rated, and the content may be relatively old or recent. Conflicting results have been obtained (Revelle & Loftus, 1992). Some findings indicate that retention is primarily a function of intensity of affect (Bock, 1980). Others concludes that it depends on the polarity of affect, with positive, negative, and neutral affect remembered in descending order (Koch, 1930; Thompson, 1985; Waters & Leeper, 1936). Still other findings indicate that retention varies as a function of the degree of arousal (Isen, 1984).

Methodological problems of the naturalistic approach include the confounding of variables as well as failure to control changes of affect during the retention interval. In most naturalistic investigations, memory content is recorded some time after the targeted content is experienced. If diaries are used (Linton, 1975; Skowronski, Betz, Thompson, & Shannon, 1991; Wagenaar, 1986), the time lapse between occurrence and recording of the event may be only a few hours. In other investigations (Jerild, 1931), the lapses may be much longer. Intensity and polarity of affect associated with a given memory content may change over time (Holmes, 1970) and delayed ratings may therefore no longer reflect the affect at the time of the experience. Specifically, it has been shown that negative affect may change to neutral or positive affect (Gilbert, 1938; Holmes, 1970), and that intensity of affect judged retrospectively is often diminished. Our investigation (Bahrick et al., 1996) showed that ratings of satisfaction (implying positive affect) associated with grades obtained 1 to 5 years earlier reflected the inflated, reconstructed grades, not the veridical, lower grades. This finding supports the conclusion that delayed ratings of affect may systematically change in a more positive direction. Historically, the question of whether emotions can be revived in memory has been questioned (Linton, 1982), and the most common view holds that memory for emotion is indirect and takes the form of feelings attached to revived cognitions (Ross, 1991).

Problems of confounding involve both independent and dependent variables. Affective intensity is frequently confounded with significance or consequentiality of the content (Neisser, 1982; Yuille & Tollestrup, 1992). Affectively neutral content is generally also less significant; that is, it has little impact on the life of the individual. Inconsequential content is less well retained (Rubin & Kozin, 1984) because it is likely to be less well encoded and rehearsed than significant content. Similar effects have been attributed to the emotional impact of the content (Christianson, 1992). Diminished retention based on inconsequentiality of content may then be erroneously attributed to affective neutrality or low intensity of affect (Bahrick et al., 1996).

Another kind of confounding can occur if affect induces systematic errors of perceptual organization of the input. If this happens, distortion is a phenomenon of perception rather than memory, because it does not involve changes of the input–output correspondence during the retention interval.

Confounding of dependent variables may occur if the retention score reflects the combined effects of replicative and reconstructive processing. Replicative processing favors the retention of content generating positive affect. Reconstructive processing introduces systematic errors of inference. The direction and amount of error depend on relevant generic memories and other individual difference variables (Bahrick et al., 1996). As a result, inferential bias can augment or diminish retention of content generating positive affect, and the relative contributions to retention by replicative and reconstructive processing will determine the net effect of affect on retention.

RECOMMENDED RESEARCH STRATEGIES

To clarify the relation between replicative and reconstructive processing of memory content we need tasks and research designs that yield indicants of systematic and nonsystematic error components for the same individuals. Such designs require archival records to score errors, and segmented tasks that yield a distribution of retention scores for each individual. I have assumed that only inferential-reconstructive processing introduces distortions of content (systematic error components) and that these components reflect interactions of individual difference variables and affect associated with the content.

To clarify the effects of polarity and intensity of affect on memory, we also need to separate constant and variable error components. This will allow us to distinguish the longevity effect from the distortion effect. To avoid confounding the effects of affect with the effects of consequentiality of content, we must select content that varies in affect, but not in consequentiality. This can be achieved by selecting homogeneous content domains (e.g., grades received in school, money contributed to charity, scores in successive athletic contests), instead of comparing the retention of participant-selected autobiographical content belonging to various content categories.

To control retrospective changes in ratings of the polarity or intensity of affect, one option is to avoid such ratings altogether and to infer affect from the nature of content (grades of A, B, C, or D; contests that are won or lost). Another possibility is to obtain ratings immediately after the respective content is experienced (Brewer, 1988). These strategies are likely to improve our understanding of the extraordinarily complex relations between affect and memory.

SUMMARY

Replicative and reconstructive-inferential processing of memory content are found to be sequential and supplementary, not interactive. Inferential processing is invoked when replicative processing fails to retrieve the desired content. Distortions of memory content are the result of faulty inferential processing and an analysis of the relation between constant and variable errors of retention can be used to investigate the relation between the two types of processes. Memory content that generates positive affect leads to rehearsals that prolong the life span of such content. Distortions induced by inferential processing are likely to be in a direction that enhance positive affect. As a result, positive affect is associated with reduced variable errors and enhanced systematic errors of memory.

ACKNOWLEDGMENTS

Preparation of this manuscript was supported by National Science Foundation Grant BNS-9119800. I wish to thank Cathleen O'Toole for many valuable suggestions.

REFERENCES

Bahrick, H. P. (1984a). Associations and organization in cognitive psychology: A reply to Neisser. *Journal of Experimental Psychology: General, 113,* 36–37.

Bahrick, H. P. (1984b). Replicative, constructive and reconstructive aspects of memory — Implications for human and animal research. *Physiological Psychology, 12*(2), 53–58.

Bahrick, H. P. (1985). Associationism and the Ebbinghaus legacy. *Journal of Experimental Psychology, 11*(3), 439–443.

Bahrick, H. P., Hall, L. K., & Berger, S. A. (1996). Accuracy and distortion in memory for high school grades. *Psychological Science, 7*(5), 265–271.

Bartlett, F. C. (1932). *Remembering.* Cambridge, UK: Cambridge University Press.

Bock, M. (1980). Angenehme und unangenehme Erfahrungen aus gedaechtnispsychologischer Sicht — Bilanz einer 80jaehrigen Forschung. [Pleasant and unpleasant experiences from the perspectives of the psychology of memory — Evaluation of 80 years of research]. *Psychologische Beitraege, 22,* 280–292.

Brewer, W. F. (1988). Memory for randomly sampled autobiographical events. In U. Neisser & E. Winograd (Eds.), *Remembering reconsidered: Ecological and traditional approaches to the study of memory* (pp. 21–90). Cambridge, UK: Cambridge University Press.

Bruce, D., & Van Pelt, M. (1989). Memories of a bicycle tour. *Applied Cognitive Psychology, 3*(2), 137–156.

Christianson, S. (1992). Remembering emotional events: Potential mechanisms. In S. Christianson (Ed.), *The handbook of emotion and memory: Research and theory* (pp. 307–340). Hillsdale, NJ: Lawrence Erlbaum Associates.

Dooling, J. D., & Christiaansen, R. E. (1977). Episodic and semantic aspects of memory for prose. *Journal of Experimental Psychology: Human Learning and Memory, 3*(4), 428–436.

Edwards, A. (1942). The retention of affective experiences — A criticism and restatement of the problem. *Psychological Review, 49,* 43–53.

Fischoff, B. (1975). Hindsight ≠ foresight: The effect of outcome knowledge on judgement under uncertainty. *Journal of Experimental Psychology: Human Perception and Performance, 1,* 288–299.

Freud, S. (1962). *The standard edition of the complete works of Sigmund Freud* (Vol. 3, J. Sprachey, Trans.). Toronto: Hogarth. (Original work published 1899)

Gilbert, G. M. (1938). The new status of experimental studies on the relationship of feeling to memory. *Psychological Bulletin, 35,* 26–35.

Gordon, K. (1905). Ueber das Gedaechtnis fuer affektiv bestimmte Eindruecke [Memory for experiences characterized by affect]. *Archiv fuer die gesamte Psychologie, 4,* 337–458.

Hall, J. F. (1990). Reconstructive and reproductive models of memory. *Bulletin of the Psychonomic Society, 28*(3), 191–194.

Hasher, L., & Griffin, M. (1978). Reconstructive and reproductive processes in memory. *Journal of Experimental Psychology: Human Learning and Memory, 4*(4), 318–330.

Holmes, D. S. (1970). Differential change in affective intensity and the forgetting of unpleasant personal experiences. *Journal of Personality and Social Psychology, 15*(3), 234–239.

Isen, A. M. (1984). Toward understanding the role of affect in cognition. In R. S. Wyer & T. K. Srull (Eds.), *Handbook of social cognition* (Vol. 3, pp. 179–236). Hillsdale, NJ: Lawrence Erlbaum Associates.

Jersild, A. (1931). Memory for the pleasant as compared with memory for the unpleasant. *Journal of Experimental Psychology, 14,* 283–388.

Kihlstrom, J. F. (1989). On what does mood-dependent memory depend? *Journal of Social Behavior and Personality, 4*(2), 23–32.

Koch, H. L. (1930). The influence of some affective factors upon recall. *Journal of General Psychology, 4,* 171–190.

Koriat, A., & Goldsmith, M. (1994). Memory in naturalistic and laboratory contexts: Distinguishing the accuracy-oriented and quantity-oriented approaches to memory assessment. *Journal of Experimental Psychology: General, 123*(3), 297–315.

Linton, M. (1975). Memory for real-world events. In D. A. Norman & D. E. Rumelhart (Eds.),

Explorations in cognition (pp. 376–404). Orlando, FL: Academic Press.

Linton, M. (1982). Transformations of memory in everyday life. In U. Neisser (Ed.), *Memory observed: Remembering in natural contexts* (pp. 77–99). San Francisco, CA: Freeman.

Loftus, E. F. (1975). Leading questions and the eyewitness report. *Cognitive Psychology, 7,* 560–572.

Loftus, E. F. (1982). Memory and its distortions. In A. G. Kraut (Ed.), *G. Stanley Hall lectures* (pp. 119–154). Washington, DC: American Psychological Association.

Mandler, G. (1992). Memory, arousal and mood: A theoretical integration. In S. Christianson (Ed.), *The handbook of emotion and memory: Research and theory* (pp. 93–110). Hillsdale, NJ: Lawrence Erlbaum Associates.

McCloskey, M., & Zaragoza, M. (1985). Misleading post-event information and memory for events: Arguments and evidence against the memory impairment hypotheses. *Journal of Experimental Psychology: General, 114*(1), 1–16.

Murphy, K. R., & Balzer, W. K. (1986). Systematic distortions in memory-based behavior ratings and performance evaluations: Consequences for rating accuracy. *Journal of Applied Psychology, 71*(1), 39–44.

Neisser, U. (1982). Snapshots or benchmarks? In U. Neisser (Ed.), *Memory observed: Remembering in natural contexts* (pp. 43–48). San Francisco, CA: Freeman.

Revelle, W., & Loftus, D. A. (1992). The implications of arousal effects for the study of affect and memory. In S. Christianson (Ed.), *The handbook of emotion and memory: Research and theory* (pp. 113–149). Hillsdale, NJ: Lawrence Erlbaum Associates.

Ross, B. M. (1991). *Remembering the personal past.* New York: Oxford University Press.

Ross, M. (1989). Relation of implicit theories to the construction of personal histories. *Psychological Review, 96*(2), 341–357.

Rubin, D. C., & Kozin, M. (1984). Vivid memories. *Cognition, 16,* 81–95.

Sharp, A. A. (1938). An experimental test of Freud's doctrine of the relation of hedonic tone to memory revival. *Journal of Experimental Psychology, 22,* 395–418.

Skowronski, J. J., Betz, A. L., Thompson, C. P., & Shannon, L. (1991). Social memory in everyday life: Recall of self-events and other-events. *Journal of Personality and Social Psychology, 60*(6), 831–843.

Thompson, C. (1985). Memory for unique personal events: Effects of pleasantness. *Motivation and Emotion, 9,* 277–289.

Wagenaar, W. A. (1986). My memory: A study of autobiographical memory over six years. *Cognitive Psychology, 18,* 225–252.

Waters, R., & Leeper, R. (1936). The relation of affective tone to the retention of experiences of daily life. *Journal of Experimental Psychology, 19,* 203–215.

Woodworth, R. (1938). *Experimental psychology.* New York: Holt.

Wulf, F. (1922). Ueber die Veraenderung von Vorstellungen (Gedaechtnis und Gestalt). [Concerning changes of imagery (Memory and Gestalt)]. *Psychologische Forschung, 96*(2), 341–357.

Yuille, J. C., & Tollestrup, P. A. (1992). A model of the diverse effects of emotion on eyewitness memory. In S. Christianson (Ed.), *The handbook of emotion and memory: Research and theory* (pp. 201–216). Hillsdale, NJ: Lawrence Erlbaum Associates.

6

Gendered Narratives: Elaboration, Structure, and Emotion in Parent–Child Reminiscing Across the Preschool Years

Robyn Fivush
Emory University

The ways in which we each experience and understand the events of our lives is an integral part of who we are; through our autobiographical memories each of us creates a narrative self (Bruner, 1987; Fivush, 1988; Linde, 1993; Neisser, 1988). Moreover, these narratives are created in social interaction. Through sharing our experiences with others, we come to understand and organize our experiences in ever more meaningful ways (Fivush, Haden, & Reese, 1995; Middleton & Edwards, 1990; Miller, 1994). It is in this sense that our autobiographical memories can be said to be socially constructed (Nelson, 1993; Pillemer & White, 1989). The ways in which we reminisce with others about our life experiences influence the ways in which we come to understand and represent those experiences to ourselves.

Given this theoretical framework it is intriguing that there is growing evidence of gender differences in adults' autobiographical memories. Adult females report more memories from early childhood than do adult males, and they report earlier memories than do males (Cowan & Davidson, 1984; Friedman & Pines, 1991; Mullen, 1994). Women's memories also seem to be more detailed and vivid than those of males. Women's reports of early childhood memories are longer and more elaborated than those of males (Friedman & Pines, 1991), and, in a study of married couples, Ross and Holmberg (1990) found that independent raters judged women's memories to be more accurate and more vivid than the memories of their male counterparts. Women's autobiographical memories may also be more emotionally laden than are males' (Davis, 1991).

That women's autobiographical reports are more elaborate, vivid, and emotional than those of males is not surprising given the large literature on gender differences in language and communication (see Graddol & Swann, 1989, for a review). In virtually all types of social interaction, women have been found to be more communicatively fluent than men. Women talk more, they talk about more intimate topics (Aries & Johnson, 1983; Balswick & Avertt, 1977; Wheeler & Nezlek, 1977), and they talk in more emotionally disclosing ways than men. Interestingly, these gender differences can be seen as early as 6 years of age (Tannen, 1990). Much of this literature has been interpreted from the feminist notion of "voice" (Belenky, Clinchy, Goldberger & Tarule, 1986; Gilligan, 1982). Women are posited to be more relationally oriented than men (e.g., Chodorow, 1978), in that they value interpersonal relationships and work to maintain those relationships more than do men. Concerns with interpersonal relatedness lead women to value communication and emotional disclosure more than men do, which in turn leads to differences in communicative styles or voices. Thus, gender differences in autobiographical recounts may reflect these more overarching gender differences in relationships and discourse.

Even so, gender differences in autobiographical recounts may have particular implications for one's understanding of one's life and one's self. Because women talk about their autobiographical experiences in more elaborated and detailed ways than do men, women may come to think about and represent their experiences in more elaborated and emotional ways as well. Following from Vygotskian notions of cognitive socialization (Vygotsky, 1978; Wertsch, 1985), the tools one has available for sharing cognitive skills with others come to be internalized and used for representing these skills intrapsychically. In this way, the ways in which women and men reminisce with others come to reflect the ways in which they represent their autobiographical experiences to themselves. Through a richer understanding of their past experiences, women may come to have a richer understanding of their narrative self; indeed, women's sense of self may be more heavily based on their autobiographical narratives than are men's.

EXPLORING GENDER DIFFERENCES IN AUTOBIOGRAPHICAL MEMORY

Although intriguing, arguments about gender differences in autobiographical memory are still quite speculative. In this chapter, I explore possible gender differences in autobiographical memory and narrative more explicitly by examining the ways in which mothers and fathers reminisce with their daughters and sons across the preschool years. By examining families, and by examining patterns of reminiscing both developmentally and longitudinally, I can begin to address some of the important questions about gender differences in autobiographical recounts. First, participants are assessed in familiar and personally meaningful contexts. Many gender differences in communication are attenuated when males and females are assessed in more intimate situations. For example, although women generally talk about emotions more than do men, when men are conversing with intimate partners (especially female partners) they are as emotionally open as females (Dosser, Balswick, & Halverson, 1983). This suggests that males may be more sensitive to context in revealing their emotions than are females. Virtually all of the data on gender differences in autobiographical remembering have been gathered through experimental interviews, a context in which participants are asked to recount their past experiences to a virtual stranger. Perhaps in the context of talking about the past with close family members, males would be as elaborative and emotional as females.

More important, by examining parent–child reminiscing, I can begin to examine possible antecedents to the adult gender differences. Are parents talking about the past differently with daughters than with sons? Are girls and boys talking about the past in different ways? Further, by examining parent-child talk about the past longitudinally across the preschool years, I can also examine how gender-related patterns of reminiscing may develop over time. Thus I can examine how possible gender differences in parent–child reminiscing might relate to the gender differences we see in adults.

Given the gender differences in adult autobiographical remembering, I was centrally concerned with three aspects of parent–child talk about the past. First, how elaborative are parents and children in these conversations? Elaborations are essentially a measure of how much information is included in the recall, and how detailed that information is. Second, how coherently structured is the narrative? In recounting a past event, one must go beyond telling what occurred. One must orient the listener to the who, where, and when of an event, as well as tell the listener why the event was interesting or important to recall at all (Labov, 1982; McCabe & Peterson, 1991; Neisser, 1982). Although gender differences in this aspect of recounting the past have not been explicitly studied, the fact that adult females are judged to have more accurate and vivid memories than adult males might suggest that their recall is more narratively coherent as well. Finally, I was interested in the emotional content of these narratives. How do parents and children talk about emotional aspects of past events?

These questions must be considered in light of previous research on parent–child talk about the past. Personal narratives are the most prevalent and the earliest form of narrative discourse (Miller, 1994). Children begin talking about the past almost as soon as they begin to talk (Eisenberg, 1985; Engel, 1986; Miller & Sperry, 1988). However, in these early conversations, it is the adult who provides much of the content and the structure of the recall, and the child participates by confirming or repeating what the parent said. Between the ages of 2 and 3 years, children become more competent participants in these conversations; they recall increasing amounts of information about the past, and even begin to bring up past events as topics of conversations, although they are still somewhat dependent on adults to help retrieve and organize remembered information. With increasing age, children become increasingly able to recount past events as coherently organized narratives. By the age of about 5, most children are able to narrate their personal experiences effectively, although these skills obviously continue to develop throughout childhood (Hudson & Shapiro, 1991; Peterson & McCabe, 1983).

Recent research indicates that children are learning autobiographical recall skills through participating in early adult-guided conversations about the past. Reese, Haden, and Fivush (1993) showed that mothers who engage in highly elaborated and detailed talk about the past with their young children facilitate their children's developing abilities to recount details about their personal experiences. Along similar lines, several studies have demonstrated that mothers who use particular types of narrative devices in reminiscing with their very young children, such as attention to spatial orientation or emotional evaluation, have children who begin to focus on these aspects of narrative in their own independent accounts later in development (Fivush, 1991b; McCabe & Peterson, 1991; Peterson, 1990). These kinds of results point to the important role that early adult guidance plays in children's developing abilities to recount their past experiences in more detailed and coherent ways.

PARENT–CHILD REMINISCING

In the study reported here, I was particularly interested in documenting the ways in which mothers and fathers might differentially discuss the past with their daughters and their sons, and how these patterns might relate to children's developing autobiographical remembering. To address this concern, White middle-class two-parent families were visited in their homes when the target child was 40 months of age and again when the child was 70 months of age. The analyses reported here are part of a larger longitudinal study of parent–child narrative interactions throughout the preschool years. The original group consisted of 24 families. However, by the 70-month age point, only 17 families were still able to participate. Thus all analyses reported here are based on these 17 families. Eight of the children were females and nine were males. At each of the time points, each parent was asked to sit in a quiet place in the home alone with the child and discuss several special past events that the parent and child had experienced together. Other than these very unstructured directions, parents were free to select events for discussion, and to structure the conversations in any way that seemed appropriate. Thus the style, content, and length of the conversations were determined by the dyad. All conversations were tape recorded and transcribed verbatim for coding and analysis.

Event Selection

Because parents were free to select events to reminisce about, there was little control over the type of events discussed. Still, there was a great deal of similarity in the events that families selected. Virtually all of the events were quite positive and most were child centered. Most frequently discussed events included trips to amusement parks, theme parks such as Disney or SeaWorld, science museums, zoos, and aquariums. There were no apparent differences in the kinds of events that mothers and fathers selected to recall, with the exception that only father–son dyads discussed sporting events. The dyad also determined the length of the conversation. As shown in Table 6.1, there were no statistical differences in the number of conversational turns, measured as the number of shifts between conversational partners (a standard measure of conversational length), between mothers and fathers with daughters or with sons.

Parent–Child Elaborativeness

The first question of interest was the level of elaboration and detail in these conversations. As already discussed, elaborativeness was conceptualized as

TABLE 6.1
Mean Number of Conversational Turns in Parent–Child Conversations at Each Time Point

	Time Point	
	40 Months	70 Months
Mother–daughter	54.42	56.62
Mother–son	44.75	44.37
Father–daughter	62.91	58.57
Father–son	41.10	67.02

the amount of unique information provided by either the parent or the child. Related to this is the level of confirmation. Confirmation refers to the feedback provided by the parent when the child provides information about the event under discussion. (Note that although children often confirmed their parent's memory elaborations, these confirmations did not function in the same way as adults' confirmations. Children's confirmations were essentially responses to yes–no questions, rather than the provision of feedback about their parent's responses. Thus it did not make sense to examine children's confirmations in this context.) A few examples illustrate these concepts. The first is a father and daughter discussing a trip to the beach:

Father: Do you remember what shoes we wore?
Daughter: Watershoes.
Father: What was fun about the watershoes?

Here we see that the child provides an elaborative response to the father's question. The father then further elaborates on this response by incorporating more information about the watershoes (they were fun) into his following question. The next example is a mother–daughter dyad discussing a trip to Bermuda:

Mother: Do you remember what we did on Christmas when we went to Bermuda?
Daughter: We went to the beach.
Mother: We sure did.

Again, the child provides an elaborative response to the mother's question, which the mother then confirms. Confirmations function both to inform the child about the accuracy of his or her response and also to praise the child for participating in the reminiscing. In this way, confirmations inform the child that his or her participation is valued, that the parent is interested in what the child has to say about the event being recalled.

Analyses focused on how mothers and fathers elaborated and confirmed with daughters and with sons (see Reese, Haden, & Fivush, 1996, for details). Given the previous research on gender differences in adults' autobiographical memories, it seemed possible that mothers would elaborate and confirm more than fathers regardless of gender of the child. On the other hand, because fathers are reminiscing with a close family member, it also seemed possible that fathers would be as elaborative and confirming as mothers in this situation. Perhaps more interesting are possible parental differences with daughters and with sons. If parents are more elaborative and confirming with daughters than with sons, then we would have some evidence for differential socialization that might be related to the gender differences we see among adults. Moreover, by examining these patterns over time, we can examine consistency in parental reminiscing styles, and how any such differences might be related to children's developing ability and/or interest in participating in reminiscing with their parents.

The mean number of elaborations mothers and fathers provided per event discussed with daughters and with sons at 40 months and at 70 months is shown in Fig. 6.1. Overall, mothers and fathers did not differ significantly from each other, but both mothers and fathers were somewhat more elaborative with daughters than with sons, $F(1,15) = 6.86$, $p = .07$. This was particularly true at 40 months of age. Moreover, whereas mothers do not substantially change their level of elaborativeness over time, fathers become more elaborative with sons, but not with daughters. Figure 6.2 shows the mean number of confirmations per event used by mothers and fathers at each time point. Again, mothers and fathers do not differ from each other, but they do differ depending on the gender of the child with whom they are reminiscing. Mothers are using more confirmations with daughters than with sons at both 40 months and 70 months of age. Fathers also use more confirmations with daughters than with sons at 40 months of age, but not at 70 months of age, $F(1, 15) = 6.20$, $p < .05$. Note that although it appears that fathers use more confirmations with sons than with daughters at 70 months, this effect did not reach statistical significance, probably due to the extremely high variability in the data and the small sample size.

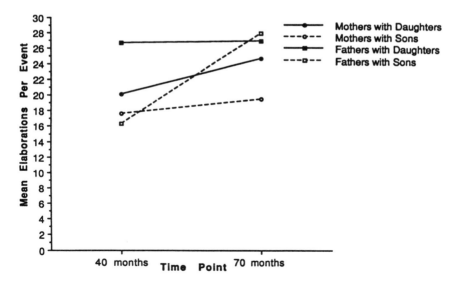

FIG. 6.1.   Mean frequency of elaborations used by mothers and fathers with daughters and sons over time.

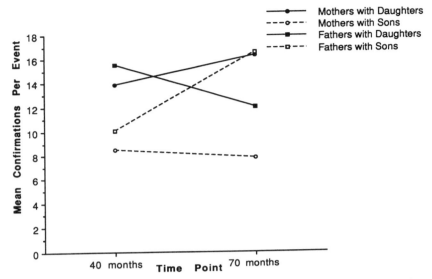

FIG. 6.2. Mean frequency of confirmations used by mothers and fathers with daughters and sons over time.

Although somewhat complex, the pattern indicates that gender of child is more important in influencing these conversations than gender of parent. When the children are 40 months of age, the patterns are quite clear; both mothers and fathers are significantly more elaborative and more confirming with daughters than with sons, and there are no systematic differences between mothers and fathers. At 70 months of age, mothers are still more elaborative and more confirming with daughters than with sons, but fathers show no significant differences in elaborations or confirmations between daughters and sons. Overall, it seems that, especially early in development, parents are engaging in highly embellished reminiscing with daughters and are working to encourage their daughters' participation in these conversations. In contrast, reminiscing with sons is less detailed and less engaging than with daughters.

However, we need to consider the child's role in these conversations. Figure 6.3 displays the mean number of elaborations provided by girls and boys with mothers and fathers at each time point. Intriguingly, at both ages girls are recalling more information about past events than are boys, $F(1,15) = 8.22$, $p < .01$. Somewhat unexpectedly, both boys and girls are also recalling more information with their fathers than with their mothers at both ages, $F(1,15) = 4.71$, $p < .02$. It is not immediately apparent why children might recall more information when reminiscing with their fathers than with their mothers. What is interesting, however, is that we are seeing gender differences in amount of information recalled about past events as

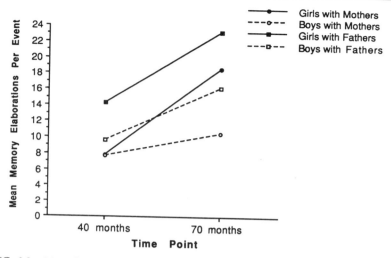

FIG. 6.3. Mean frequency of elaborations used by daughters and sons with mothers and fathers over time.

early as 40 months of age. The fact that parents, and especially mothers, are more elaborative and more confirming with daughters than with sons might suggest that parents are socializing their daughters to engage in reminiscing to a greater extent than they do their sons. On the other hand, that girls are recalling more information about their past experiences than boys even at 40 months of age might suggest that daughters are eliciting elaborations and confirmations from their parents to a greater extent than are sons. At this point, we can only conclude that parent–child reminiscing is more detailed in parent–daughter dyads than in parent–son dyads, and this is true for both the parent and the child. Why this might be so is discussed further after the additional analyses are presented.

Parent–Child Narrative Structure

As alluded to earlier, giving a coherent account of a past experience involves more than simply reporting what happened. One must also provide information that places the event in an appropriate context. In order to accomplish this, autobiographical accounts often conform to canonical narrative structures (Bruner, 1987; Fivush & Haden, 1997; Nelson, 1993). Narratives give form and meaning to experience through the use of specific narrative devices (Labov, 1982; Peterson & McCabe, 1983). Of course, the narrator must tell what happened during the event, through the use of referential statements ("We went on the biggest roller coaster," "We watched the parade."). But in addition, narratives provide a spatial-temporal framework for the event through the use of orientations. Orientations include information about when and where the event occurred ("It was last winter," "When we went to Baltimore . . ."), as well as introducing the major participants (" . . . and my brother came with us," "My best friend was at the party."). Orientations can further provide information that link this event to other significant events and people in the narrator's life. For example, in recounting a trip to the beach, the narrator can talk about how this event is related to other vacation experiences, and explicitly link events as related and important because of the people involved (e.g., "We had fun at the beach just like we did when we went camping because Grandma was there. We always have fun with Grandma."). This example further demonstrates a second critical element of narrative structure: Narratives provide subjective or personal meaning to the event through the use of evaluations. Evaluative devices include ways of linguistically marking intensity ("It was the best thing that ever happened to me." "She was very naughty."), suspense ("And then guess what happened."), emphasis ("It was so cold, it was freezing." "And we ran and ran and ran."), and internal states ("And my mother didn't know where SeaWorld was." "I really wanted to go to her party."). Through the use of evaluative devices, narrators convey their responses to and perspectives on the experience.

In these parent–child conversations, I was able to examine how these various narrative devices were used by mothers, fathers, daughters, and sons. If we assume that more vivid and detailed narratives are also more coherently organized, then we might expect mothers to use more orientations and evaluations than fathers. And again, it was of interest to determine if mothers and fathers used more orientations and evaluations with daughters than with sons, as well as how these patterns might change developmentally, and how they might relate to the ways in which girls and boys used these narrative devices in their own reminiscing.

All of the parents' and children's utterances were categorized as orientations, referentials, or evaluations. Table 6.2 displays the mean number of each utterance type used by mothers and fathers with daughters and sons at each time point, and Table 6.3 displays these means for the children. Statistical analyses reveal that parental narrative structure shows little difference between mothers and fathers, talking with daughters or with sons, at either 40 months or 70 months. The means indicate that even early in development, parents are using a variety of narrative devices, and are placing events discussed in both a spatial-temporal and evaluative context, although both mothers and fathers increase in their use of referentials, $F(1, 13) = 3.65$, $p = .08$, and evaluations, $F(1,13) = 10.13$, $p < .01$, as their children become more competent participants in these conversations.

In contrast to the parental patterns, children show significant differences

TABLE 6.2
Mean Number of Each Narrative Utterance Used by Parents at
Each Time Point

Parent	Narrative Utterance Type		
	Orientations	Referentials	Evaluations
Time 1: 40 Months			
Mothers			
With daughters	6.52	7.95	6.10
With sons	5.25	9.69	6.99
Fathers			
With daughters	9.16	11.52	9.47
With sons	6.66	6.42	3.37
Time 2: 70 Months			
Mothers			
With daughters	8.52	10.19	12.75
With sons	7.28	11.21	12.25
Fathers			
With daughters	7.71	13.09	13.86
With sons	8.40	15.85	10.57

in their narrative structure both across time and by gender. Not surprisingly, children are recounting more information in these conversations at 70 months than at 40 months of age, and there is an increase in all three categories of narrative information, $F(1,13) = 43.25$, $p < .001$. More interesting, although girls and boys are providing referential information, which is the bare bones of the narrative, with equal frequency, girls are placing their accounts in spatial-temporal and evaluative perspective to a greater extent than are boys. Girls use more orientations, $F(1,13) = 8.82$, $p < .01$, and more evaluations, $F(1,13) = 3.87$, $p = .07$, at both ages than do boys. And again, both girls and boys are reminiscing differently with fathers than with mothers. Specifically, children use more referentials, $F(1,13) = 5.86$, $p < .01$, and more evaluations, $F(1,13) = 3.45$, $p < .05$, with fathers than with mothers. This finding is obviously related to the earlier finding that children recount more information overall with fathers than with mothers, but provides additional information about exactly what kinds of information are being differentially recalled.

In summary, there is little evidence of differences between mothers and fathers in either their narrative structure of reminiscing or in how they reminisce with their daughters and their sons. Yet, as early as 40 months of age, we are again seeing differences in how girls and boys reminisce. Girls are providing more of a framework for placing events discussed in context than are boys. So although there is little evidence of parental socialization of gender differences in autobiographical recounts, there is evidence of

TABLE 6.3
Mean Number of Each Narrative Utterance Used by Children at Each
Time Point

Child	Narrative Utterance Type		
	Orientations	*Referentials*	*Evaluations*
	Time 1: 40 Months		
Daughters			
With mothers	2.00	1.67	1.52
With fathers	3.64	4.36	3.64
Sons			
With mothers	1.71	2.35	1.97
With fathers	2.46	3.29	2.25
	Time 2: 70 Months		
Daughters			
With mothers	4.95	7.71	9.19
With fathers	6.58	10.19	10.19
Sons			
With mothers	2.67	4.71	4.01
With fathers	3.89	7.79	6.59

child gender differences in autobiographical memory emerging very early in development.

Parent–Child Talk About Past Emotions

A third aspect of these conversations that was of interest was the ways in which parents and children talked about emotions associated with their past experiences. Although little research has focused on talk about past emotions, there is a substantial body of literature on emotion discourse in general. As mentioned at the beginning of this chapter, women are more emotionally expressive overall than men (see Brody & Hall, 1993, for a review). Women talk more about emotional experience than men, women report valuing emotions more than men, and women express more non-verbal emotions than men. Notably, these patterns hold for the emotions of happiness, sadness, and fearfulness, but it is somewhat reversed for anger. Women seem to express less anger than men, and certainly report feeling less comfortable expressing anger than do men.

Whereas gender differences in emotion experience in adults is quite robust, there is less evidence of gender differences in children's emotion understanding (see Brody, 1985, for a review), and limited research on the development of talk about emotion. Children begin to use emotion words very early in development, perhaps as early as 13 months of age (see

Bretherton, Fritz, Zahn-Waxler, & Ridgeway, 1986, for a review). Between 24 and 28 months of age, children are talking about both their own and others' emotional states. Parents who talk more about emotions have children who talk more about emotions, and parental talk about emotion is strongly linked to other measures of children's developing socioemotional skills (Denham, Zoller, & Couchoud, 1994; Dunn, Brown, & Beardsall, 1991). There is also some suggestion that mothers may talk about emotions more with daughters than with sons (Dunn, Bretherton, & Munn, 1987).

The inclusion of emotional aspects of past events may serve a very special function in reminiscing. By including emotional states and reactions in our narratives about the past, we provide information about our involvement with an event. In this way, emotions are similar to narrative evaluations (and, indeed, there is some overlap in the categories). However, explicit mention of emotion conveys information about the meaning of an event that is deeper and more personal than many of the narrative evaluative devices discussed previously. Emotions are really what tie our autobiographical narratives to our self-concept. It is the emotional tone and texture of an event that gives it personal meaning, that moves the narrative beyond an interesting story to a self-defining one. Moreover, by selecting particular emotions to focus on in discussing the past, the narrator is conveying information about enduring aspects of the self. For example, a person who recounts many experiences with anger conveys a very different sense of self than one who recounts many sad experiences (see Fivush, 1993, for a full discussion of these issues).

In looking at how emotions were discussed in these parent–child conversations about past events, then, I was interested in two major issues. First, of course, is the possibility that mothers and fathers would differ in how much emotions are incorporated into their reminiscing. Related to this is whether parents talk more about emotional aspects of the past with their daughters than with their sons, and whether girls and boys talk about emotions differentially. The second major issue was the kind of emotions talked about. Even if there are no gender differences in the overall amount of emotion talked about during reminiscing, mothers, fathers, daughters, and sons might talk about qualitatively different emotions.

All emotion words used by mothers, fathers, daughters, and sons were counted and these means are displayed in Fig. 6.4 for parents at each time point and in Fig. 6.5 for children at each time point (see Adams, Kuebli, Boyle, & Fivush, 1995, for details). The results are straightforward. Although mothers and fathers did not differ significantly from each other, both mothers and fathers used substantially more emotion words in reminiscing with their daughters than with their sons at both time points, $F(1,15) = 5.92$, $p < .05$. For children, there were no differences between girls and boys in the number of emotion words used in these conversations

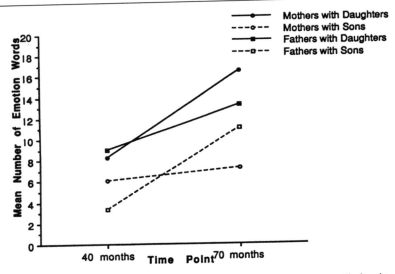

FIG. 6.4.   Mean number of emotion words used by mothers and fathers with daughters and sons over time.

at 40 months of age, but by 70 months of age, girls are using significantly more emotion words than are boys, especially when conversing with their mothers, $F(1,15) = 4.31$, $p = .055$. However, overall, children, especially boys, use more emotion words with their fathers than with their mothers, $F(1,15) = 4.98$, $p < .05$, a finding similar to the one reported earlier that children are recounting more information overall with fathers than with mothers. I return to this finding in interpreting the overall results.

The overall pattern is one that suggests that parents are facilitating children's discussion of past emotions. That there were no child gender differences early on indicates that the parental differences are not a simple response to child differences or elicitation. The emerging gender difference between girls and boys suggests that girls may begin to talk about emotional aspects of the past to a greater extent than boys because they have been exposed to more of this type of talk earlier in development.

An examination of what emotions were discussed in these conversations is quite revealing. All emotion words were categorized as expressing sadness (sad, unhappy), fear (afraid, scared), anger (angry, mad), general negative state (cranky, upset, fussy), or general positive state (happy, joyful). The number of times each of these emotional states were referenced by mothers and fathers with daughters and sons across time is shown in Table 6.4. (Children's use of emotion words was too low overall to make division into these categories meaningful.) Recall that the vast majority of events discussed by parents and children were positive, child-centered events such as going to the circus, the zoo, SeaWorld, and so on. Thus it is not

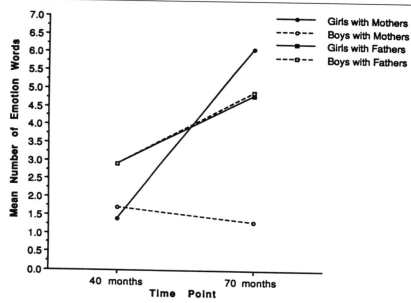

FIG. 6.5. Mean number of emotion words used by daughters and sons with mothers and fathers over time.

surprising that the overwhelming majority of emotion words used in these conversations expressed general positive emotion. Still, even given the types of events discussed, negative emotions were referenced, and as can be seen, negative emotions are discussed differently with daughters than with sons. Parents talk about sadness more than twice as much with daughters than with sons. Parents also talk about general negativity significantly more with daughters than with sons. Perhaps because of the reminiscing context, anger was rarely mentioned at all, and there were no apparent differences in the mention of anger with daughters versus sons. That parents talk more frequently about sadness and negative emotion with daughters than with sons is important because other research indicates that the sheer frequency,

TABLE 6.4
Frequency of Mention of Specific Emotion Terms by Parents With Daughters and Sons Across Time

	With Daughters	With Sons
Sadness	29	12
Fear	24	17
Anger	6	3
Negative emotion	37	23
Positive emotion	269	193

rather than the proportion, with which children are exposed to specific types of language influences the kind of language children come to use independently (Fivush, 1991b; Hoff-Ginsburg, 1991; McCabe & Peterson, 1991).

In summarizing this set of analyses, once again, there is little evidence of differences between mothers and fathers in how they discuss emotional aspects of the past. However, both mothers and fathers discuss the past in more emotionally laden ways with daughters than with sons. Parents also focus more on sadness and negativity with daughters than with sons. Although there are no differences between girls and boys early in development, by the end of the preschool years, girls are referring to emotional aspects of past events significantly more than are boys.

PUTTING IT ALL TOGETHER: THE STRUCTURE OF PARENT–CHILD REMINISCING

In these analyses, I have examined parent–child conversations about past events from three different vantage points: the level of elaboration and confirmation in these conversations, the narrative structure and the emotional content. Although some of the findings are a bit complex, several major themes emerge. First, in no analysis were there significant differences between mothers and fathers in how they reminisced with their preschool children. Thus, contrary to some of the previous literature (Cowan & Davidson, 1984; Davis, 1991; Friedman & Pines, 1991; Mullen, 1994; Ross & Holmberg, 1990), I found no evidence of adult gender differences in autobiographical reminiscing. However, the second major theme to emerge was strong gender differences between preschool girls and boys in their autobiographical reminiscing. Girls recalled more information than boys, placed their autobiographical recounts in spatial-temporal and evaluative context to a greater extent than boys, and recounted emotional aspects of their past experiences more than did boys.

Related to the obtained gender differences between girls and boys, there was evidence that mothers and fathers reminisced differently with daughters than with sons. In particular, parents elaborated more with daughters than with sons, and they confirmed their daughters' participation to a greater extent than their sons'. This was especially true earlier in the preschool years and for mothers. In addition, parents discussed emotional aspects of the past to a greater extent with daughters than with sons, and this remained stable across the preschool years for both mothers and fathers. More specifically, parents discussed sadness and general negativity more with daughters than with sons. However, parents did not show any differential use of narrative structure with daughters than with sons at either age point.

That parents reminisced differently with daughters and sons might support the notion that parents are socializing girls to reminisce differently than boys. Through more elaborative, confirming, and emotional reminiscing with daughters, parents might be teaching their daughters to value and to engage in more detailed, more emotional reminiscing than their sons. Yet this conclusion is not completely warranted given the findings. Even at 40 months of age, girls are recalling more information and more narratively coherent information than are boys. Thus it is just as likely that girls are eliciting a particular type of reminiscing from their parents as that parents are socializing girls to reminisce in particular ways. Perhaps the most surprising finding in this study is that gender differences in autobiographical memory are already apparent at 40 months of age. Yet, these gender differences are no longer apparent when we look at the adults in this study. Thus we are left with two issues to resolve. First, how can we explain the gender differences in children's autobiographical reminiscing? And, second, given this finding, how can we explain the lack of gender differences between mothers and fathers?

UNDERSTANDING THE DEVELOPMENT OF GENDER DIFFERENCES IN AUTOBIOGRAPHICAL MEMORY

Why might we see gender differences in autobiographical narratives so early in development? One possibility has to do with language development. Reminiscing is clearly a verbal task, and children who are more advanced in their linguistic abilities would most likely be able to engage in reminiscing in more sophisticated ways. There are two reasons why this explanation is probably not correct. First, although there is a general perception that females are more advanced in language than males, recent meta-analyses of this literature suggest that the actual differences in language development are quite small, accounting for very little of the variance (Hyde & Linn, 1988). Second, we were able to assess the language abilities of the children in this study. Girls and boys did not differ in mean length of utterance (MLU), a well-accepted measure of grammatical development, at 40 months. Nor did they differ in their vocabulary, as measured by the Peabody Picture Vocabulary Test, at 70 months of age.

Still, there are other aspects of language use and discourse that might be particularly important for reminiscing. As I discussed at the beginning of this chapter, there are gender differences in communicative fluency. Fluency refers to the pragmatics of language, the ability to take turns, maintain topic, and communicate effectively. These skills are not as heavily studied in the language learning literature as grammar and vocabulary, and we simply do not know at this point if there are gender differences in the development of these abilities. However, there is some suggestion that young females are better able to engage in, or at least enjoy conversational interaction more than young males. Simply looking at the amount of time girls spend in conversation with others as compared with boys indicates that girls converse in one-on-one interaction more than boys (Lever, 1976; Tannen, 1990).

Indeed, these patterns begin very early in development, with parents spending more time in face-to-face verbal communication with daughters than with sons (Caldera, Huston, & O'Brien, 1989). Even before girls are able to participate verbally in conversation, parents spend more time vocalizing to daughters than to sons, and they work harder to get their daughters to "respond" with a gurgle or a coo than they do their sons (Goldberg & Lewis, 1969). What these findings suggest is that from the very beginning of development, girls are engaging in more conversational interaction than are boys. Because they are conversing more in general, perhaps girls are also conversing about the past more than boys from an early age. If this were true, then it would not be surprising that girls are more advanced in their autobiographical reminiscing than boys by the age of 40 months.

This discussion raises the perennial question of "nature versus nurture." Are girls conversing more than boys because they are inherently better able to do so? Or are girls conversing more than boys because of their socialization environment? As with all such dichotomies, the answer must be an interaction of the two. Girls and boys are already somewhat different in their temperament at birth (Davis & Emory, 1995), with female infants better able to maintain a steady, alert state for longer periods of time than male infants. Related to this, male infants are more irritable and have more difficulty returning to a state of equilibrium following arousal than do female infants. Female infants are also better able to maintain eye gaze than male infants. Thus males, who need to be comforted more, will most likely be held close to the body with their face on the adults shoulder, whereas females are likely to be held cradled along the arm in face-to-face gaze with the adult. What all this means is that female infants engage in face-to-face interaction more frequently than males beginning at birth.

These slight temperamental differences (and of course, there is great variability within each gender group as well as variability between genders) are exacerbated by parental gender-typed beliefs. Parents expect their female infants to be more interested in face-to-face communication and they work harder to maintain face-to-face communication with daughters than with sons. In this way, girls may come to engage in face-to-face communication more and more frequently as they develop than do boys.

And because of this exposure, girls may come to develop better skills for communication than boys, and may even come to enjoy this kind of activity more than do boys. Thus, when reminiscing becomes part of conversational interaction, girls may be better prepared to engage in this activity and may even enjoy this activity more than boys.

Moreover, once parents and children begin to reminisce together, parents seem to engage girls in this activity in somewhat different ways than boys. Although there were no differences in how parents structured their narrative recounts of past events with daughters or with sons, parents did elaborate more with girls, confirm more, and talk about more emotional aspects of the past with girls than with boys. In all of these ways, parents may be helping girls to engage in reminiscing to a greater extent than boys. Especially by including more emotions in reminiscing with girls than with boys, parents may be highlighting the personal meaning of the past more, and making more explicit links between past experiences and self-concept with girls than with boys. In this light, the different emotions discussed with girls and boys are especially intriguing. By focusing on sadness and general negativity with daughters more than with sons, parents may be implicitly highlighting these emotions as important self-defining emotions. Through participating in these conversations, girls may be learning to define themselves more emotionally, and perhaps more negatively, than do boys (see Fivush, 1991a, for a discussion of how this might relate to gender differences in depression).

Regardless of why girls and boys may come to reminisce differently, the fact that they do may have important implications for the development of autobiographical memory and self-concept. As argued earlier in the chapter, the ways in which we reminisce with others about our past experiences may come to influence the ways in which we think about and represent those experiences to ourselves. Because girls are recounting their past in more detailed, more narratively coherent and more emotionally laden ways than boys, girls may come to have more detailed, coherent, and emotional memories of their personal past than boys. Moreover, if we assume that girls engage in reminiscing more frequently than boys, which seems warranted given their better skills at this task, then we might also assume that girls come to value reminiscing to a greater extent than boys. That is, there is a dialectical relationship between the frequency with which we engage in particular activities and the value we place on them. Activities that are engaged in frequently come to be highly valued, and as their value increases, so does their frequency (see Rogoff, 1990, for related arguments). In this way, it is possible that females come to value reminiscing, both with others and to themselves, more than do males (e.g., Ross & Holmberg, 1990). The ultimate outcome may be that females define themselves more strongly in terms of their autobiographical experiences than do males.

UNDERSTANDING CONTEXT EFFECTS ON GENDER DIFFERENCES IN AUTOBIOGRAPHICAL MEMORY

Given these arguments, the second issue we need to address is why there were no differences between mothers and fathers in this study. Certainly, we would have expected mothers to reminisce in more elaborated, more coherent, and more emotional ways than fathers, yet they did not. Thus the arguments about how females and males might reminisce about and represent their past experiences in different ways needs to be modified to account for this finding.

An emerging theme in the literature on gender focuses on the contextual specificity of gender-related behaviors (Deaux & Major, 1987). Rather than arguing for essentialist, often biologically given differences between males and females, it is becoming quite clear that gender differences reflect a complex interplay of biology, culture, and situation specificity (Golombok & Fivush, 1994). Moreover, many gender differences are better conceptualized as differences in preferences or styles, rather than as differences in inherent abilities. In order to understand when and why gender differences might and might not emerge in reminiscing, then, we need to understand how this activity relates to other aspects of gender-related activities.

Reminiscing is an activity that closely resembles personal disclosure. Indeed, conversations that include reminiscing are clearly those conversations in which people are revealing personal information. Although it is quite clear that females engage in personal disclosure more frequently than males, it is also the case that males do engage in personal disclosure in some situations. In particular, males will disclose in situations in which they are conversing with a close intimate, usually a female (Aukett, Ritchie, & Mill, 1988). The conclusion to be drawn from this literature is that females disclose in a wide variety of contexts, whereas males only display this behavior in a more circumscribed set of contexts. By analogy then, it seems quite likely that females engage in elaborated reminiscing in a wide variety of contexts, but males only engage in this activity in the presence of a close other, such as a family member. What this means is that males are capable of engaging in elaborated reminiscing, but they choose not to do so as frequently or with as many partners as females.

Thus adult gender differences in reminiscing may be very context dependent. However, this raises an additional paradox. If preschool girls and boys are already showing substantial differences in reminiscing, when and where are boys learning the skills of elaborated reminiscing that they display as fathers? There is no clear answer from the data presented here, but the fact that children reminisce differently with fathers than with mothers poses an intriguing possibility. Recall that both boys and girls recall more information, place recalled information in evaluative context to a greater extent, and recall more emotional information with fathers than with mothers. This holds despite the fact that overall conversations are no longer with fathers than with mothers, nor do mothers and fathers differ on any other dimension. That is, children are recalling differently with fathers than with mothers even though fathers are not recalling differently than mothers.

This pattern indicates that gender differences in autobiographical reminiscing may not be attributed simply to one conversational partner or the other, but reflect interactive influences of the dyad. Just as parents' reminiscing was dependent on the gender of the child, children's reminiscing was dependent on the gender of the parent. Children may reminisce in more elaborated, evaluative, and emotional ways with their fathers than their mothers for at least two reasons. First, conversing one-on-one with the father about any topic may be a less frequent, and therefore more special activity than conversing with the mother. This, in turn, may lead children to be more engaged in conversation with the father than the mother, leading to the differences in recall. Second, mothers may be better than fathers at reading their children's nonverbal cues, such as emotional expression and gestural communication. This seems likely both because females are substantially better than males at reading nonverbal communication (Brody & Hall, 1993), and because mothers spend more time and are therefore more familiar with their children than fathers. (This is true in general, and is true in our families, in which the mothers were all the primary caregivers.) Thus, children may have to recall more verbally with fathers than with mothers because less of their nonverbal communication is being understood.

In any case, the fact that children are recounting more information, more evaluative information, and more emotional information with fathers than with mothers suggests the possibility that fathers are responding to their child's reminiscing style. Because children are reminiscing in such rich ways, fathers reminisce in rich ways. Mothers do not need as much from their children to elicit rich reminiscing. Thus fathers may be able to reminisce in richly elaborated, coherent, and emotional ways in conversations with close family members who facilitate this style of reminiscing through their own elaborated participation. Note that although fathers are capable of reminiscing in ways similar to mothers in this highly intimate situation, the argument is that they need the support of a conversationally rich partner to elicit and maintain this level of reminiscing. That females display this style of reminiscing in a wide variety of contexts with a wide variety of partners

supports the earlier interpretation that females seem to have more elaborated and emotional autobiographical memories than males, and that they
value this style of rich reminiscing to a greater extent than males.

CONCLUSIONS

In this chapter, I explored gender differences in mothers and fathers
reminiscing with their daughters and sons. Contrary to previous research
with adults, I found little evidence of differences in the ways in which
mothers and fathers talked about past events with their preschool children,
indicating that adult gender differences in autobiographical remembering
may be quite context dependent. However, both mothers and fathers
reminisced differently with daughters than with sons. Parents were more
elaborative, more confirming, and more emotional in discussing the past
with daughters than with sons. In turn, girls and boys also differed
markedly. Girls recalled more information overall, placed that information
in a more coherent spatial-temporal and evaluative context, and incorporated emotional aspects of the past into their discussions to a greater extent
than boys. That gender differences in autobiographical memory emerged so
early in development was somewhat surprising and it suggests that girls and
boys may be developing different understandings of their personal pasts
and of themselves.

ACKNOWLEDGMENTS

Many people collaborated on the research reported in this chapter. I
especially want to thank Catherine Haden, Elaine Reese, Janet Kuebli,
Susan Adams, and Patricia Boyle for their conceptual input and insightful
comments during all phases of this research, as well as their hard work in
collecting, transcribing, coding, and analyzing data. The research project
was funded by the Spencer Foundation.

REFERENCES

Adams, S., Kuebli, J., Boyle, P., & Fivush, R. (1995). Gender differences in parent–child
conversations about past emotions: A longitudinal investigation. *Sex Roles, 33*, 309–323.
Aries, E., & Johnson, F. (1983). Close friendship in adulthood: Conversational content
between same-sex friends. *Sex Roles, 9*, 1183–1196.
Aukett, R., Ritchie, J., & Mill, K. (1988). Gender differences in friendship patterns. *Sex Roles,*

19, 57–66.

Balswick, J., & Avertt, C. P. (1977). Differences in expressiveness: Gender, interpersonal orientation and perceived parental expressiveness as contributing factors. *Journal of Marriage and the Family, 38*, 121–127.

Belenky, M. F., Clinchy, B. M., Goldberger, N. R., & Tarule, J. M. (1986). *Women's ways of knowing: The development of self, voice and mind.* New York: Basic Books.

Bretherton, I., Fritz, J., Zahn-Waxler, C., & Ridgeway, D. (1986). Learning to talk about emotions: A functionalist perspective. *Child Development, 57*, 529–548.

Brody, L. (1985). Gender differences in emotional development: A review of theories and research. *Journal of Personality, 53*, 102–149.

Brody, L. R., & Hall, J. A. (1993). Gender and emotion. In M. Lewis & J. M. Haviland (Eds.), *Handbook of emotions* (pp. 447–460). New York: Guilford.

Bruner, J. (1987). Life as narrative. *Social Research, 54*, 11–32.

Caldera, Y. M., Huston, A. C., & O'Brien, M. (1989). Social interactions and play patterns of parents and toddlers with feminine, masculine and neutral toys. *Child Development, 60*, 70–76.

Chodorow, N. (1978). *The reproduction of mothering.* Berkeley: University of California Press.

Cowan, N., & Davidson, G. (1984). Salient childhood memories. *The Journal of Genetic Psychology, 145*, 101–107.

Davis, M., & Emory, E. (1995). Sex differences in neonatal stress reactivity. *Child Development, 66*, 14–27.

Davis, P. (1991, July). *Gender differences in autobiographical memory.* Paper presented at the NATO Advanced Research Conference: Theoretical perspectives on autobiographical memory, LaGrange, UK.

Deaux, K., & Major, B. (1987). Putting gender into context: An interactional model of gender-related behavior. *Psychological Review, 94*, 369–389.

Denham, S. A., Zoller, D., & Couchoud, E. A. (1994). Socialization of preschoolers' emotion understanding. *Developmental Psychology, 30*, 928–936.

Dosser, D. A., Jr., Balswick, J. O., & Halverson, C. F., Jr. (1983). Situational context of emotional expressiveness. *Journal of Counseling Psychology, 30*, 375–387.

Dunn, J., Bretherton, I., & Munn, P. (1987). Conversations about feeling states between mothers and their young children. *Developmental Psychology, 23*, 132–139.

Dunn, J., Brown, J., & Beardsall, L. (1991). Family talk about feeling states and children's later understanding of others' emotions. *Developmental Psychology, 27*, 448–455.

Eisenberg, A. R. (1985). Learning to describe past experiences in conversation. *Discourse Processes, 8*, 177–204.

Engel, S. (1986). *Learning to reminisce: A developmental study of how young children talk about the past.* Unpublished doctoral dissertation, City University of New York, New York.

Fivush, R. (1988). The functions of event memory: Some comments on Nelson and Barsalou. In U. Neisser & E. Winograd (Eds.), *Remembering reconsidered: Ecological and traditional approaches to memory* (pp. 277–282). New York: Cambridge University Press.

Fivush, R. (1991a). Gender and emotion in mother–child conversations about the past. *Journal of Narrative and Life History, 1*, 325–341.

Fivush, R. (1991b). The social construction of personal narratives. *Merrill-Palmer Quarterly, 37*, 59–82.

Fivush, R. (1993). Emotional content of parent–child conversations about the past. In C. A. Nelson (Ed.), *The Minnesota Syposium on child psychology: Memory and affect in development* (pp. 39–77). Hillsdale, NJ: Lawrence Erlbaum Associates.

Fivush, R., & Haden, C. (1997). Narrating and representing experience: Preschoolers' developing autobiographical recounts. In P. van den Broek, P. A. Bauer, & T. Bourg (Eds.), *Developmental spans in event comprehension and representation: Bridging fictional and actual events* (pp. 169–198). Hillsdale, NJ: Lawrence Erlbaum Associates.

Fivush, R., Haden, C. A., & Reese, E. (1995). Remembering, recounting and reminiscing: The development of autobiographical memory in social context. In D. C. Rubin (Ed.), *Reconstructing our past: An overview of autobiographical memory* (pp. 341–359). Cambridge, UK: Cambridge University Press.

Friedman, A., & Pines, A. (1991). Sex differences in gender-related childhood memories. *Sex Roles, 25,* 25–32.

Gilligan, C. (1982). *In a different voice: Psychological theory and women's development.* Cambridge, MA: Harvard University Press.

Goldberg, S., & Lewis, M. (1969). Play behavior in the year old infant: Early sex differences. *Child Development, 40,* 21–32.

Golombok, S., & Fivush, R. (1994). *Gender development.* New York: Cambridge University Press.

Graddol, D., & Swann, J. (1989). *Gender voices.* Cambridge, MA: Blackwell.

Hoff-Ginsburg, E. (1991). Mother–child conversations in different social classes and communicative settings. *Child Development, 62,* 782–796.

Hudson, J. A., & Shapiro, L. (1991). Effects of task and topic on children's narratives. In A. McCabe & C. Peterson (Eds.), *New directions in developing narrative structure* (pp. 89–136). Hillsdale, NJ: Lawrence Erlbaum Associates.

Hyde, J. S., & Linn, M. C. (1988). Gender differences in verbal ability: A meta-analysis. *Psychological Bulletin, 104,* 299–324.

Labov, U. (1982). Speech actions and reactions in personal narrative. In D. Tannen (Ed.), *Analyzing discourse: Text and talk* (pp. 219–247). Washington, DC: Georgetown University Press.

Lever, J. (1976). Sex differences in the games children play. *Social Problems, 23,* 478–487.

Linde, C. (1993). *Life stories; The creation of coherence.* New York: Oxford University Press.

McCabe, A., & Peterson, C. (1991). Getting the story: A longitudinal study of parental styles in eliciting narratives and developing narrative skill. In A. McCabe & C. Peterson (Eds.), *Developing narrative structure* (pp. 217–253). Hillsdale, NJ: Lawrence Erlbaum Associates.

Middleton, D., & Edwards, D. (1990). Conversational remembering: A social psychological approach. In D. Middleton & D. Edwards (Eds.), *Collective remembering* (pp. 23–45). London: Sage.

Miller, P. J. (1994). Narrative practices: Their role in socialization and self-construction. In U. Neisser & R. Fivush (Eds.), *The remembering self: Construction and accuracy in the life narrative* (pp. 158–179). New York: Cambridge University Press.

Miller, P., & Sperry, L. L. (1988). Early talk about the past: The origins of conversational stories of personal experience. *Journal of Child Language, 15,* 293–315.

Mullen, M. K. (1994). Earliest recollections of childhood: A demographic analysis. *Cognition, 52,* 55–79.

Neisser, U. (1982). Snapshots or benchmarks? In U. Neisser (Ed.), *Memory observed* (pp. 43–48). San Francisco, CA: Freeman.

Neisser, U. (1988). Five kinds of self-knowledge. *Philosophical Psychology, 1,* 35–59.

Nelson, K. (1993). The psychological and social origins of autobiographical memory. *Psychological Science, 1,* 1–8.

Peterson, C. (1990). The who, when and where of early narratives. *Journal of Child Language, 17,* 433–455.

Peterson, C., & McCabe, A. (1983). *Developmental psycholinguistics: Three ways of looking at a child's narrative.* New York: Plenum.

Pillemer, D. B., & White, S. H. (1989). Childhood events recalled by children and adults. *Advances in Child Development and Behavior, 21,* 297–340.

Reese, E., Haden, C. A., & Fivush, R. (1993). Mother–child conversations about the past: Relationships of style and memory over time. *Cognitive Development, 8,* 403–430.

Reese, E., Haden, C., & Fivush, R. (1996). Mothers, fathers, daughters, sons: Gender differences in autobiographical reminiscing. *Research on Language and Social Interaction, 29,* 27–56.

Rogoff, B. (1990). *Apprenticeship in thinking.* New York: Oxford University Press.

Ross, M., & Holmberg, D. (1990). Recounting the past: Gender differences in the recall of events in the history of a close relationship. In M. P. Zanna & J. M. Olson (Eds.), *The Ontario Symposium: Vol. 6, Self- inference processes* (pp. 135–152). Hillsdale, NJ: Lawrence Erlbaum Associates.

Tannen, D. (1990). Gender differences in topical coherence: Creating involvement in best friend's talk. *Discourse Processes, 13,* 73–90.

Vygotsky, L. S. (1978). *Mind in society: The development of higher psychological processes.* Cambridge, MA: Harvard University Press.

Wertsch, J. (1985). *Vygotsky and the social formation of mind.* Cambridge, MA: Harvard University Press.

Wheeler, L., & Nezlek, J. (1977). Sex differences in social participation. *Journal of Personality and Social Psychology, 35,* 742–754.

7

The Effects of Aging on Autobiographical Memory

Gillian Cohen
The Open University

Although it is interesting and important to identify and describe the effects of aging on autobiographical memory, it is much more illuminating if we try to understand these changes by asking how and why such changes occur. Accordingly, this chapter adopts a functional approach and is mainly concerned with age-related changes in the function of autobiographical memory and age-related changes in the nature and quality of the memories. The goal is to achieve some insight into the relationship between the function of autobiographical memory and the quality of these memories.

AGE-RELATED CHANGES OF FUNCTION

It is of particular interest to consider how the function of autobiographical memory might change with the approach of old age because any such changes affect the way that we interpret and evaluate changes in the quality of the memories. With this approach we can consider whether the effects of aging on autobiographical memories are adaptive and appropriate for the changed functions.

Autobiographical memory serves a wide range of different functions that may vary in importance across individuals and across the life span. Some researchers (e.g., Robinson, 1992) have divided these into interpersonal functions and intrapersonal functions. Further distinctions can be made within each category and an additional category of knowledge-based functions can also be identified.

Interpersonal Functions

Interpersonal functions dominate when remembering occurs in a social context and can be further classified into the following subcategories.

Social Interaction. Autobiographical memories serve as material for conversations. Exchanging experiences helps to maintain interest in current interactions and allows the individual to participate in the group.

Self-Disclosure. Sharing autobiographical memories is a means to establish relationships and develop intimacy and friendship. It is interesting in this context to note that negative memories may serve this function more effectively than positive ones. In general, we only disclose negative memories in a relationship of trust and intimacy or when we intend to increase the existing level of intimacy.

Empathy. Autobiographical memories provide a basis for interpreting other people's behavior, inferring their emotions and opinions, and guiding responses. We understand how people feel about their experiences by remembering how we ourselves felt about similar experiences.

Intrapersonal Functions

Intrapersonal functions are served when autobiographical remembering takes the form of private reminiscence.

Mood Regulation. Selection of appropriate autobiographical memories to contemplate can serve to sustain a good mood or alter a poor mood and so to regulate emotional state. The emotions and affect connected with relationships may be moderated by rehearsing the history of those relationships.

Self-Concept Formation. Review of autobiographical memories operates to construct, preserve, or edit the self-concept, to create a self-history, and to carry out self-assessment against long-term goals. It may be a means to deal with unresolved conflicts or to reconcile differences between the ideal self and the actual self.

Knowledge-Based Functions

In addition to these two types of function we can also add knowledge-based functions. The information contained in episodic autobiographical memories may be entered into semantic memory and become part of the store of general knowledge that is utilized in many everyday situations.

General Knowledge. The accumulation of general knowledge occurs when general event knowledge representations are constructed by processes of abstraction or inductive inference from specific autobiographical memories.

Problem Solving. Autobiographical memories provide analogical experiences of past problems that can offer possible strategies and solutions for current problems and guide plans for future actions.

There is some indication that the relative importance of these functions changes with age, although the evidence is scanty, and information about the frequency, nature, and purpose of intrapersonal reminiscence is necessarily dependent on the accuracy of self-reports. A study by Lieberman and Falk (1971) supports the intuition that the middle-aged use reminiscence primarily for problem solving, whereas, for the elderly, the intrapersonal functions predominate. Similarly, Webster and Cappeliez (1993) reported that in the first three decades of life, reminiscence serves primarily for problem solving or identity construction. In late old age there is an accelerated increase in a form of life review described as "death preparation." However, as Fitzgerald (1996) pointed out, the evidence that the nature of reminiscence changes across the life span is far from being clear cut.

Intuition also suggests that the social functions of autobiographical memory are important in old age when the maintenance of social interactions is particularly necessary for well-being, but there is also evidence that these functions are less effective as social skills often decline in old age (Gold, Arbuckle, & Andres, 1994). In conversation, old people may offer autobiographical memories but tend to indulge in long and boring monologues, sometimes called *habitual narratives*, with little regard for whether their listener is interested or has heard it before. This behavior, labeled by Gold et al. as *off-target verbosity*, makes it less likely that the memories will serve to develop or maintain satisfying social interactions. The increased incidence of depression in old age (Cohen, 1990) also suggests that the mood-regulating function of autobiographical memory is more necessary, or perhaps less effective.

Holland and Rabbitt's (1991) study comparing reminiscence in community- dwelling elderly people and a group of elderly people, matched for age and IQ, living in residential care institutions, also sheds light on the function of autobiographical memory.The striking difference between these groups was that the community dwelling group, like young people, recall and rehearse more recent memories than remote ones. By contrast, the institutionalized elderly recalled and rehearsed more remote memories than recent ones. People who are out and about in the world, leading busy active lives, do not have so much occasion for mulling over old memories. On the other hand, it is reasonable to surmise that people who are in residential care do not think about the present and the recent past so much because they have no need to plan and manage their daily lives and because their current lives are probably monotonous and unimportant. Rabbitt and Winthorpe (1988) expressed this in a memorable phrase: "Remote events may be more often rehearsed in memory as the theatre of the mind becomes the only show in town" (p. 302). Holland (1992) made the same point:

> If an elderly person readily recalls many early events and few recent ones . . .
> then we have some idea that this person no longer has need to maintain him
> or herself in the present and has greater need to preserve his or her identity by
> remembering and recounting what they used to do, and also has more need to
> remember more active, perhaps happier days. (p. 203)

Two conclusions can be drawn from Holland and Rabbitt's (1991) study. First, the shift toward greater rehearsal of remote events is consistent with increased importance of the self-concept and self-history functions of autobiographical memory. Second, this shift is not necessarily a consequence of age per se, but rather a secondary consequence of the restricted lifestyle that is often associated with old age. Taken together, the introspective evidence, observations, and intuitions all point to age-associated changes in the relative importance of the different functions of autobiographical memory.

AGE-RELATED CHANGES IN MEMORY QUALITY

Conflicting results have characterized research into age-related changes in memory quality. Of the studies outlined in the following, some have produced results showing that there are no age differences in the quality of autobiographical memories; others have shown an age-related deterioration in memory quality. This conflict can be resolved if it is recognized that, in old age, autobiographical memory diverges to form two distinct classes of memory. One type of memory is clear and detailed; the other type of memory is overgeneral, imprecise, and lacking in detail. Different studies, using different methods of eliciting recall, are tapping into these different types of autobiographical memory. In this section I review some of these studies and show how the methods employed affect the results obtained.

A number of different methods have been used in autobiographical memory research and one of the most crucial differences between them is whether the memories that are elicited are self-selected or experimenter-designated. The word cuing method (Rubin, Wetzler & Nebes, 1986) elicits self-selected memories because it allows participants to select any memory that is associated with the cue. In some studies participants are asked to recall any memories from designated life periods (e.g., Rabbitt & Winthorpe, 1988) or simply to recall a subset of their most vivid memories (Cohen & Faulkner, 1988). These methods vary in the degree of constraint they impose on self-selection, but, by and large, they allow participants to choose which memories to report.

Experimenter-designated memories are elicited when participants are asked to recall specific events, as in eyewitness testimony or flashbulb memory studies or studies that ask for recall of specific events such as the birth of a sibling or details of old TV shows. Holland and Rabbitt (1990) designated the type of event and life period, asking participants to describe specific events such as "an incident when you first started work" or "an incident from when you were first married." This instruction allows some freedom of choice but within a fairly restricted set. The degree of self-selection that is allowed is an important factor because, given a free choice, the memories people select for report will tend to be those that are particularly accessible, vivid, and significant and these may be quite unrepresentative of the rest of their autobiographical memories.

Self-Selected Memories

When memories are self-selected, as opposed to being experimenter desig-nated, the general pattern of results is that there are no age differences in vividness and detail. In Cohen and Faulkner's (1988) study, which com-pared 154 people between 20 and 87 years old, self-selected memories were rated for vividness, with *vivid* being defined as clear and detailed. The unexpected finding was that the elderly group rated their memories as more vivid than did the young and middle-aged. Furthermore, vividness declined with the age of the memory (i.e. the retention interval) for the young and middle-aged but, for the elderly, remote memories were not significantly less vivid than recent memories. Regression analyses showed that the age groups differed in which variables were significant predictors of vividness. For the young and middle-aged, vividness was predicted by the emotionality of the event, by the retention interval, and by how old they were when the event occurred. For the elderly group, however, the predictors of vividness were different. For the elderly people the vividness of their memories was predicted by the frequency with which they were rehearsed and how important they were judged to be.

These results suggested that older adults were sampling from a pool of personally significant memories that had been maintained by frequent rehearsal. Because they had been so often rehearsed, these self-selected memories were highly accessible and were preserved in their original vividness and detail. As can be seen from the examples shown in Table 7.1, there was no indication that these very remote memories were overgeneral and lacking in specificity. Almost all the memories elicited were of unique events, and, although participants were only asked to supply a brief description of two or three sentences, this is sufficient to show that these memories are highly specific even though they have survived for over 50 years.

Similar findings emerged from Rabbitt and Winthorpe's (1988) study. They also found that frequency of spontaneous everyday rehearsal was the strongest predictor of memory quality, especially for the oldest participants. Indeed, they concluded that "the old, increasingly, could *only* produce well rehearsed memories" (p. 306).

A particularly impressive example of this kind of well-maintained memory has been reported by Hoffman and Hoffman (1990) . Howard Hoffman produced a 44-page transcript of his memories of his experiences in World War II and reproduced the same memories 4 years later. The content and organization were virtually unchanged. The Hoffmans concluded:

There is a subset of autobiographical long-term memory which is so permanent and largely immutable that it is best described as archival. From this

TABLE 7.1
Examples of Highly Specific Remote Memories From Early Life Recalled by Elderly People 50–70 Years After the Event (Cohen & Faulkner, 1988)

Being wrapped in a blanket and taken down to the cellar by my mother as zeppelin raids were on. (69 years ago)

Opening a sea-chest full of carpenters' tools stored in the larder without permission. (60 years ago)

The shame of wetting myself when I stood up at prayers in my infant school. I was too timid to ask to leave the room. (65 years ago)

My sailor uncle returned home in the middle of the night, woke me up to see glow worms all round his cap. (65 years ago)

Father taking me to the park to see rabbits, poking my finger through the wire, and having it bitten. (50 years)

perspective archival memory consists of recollections that are rehearsed, readily available for recall and selected for preservation over the lifetime of the individual . . . they define the self and constitute . . . the sense of identity over time. (p. 145)

The general conclusion is that self-selected memories form a subset of autobiographical memories consisting of highly specific, vivid memories that are of particular significance in the individual's life history and are frequently rehearsed.

Experimenter-Designated Memories

By contrast, a different picture emerges when age differences are examined for memories that are designated by the experimenter and that may not have been rehearsed very frequently. Here there is evidence of loss of specificity, confusions, and confabulation. Studies of age differences in eyewitness testimony (e.g., Cohen & Faulkner, 1989; Yarmey & Bull, 1978) have shown that the elderly are less accurate and are more susceptible to misleading information. The loss of detail and accuracy are shown particularly strikingly in a study of age differences in flashbulb memory by Cohen, Conway, and Maylor (1994). In this study, a younger group, 18 to 55 years old, and an older group, 64 to 84 years old, were asked to fill in a detailed questionnaire recording how they had heard the news of the resignation of the British prime minister Margaret Thatcher in 1992. They supplied a short narrative description of the reception event and answered specific questions about the event attributes including location (where they were), activities (what they were doing at the time), people (who was present), and source of the information (e.g., another person, radio, television). The questionnaire was administered within 10 to 14 days of the event and no age differences were apparent in the responses.

Eleven months later, all the participants were asked to complete the same questionnaire again. Consistency between original and retest responses was used as a measure of accuracy. The responses at this delayed retest were scored according to the degree of match with the initial responses. For example, a score of 2 was awarded if the original and retest responses mentioned identical information and the retest response included all the original information. A score of 1 was given to a response that was basically but not exactly the same. For example, the participant might have responded originally "in my kitchen at home" and responded at retest with the less specific "at home." Scores of 0 were given if a response was omitted or if it was completely different at retest. Using this scoring procedure and combining scores for all five responses, overall scores fell between 0 and 10.

Figure 7.1 shows the distribution of the scores for the young and elderly age groups.

For the purposes of this study, scores of 9 and 10 were classified as flashbulb memories. Of the younger participants, 90% achieved scores of 9 or 10 and were therefore classed as having flashbulb memory. Only 42% of the elderly group produced the same level of highly detailed and accurate recall.

It is interesting to compare the narrative descriptions produced by the respondents and to note the kind of errors and confabulations that characterized the recall of some of the older participants. Table 7.2 shows examples of descriptions supplied by young and elderly participants.

This recall of the event contains both confabulation (being at home instead of out shopping) together with omission of the critical details of source, people, and activity, and substitution of vague generalities. Other examples of recall by elderly participants contained errors that appeared to be schema-based reconstructions, such as substituting "being in the living-room" for "being in the kitchen" or "having breakfast" instead of "having

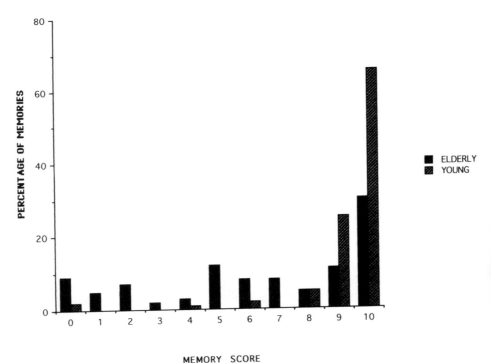

FIG. 7.1. The distribution of memory scores for young and elderly adults (from Cohen, Conway, & Maylor, 1994).

TABLE 7.2
Results From Experimenter-Designated Memories

Description Supplied by a Young Participant Classed as Having Flashbulb Memory

Initial test 10 days after the event: I was collecting a vacuum cleaner from the Miele depot in Abingdon at midday on 22nd November and heard the news broadcast giving the news that Margaret Thatcher had resigned—a radio was on in the warehouse.
Retest 11 months later: I was collecting a new vacuum cleaner from the Miele warehouse in Abingdon. Waiting for the appliance to be brought to me I could hear the 12.00 news which was coming from a radio.

Description Supplied by an Elderly Participant Classed as Having Non-Flashbulb Memory

Initial test 10 days after the event: My wife and I were shopping on Thursday morning and we were just about to go into Sainsbury's store when we met a neighbour and the first thing she said to us was "Have you heard the news?" We both said at the same time "What news?" and she then told us that a flash had just come on the radio that Margaret Thatcher had resigned.
Retest 11 months later: When Margaret Thatcher resigned I was at home. Previously we had heard on TV that there was some disturbance amongst the higher-ups in the government and when Geoffrey Howe made his speech in the Commons we saw and heard it on TV, I was flabbergasted at the idea of any of her own party (except Heath) being against her and when she was urged to resign I could hardly believe it.

lunch." Overall, the responses illustrated a very marked age-related increase in inaccuracy and loss of detail. Interestingly, those of the elderly who did report flashbulb memories, recalling the event in detail, were those who had rehearsed it most frequently. Cohen et al. (1994) concluded that although in younger people the strong emotion and surprise engendered by a dramatic event was sufficient to produce vivid and long-lasting memories, in older people the retention of detailed memories is critically dependent on rehearsal.

Overgeneral Memories

Memories that show the loss of specific details are known as overgeneral memories, although the concept of overgenerality is itself not very clearly defined. Holland (1992) distinguished between specificity and detail. Albeit closely linked, these two concepts are different. A person may recall a specific event (e.g., moving to a new house) as opposed to a general event (e.g., we used to go to the seaside). The specific event memory may be more or less detailed but general event memories, by their nature, are usually lacking in detail. Holland and Rabbitt (1990) interviewed elderly people and asked them to recall designated specific incidents from their past lives. At a second, follow-up interview they were pressed to produce additional details. Participants in their 70s were less able to recall thematically relevant details than a matched group of people in their 60s, but there was no age difference in specificity of recall. So in this example there appeared to be an age deficit for detail but not for specificity. However, other researchers, such as Williams (1996), do not distinguish between loss of specificity and loss of detail and simply identify the phenomenon as overgeneral memory. To illustrate the nature of overgeneral memories, Williams (1996) quoted an example from a psychotherapy interview with an emotionally disturbed patient.

This kind of exchange is interpreted as the patient being unable or unwilling to recall a specific memory. Of course, many people have memories for this type of repeated experience that cannot be decomposed into particular occasions. Linton (1982) reported that, over time, multiple memories of repeated trips to attend meetings had coalesced into a single generic memory so that she could not recall specific occasions. Nevertheless, there is evidence that this process of generalization is exaggerated by the effects of age and trauma. The memories of elderly people typically show characteristics of overgenerality when they are not drawn from the privileged set of frequently rehearsed and personally significant memories. As well as the elderly, several other groups of people have been identified as showing indications of overgeneral memory, including those who are emotionally disturbed or severely depressed, dense amnesics, and young children. Williams (1996) reported that emotional cue words like *clumsy*, *safe*, or *angry* elicit specific memories from control participants but general

TABLE 7.3
Extract From an Interview in Which the Patient is Producing Overgeneral Memories

Therapist: When you were young what sort of things made you happy?
Patient: Well, things used to be alright then: I mean better than they are now, I think. When my dad was there, he used to take me for walks on the Common sometimes after lunch on Sunday.
Therapist: Can you tell me about one such walk?
Patient: Well, we used to go out after lunch, sometimes we would take a ball and play around. Afterwards, we might go and see my granny who lived the other side of the Common.
Therapist: When you think back, now, can you remember any particular time? I want you to try to recall any one of these times. Any time will do, it doesn't have to be particularly important or special.
Patient: I remember there used to be other children on the Common sometimes. Sometimes they would be friends of mine and I would stop and chat to them for a while.
Therapist: Can you remember any particular time when you met any of your friends?
Patient: If it was winter there weren't usually many people about.

memories from people who have recently attempted suicide. Similar findings emerge from those diagnosed as having severe depression (Williams & Broadbent, 1986). Williams and Scott (1988) noted that, although all the emotional memories of depressed people are characterized by overgenerality, the emotionally positive memories are even less specific than emotionally negative memories. Baddeley and Wilson (1986) reported that patients with frontal lobe amnesia show loss of detail in autobiographical memories although they can recall specific episodes.

It is interesting that, as Nelson and her colleagues noted, young children also display the same phenomenon of overgeneral memory to some extent. Three-year-olds find it easier to respond to general questions like "What do you do in play group?" than to specific questions like "What did you do in play group this morning?" (Hudson & Nelson,1986; Morton, 1990). Nelson's (1988) earlier theory claimed that the ability to construct general event representations (GERs) precedes the ability to form specific autobiographical memories but she has since modified this view (Nelson, 1991). It is apparent that specific memories can sometimes be elicited if the right kind of specific cuing is employed and Nelson considers that new specific memories are stored briefly and transformed into a general memory if the event is repeated. The ability to form specific autobiographical memories that are more stable develops through the joint construction of narratives in conversation with caregivers who question children about their experiences and elaborate and confirm their answers Nevertheless, it is important to recognize that the tendency toward overgeneral autobiographical memory appears at both ends of the life span.

Explanations of Overgeneral Memory

A number of explanations have been proposed to account for the phenomenon of overgeneral memory. These proposed explanations can best be understood in terms of current theories about the way autobiographical memories are structured and organized. There is general consensus that memories are organized in nested hierarchies and two principles of organization have been identified: a categorical or thematic principle of organization and a temporal principle. Thus memories may be organized in terms of categories such as "holidays" or "jobs," or in terms of life periods such as "when I was at college" or "during the war." Some researchers, for example, Williams (1996), assume that the two principles generate separate hierarchies, but Barsalou (1988) suggested a plausible model, shown in Fig. 7.2, whereby these two principles are interlocked, with categories of events linked to particular time periods. In this example, for instance, the categories of "job," "vacation," and "home" are linked to the time periods

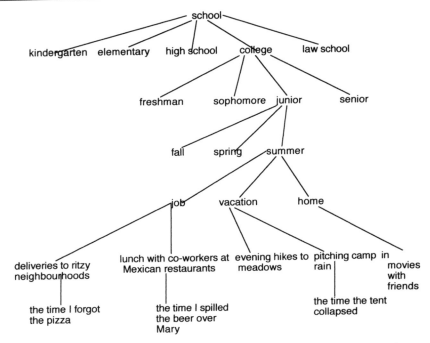

FIG. 7.2. Hierarchical organization of autobiographical memories (adapted from Barsalou, 1988).

"fall," "spring," and "summer." Barsalou's model stops short at the level of general events such as "pitching camp in the rain" and "lunch with coworkers" but it is possible to add a lower level to show some more specific events such as "the time I spilled the beer" and "the time the tent collapsed."

Possible explanations for overgeneral memory are listed in the following. They all agree that retrieval is aborted at too high a level in the hierarchy, but truncated retrieval is variously attributed to different causes, although these are not all mutually exclusive.

1. A lack of cognitive resources, particularly a deficit in working memory.
2. An impairment of the central executive that has been labeled dysexecutive syndrome (Baddeley & Wilson, 1988).
3. Repression—a learned response to block specific memories that are painful.
4. Loss of the distinctive details that give access to specific memories.
5. Failure to encode the spatial and temporal context of events.
6. Deadlock at the general event level.

7. Transmission deficit.

It is useful to consider the evidence and arguments for and against each of these explanations.

A Cognitive Resource Deficit. This explanation rests on the assumption that working memory capacity is required to carry out the operations of search and retrieval to recover autobiographical memories and that retrieval of lower level specific memories needs more working memory capacity than retrieval of higher level general ones.There is a good deal of evidence in support of this idea. Holland and Rabbitt (1990) found that recall of details correlated with scores on the AH4 intelligence test, which they used as an index of fluid cognitive resources, and also with sentence span. Those with lower scores for cognitive resources produced overgeneral descriptions of their autobiographical memories. C. A. Holland and L. Gallant (personal communication June, 1995) studied a group of severely depressed elderly people and found that the rated specificity of memories covaried with measures of depression and of working memory capacity. The more depressed patients were, the less specific their autobiographical memories. Holland and Gallant suggested that the link between severe depression and overgeneral memory is mediated by the cognitive deficits that are correlated with the depression. It is possible that one of the factors contributing to overgeneral memory in young children is their lower working memory capacity. (Whereas normal young adults have a working memory span of about 7–8 digits, 3-year-olds have a span of only 2 items and 5-year-olds of 4 items; Pascal-Leone, 1970). This explanation can therefore extend to the very old, the very young, and the depressed groups. In Holland's view, autobiographical memory is not a special case: The deficit in cognitive resources can also be shown to account for age effects in other forms of memory such as the loss of detail in elderly people's text recall.

The Dysexecutive Syndrome. This explanation rests on the assumption that executive control is mediated by the frontal lobes. The central executive, or supervisory attentional system (Norman & Shallice, 1980), is considered to incorporate the self-concept, to organize goals and plans, and to control search and construction processes. As such, it would necessarily be critically involved in the retrieval of autobiographical memories. Patients with damage to the frontal lobe areas of the brain typically exhibit clouding of autobiographical memory with loss of detail and a tendency to confabulate (Baddeley & Wilson, 1986). It is argued, therefore, that this overgenerality results from malfunction of the executive processes. This view is also consistent with the finding that lack of specificity correlates with poor performance on tests of executive function such as word fluency and digit cancellation (della Sala, Laiacona, Spinnler, & Trivelli, 1992). An explanation that links overgeneral memory to impairment of the frontal lobes offers a plausible account of the effects of aging on autobiographical memory because deterioration of frontal lobe functions is thought to result from normal aging (Parkin & Walter, 1991).

The Repression Explanation. Williams (1996) suggested that an important cause of overgeneral memories is a tendency to block specific memories that is learned in response to painful early experiences and is used as a means of controlling negative emotions. Williams cited evidence that early negative experiences contribute to overgeneral memory and that a tendency to produce generic memories rather than specific ones forms part of the posttraumatic stress disorder (PTSD) syndrome. The repression explanation is plausible for those who have suffered trauma and for those who are severely depressed or have attempted suicide, and it is consistent with the finding that memories retrieved to emotional cue words are particularly lacking in specificity. However it is less plausible as an account of overgeneral memory in young children or in the normal, nondepressed elderly.

Loss of Distinctive Details. In a series of ingenious experiments, Anderson and Conway (1993) showed that cuing with a distinctive detail gives rapid access to specific memories. Participants recalled autobiographical events and decomposed these memories into constituent details, subsequently identifying the most salient, distinctive detail. Comparisons of the efficacy of different details as cues for the recall of the rest of the memory showed that the distinctive detail was the most effective cue. Figure 7.3 illustrates the way the distinctive detail, "dancing with Angela," is the most effective cue for retrieving the component details of the whole experience of "meeting Angela."

This model might also be used to explain the relationship between aging and overgenerality. If aging causes distinctive details to be lost through decay, then specific memories would be harder to retrieve. As yet, the paradigm developed by Anderson and Conway (1993) has not been used to examine age differences, so the possibility that the dearth of specific autobiographical memories in old age results from loss of the distinctive details that would give access to them remains to be tested. However, this explanation is consistent with the findings from a study of age differences in very long-term retention of knowledge acquired from formal education (Cohen, Conway, & Stanhope,1992). As compared with younger adults, elderly people showed more forgetting of detailed and specific information, although there was no age difference in memory for general principles.

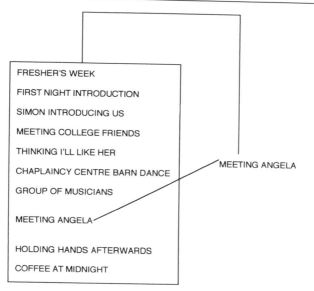

FIG. 7.3. Details of a specific memory accessed using the distinctive detail as a cue (from Anderson & Conway, 1993; reprinted by permission).

Deficit in Encoding Context. Craik (Craik & Jennings, 1992) identified age-related memory deficits with failure to encode the spatial and temporal context in which information is received or an event is experienced. This type of encoding deficit would produce overgeneral memories because overgeneral memories are, by definition, ones that lack contextual details. However, it follows that remote autobiographical memories for events that were experienced when the person was still young, and encoding was unimpaired, should not suffer from overgenerality. Holland and Rabbitt's (1990) finding that there is no difference in specificity between remote and recent memories therefore makes this explanation unlikely. Their results clearly indicated that loss of specificity originates at the retrieval stage and not at the encoding stage.

Deadlock at the General Event Level. Williams (1996) distinguished between memories that are categorically overgeneral (like "trips to the seaside") and memories that are temporally overgeneral (like "while I was at school") and claimed that, in depressed people, only categorically organized memories are abnormally overgeneral. His own view is that separate hierarchies exist for temporal and categorical organization and that search through the categorical hierarchy is deadlocked at the general event level, moving sideways to other self-referential categories instead of downward to more specific levels. According to Williams, a number of factors such as diminished cognitive resources and repression produce the deadlock. There-fore, this is not a stand-alone explanation but rather a restatement of the problem that invokes some of the mechanisms already discussed.

Transmission Deficit. Mackay and Burke (1990) in their node structure theory located the effects of aging within an interactive activation model of memory in which activation spreads through a network of interconnected nodes representing concepts. Retrieval occurs when activation of a node reaches threshold level. Activation spreads along connecting links between the nodes and the amount of activation transmitted is governed by linkage strength. In this model, linkage strength is determined by three factors: recency, frequency, and age. It declines with age but is increased by frequent or recent activation. Mackay and Burke did not apply their model to autobiographical memory, but it can provide a plausible account of age effects. It has the advantage that it can explain why access to the repertoire of frequently rehearsed self-selected memories is preserved, but for mem-ories that have not been frequently or recently rehearsed, activation is insufficient to reach the lowest levels of the hierarchy and specific memories with accompanying details cannot be accessed.

This model can also account for age-related overgenerality in other kinds of memory besides autobiographical memory. For example, Cohen and Burke (1994) showed how it could explain the difficulty in retrieving proper names, which becomes more acute with increasing age. Proper names are highly specific and are represented at terminal nodes reached by a single direct link. Activation reaches higher levels but transmission to a terminal node fails to occur if the link is infrequently used, weakened by aging, or both. Similarly, in hierarchies of intentions and actions, activation may sometimes dwindle so that memory for general intentions represented at higher levels of the hierarchy (like going upstairs to do something) persists, but memory for a specific intention represented at a lower level (such as what you went upstairs to do) is lost.

Although this analysis indicates that some of these explanations are better supported than others, there is clearly insufficient basis for opting for any one as the definitive account of overgeneral memory. Explanations in terms of a resource deficit, an impaired central executive, or a transmission deficit locate the cause of overgeneral memory at the retrieval stage, whereas the distinctive detail explanation suggests that defective storage is also implicated. Explanations in terms of blocking and deadlocking suggest, additionally, that inappropriate search strategies are employed.

The idea that in old age some memories are preserved with undiminished specificity and detail whereas others become overgeneral can be related to the controversy between copy and constructivist theories of autobiograph-ical memory. The subset of well-preserved specific memories typically shows characteristics of copy memories such as vivid imagery and the presence of irrelevant details. When copy representations have been lost, memories have to be reconstructed, and construction processes impose a load on cognitive resources that may exceed the processing capacity of some older people. In consequence, reconstructed memories would tend to suffer from incomplete or error-prone processing, resulting in the kind of overgeneral memories that have been observed.

CONCLUSION

This overview of studies of the effects of aging on autobiographical memory has shown that elderly people preserve a selected sample of memories in their original vividness and detail. These are memories of events that are personally important and are often thought about and talked about. Other memories that have less personal significance are not often recalled, recounted, or mentally rehearsed and these memories lose specificity and detail, becoming vague and general. It seems likely that some form of cognitive impairment that is part of the aging process makes it impossible to retain the whole corpus of autobiographical memories in full specificity and detail.

It is illuminating to relate these changes to the age-related changes in the function of autobiographical memory discussed earlier. The problem-solving function of autobiographical memory is likely to be poorly served by overgeneral memories, but the evidence suggests that this function becomes less important in old age. By contrast, it was noted that intrapersonal functions tend to assume greater importance in old age. We can plausibly speculate that it is difficult for an elderly person, especially one who is institutionalized, to maintain the self-concept. The setting of home life, familiar tasks, family, and friends that provided a supporting context for the self-concept may all be absent and the individual's sense of personal identity must depend on reviewing his or her life history. The subset of memories that are preserved without loss of detail by frequent rehearsal are likely to be specially selected as ones that best serve to maintain the self-concept. These specially selected memories are also appropriate for interpersonal functions. They can be exchanged in social interactions or offered in self-disclosure. The tendency of elderly people's conversation to be repetitive reflects the relatively small size of the set of memories that can be drawn on for this purpose. Overgeneral memories are like the chapter headings in the table of contents in a book: They provide an outline plan or framework of a life history but fail to flesh out the self-concept and are not of much interest in conversational exchanges. However, in the face of diminished cognitive capacity, a mechanism that retains selcted memories in detail and generalizes those that are not selected is probably an optimal solution for maintaining the most important functions of autobiographical memory.

REFERENCES

Anderson, S.J., & Conway, M. A. (1993) Investigating the structure of autobiographical memories. *Journal of Experimental Psychology: Learning, Memory and Cognition, 19,* 1178–1196.

Baddeley, A.D., & Wilson, B.A. (1986). Amnesia, autobiographical memory and confabulation. In D. C. Rubin (Ed.,) *Autobiographical memory* (pp. 225–252), Cambridge, UK: Cambridge University Press.

Baddeley, A. D., & Wilson, B. A. (1988). Frontal amnesia and the dysexecutive syndrome. *Brain and Cognition, 7,* 212–230.

Barsalou, L. W. (1988). The content and organization of autobiographical memories. In U. Neisser & E. Winograd (Eds.), *Remembering reconsidered: Ecological and traditional approaches to the study of memory* (pp. 193–243). New York: Cambridge University Press.

Cohen, G., & Burke, D. M. (1994). Memory for proper names: A review. In G. Cohen and D. M. Burke (Eds.), *Memory for proper names* (pp. 249–263). Hove, UK: Lawrence Erlbaum Associates.

Cohen, G., Conway, M. A., & Maylor, E. (1994). Flashbulb memories in older adults. *Psychology and Aging, 9,* 454–463.

Cohen, G., Conway, M. A., & Stanhope, N. (1992). Age differences in the retention of knowledge. *British Journal of Developmental Psychology, 10,* 153–164.

Cohen, G., & Faulkner, D. (1988). Life span changes in autobiographical memory. In M. M. Gruneberg, P. E. Morris and R. N. Sykes (Eds.), *Practical aspects of memory: Current research and issues* (Vol.1, pp. 277–282). Chichester, UK: Wiley.

Cohen, G., & Faulkner, D. (1989). Age differences in source forgetting: Effects on reality monitoring and eyewitness testimony. *Psychology and Aging, 4,* 1–20.

Cohen, G. D. (1990). Psychopathology and mental health in the mature and elderly adult. In J. E. Birren & K. W. Schaie (Eds.), *Handbook of the psychology of aging* (3rd ed., pp. 359–371). San Diego, CA: Academic Press.

Craik, F. I. M., & Jennings, J. M. (1992). Human memory. In F. I. M. Craik & T. A. Salthouse (Eds.), *The handbook of aging and cognition* (pp. 51–110). Hillsdale, NJ: Lawrence Erlbaum Associates.

della Sala, S., Laiacona, M., Spinnler, H., & Trivelli, C. (1992). Is autobiographical memory impairment due to a deficit of recollection? An overview of studies on Alzheimer dements, frontal and global amnesic patients. In M. A. Conway, D. C. Rubin, H. Spinnler, & W. A. Wagenaar (Eds.), *Theoretical perspectives on autobiographical memory* (pp. 451–472). Dordrecht, The Netherlands: Kluwer Academic.

Fitzgerald, J. M. (1996). Intersecting meanings of reminiscence in adult development and aging. In D. C. Rubin (Ed.), *Remembering our past: Studies in autobiographical memory* (pp. 00–00). Cambridge, UK: Cambridge University Press.

Gold, D. P., Arbuckle, T. Y., & Andres, D. (1994). Verbosity in older adults. In M. L. Hummert, J. M. Wiemann, & J. F. Nussbaum (Eds.), *Interpersonal communication in older adulthood: Interdisciplinary theory and research* (pp.107–129). Beverly Hills, CA: Sage.

Hoffman, A. M., & Hoffman, H. S. (1990). *Archives of Memory.* Lexington: University of

Kentucky Press.

Holland, C. A. (1992). The wider importance of autobiographical memory research. In M. A. Conway, D. C. Rubin, H. Spinnler, & W. A. Wagenaar (Eds.), *Theoretical perspectives on autobiographical memory* (pp. 195-205). Dordrecht, The Netherlands: Kluwer Academic.

Holland, C. A., & Rabbitt, P. M. A. (1990). Autobiographical and text recall in the elderly: An investigation of a processing resource deficit. *Quarterly Journal of Experimental Psychology, 42A*, 441-470.

Holland, C. A., & Rabbitt, P. M. A. (1991). Aging memory: Use versus impairment. *British Journal of Psychology, 82*, 29-38.

Hudson, J. A., & Nelson, K. (1986). Repeated encounters of a similar kind: Effects of familiarity on children's autobiographic memory. *Cognitive Development, 1*, 253-271.

Lieberman, M. A., & Falk, J. (1971). The remembered past as a source of data for research on the life cycle. *Human Development, 14*, 132-141.

Linton, M. (1982). Transformations of memory in everyday life. In U. Neisser (Ed.), *Memory observed: Remembering in natural contexts* (pp.77-91). San Francisco, CA: Freeman.

Mackay, D. G., & Burke, D. M. (1990). Cognition and aging: New learning and the use of old connections. In T. Hess (Ed.), *Aging and cognition: Knowledge organization and utilization* (pp. 213-263). Amsterdam: North Holland.

Morton, J. (1990). The development of event memory. *The Psychologist 1*, 3-10.

Nelson, K. (1988). The ontogeny of memory for real events. In U. Neisser & E. Winograd (Eds.), *Remembering reconsidered: Ecological and traditional approaches to the study of memory* (pp. 244-276). New York: Cambridge University Press.

Nelson, K. (1991, July). *Toward an explanation of the development of autobiographical memory.* Keynote address to the International Conference on memory Lancaster, UK.

Norman, D. A., & Shallice, T. (1980). *Attention to action: Willed and automatic control of behavior* (CHIP Rep. No. 99). San Diego: University of California, San Diego.

Parkin, A. J., & Walter, B. M. (1991). Aging, short term memory and frontal dysfunction. *Psychobiology, 19*,175-179.

Pascal-Leone, J. (1970). A mathematical model for the transition rule in Piaget's developmental stages. *Acta Psychologica, 32*, 301-345.

Rabbitt, P. M. A., & Winthorpe, C. A. (1988). What do old people remember? The Galton paradigm reconsidered. In M. M.Gruneberg, P. E. Morris, & R. N. Sykes (Eds.), *Practical aspects of memory: Current research and issues* (Vol. 1, pp. 301-307). Chichester, UK: Wiley.

Robinson, J. A. (1992). Autobiographical memory. In M. M. Gruneberg & P. E. Morris (Eds.), *Aspects of memory: Vol. 1. The practical aspects* (2nd ed., pp.223-251). London: Routledge.

Rubin, D. C., Wetzler, S. E., & Nebes, R. D. (1986). Autobiographical memory across the life span. In D. C. Rubin (Ed.), *Autobiographical memory* (pp. 202-224). Cambridge, UK: Cambridge University Press.

Webster, J. D., & Cappeliez, P. (1993). Reminiscence and autobiographical memory: Complementary contexts for cognitive aging research. *Developmental Review, 13*, 54-91.

Williams, J. M. G. (1996). Depression and the specificity of autobiographical memory. In D. C. Rubin (Ed.), *Remembering our past: Studies in autobiographical memory* (pp. 244-267). Cambridge, UK: Cambridge University Press.

Williams, J. M. G., & Broadbent, K. (1986). Autobiographical memory in attempted suicide patients. *Journal of Abnormal Psychology, 95*, 144-149.

Williams, J. M. G., & Scott, J. (1988). Autobiographical memory in depression. *Psychological Medicine, 18*, 689-695.

Yarmey, A. D., & Bull, M. P. (1978). Where were you when President Kennedy was assassinated? *Bulletin of the Psychonomic Society, 11*, 133-135.

8

Autobiographical Memory and Self-Narratives: A Tale of Two Stories

John A. Robinson
Leslie R. Taylor
University of Louisville

Our chapter concerns the relations between autobiographical memory and self-narratives. We describe a study of adult women's life histories analyzed from two different perspectives. The first approach is based on studies of the reminiscence "bump." When autobiographical memory is sampled without restrictions on time of occurrence or kind of experience, the resulting distribution of memories departs from a simple forgetting function in an interesting way. The distribution is roughly bimodal with a concentration of memories from the recent past and another between 10 and 30 years of age (Rubin, Wetzler, & Nebes, 1986). Many interpretations have been proposed for this complex pattern (cf. Rubin, chap. 4, this volume). Fitzgerald (1988, 1992) noted that the concentration of memories in adolescence and early adulthood corresponds in time with the period when a mature personal identity is being formed. Many of the experiences of that period in life have enduring importance for individuals, for their self-concept, and for the pattern of careers and relationships they initiated during that time. Fitzgerald speculated that the memories associated with the reminiscence peak anchor the person's self-narrative, a storylike representation of self. A difference in the distribution patterns of vivid versus unrestricted memories seems to support this interpretation. Both types of memories show a concentration in the adolescence and early adulthood period, but only unrestricted memories also show a recency effect. In other words, few vivid memories are reported after early adulthood. This difference is consistent with a developmental account of self-narratives and memory if we assume that few new formative experiences occur after early adulthood.

Our study takes the difference in distributional patterns as its starting point. The difference in patterns indicates it may be important to conceptually distinguish self-narratives from autobiographical memory. Whether one is simply a subset of the other is not clear. What is evident is that people remember many things that are mundane and appear to have little relevance to their self-concepts. Thus, autobiographical memory may comprise a wide range of personal information and experience. Self-narratives, in contrast, consist of a set of temporally and thematically organized salient experiences and concerns that constitute one's identity or self-concept. Our study addresses this issue by comparing narrative life histories and a separate sample of vivid memories obtained from the same participants. This procedure allowed us to see whether a reminscence bump occurred when memory was sampled in two different ways, and whether the events reported as vivid memories were also included in the narrative life histories. If vivid memories are self-defining they should come disproportionately from adolescence and early adulthood, and should be mentioned in the life histories. In life histories, on the other hand, people may mention many other experiences that did not have the impact to produce vivid memories but are pertinent to a representative account of one's life, including recent experience.

The second perspective we explored is based on proposals by narrative theorists concerning the content and form of life stories. The distinction between autobiographical memory and self-narratives is central here as well. One's autobiography is not simply the sum of one's memories. Many theorists (e.g., Bruner, 1987; Gergen & Gergen, 1988; McAdams, 1993; Singer & Salovey, 1993) have argued that self-identity is a narrative construction based on selected life events. Put differently, autobiographies or self-narratives are not documentaries. They are versions of a life that employ cultural forms to present a persuasive and coherent account of a life. These theorists would not be surprised if life histories entailed disproportionate emphasis on certain life periods. However, they would argue that distributional analyses neglect other equally, if not more important features of self-definition. For the most part, memory researchers and narrative researchers have gone their separate ways, using different theories and methods. We wanted to explore the extent to which a common data set could be examined from these two different perspectives to determine how they may complement each other. Specifically, we examined the narrative accounts we obtained for indications of continuity bias, thematic organization, and narrative form.

One concern about memory sampling methods is the lack of information about what has been left out. There is always more that can be told about a life, but it is important to know whether any particular class of experiences is systematically underrepresented. *Continuity bias* refers to a tendency to "smooth" a life history by omitting sidetracks or interruptions, or by editing events to make them conform to a more predictable and culturally acceptable pattern. A bias of this kind would be likely to lead to underrepresentation. We explored this problem by having our participants give two separate accounts of their lives, one that encouraged an emphasis on continuity and another that focused on discontinuity. We could then compare the two accounts and assess how many new experiences were reported in a second telling, whether they tended to be minor or significant, and how the new reports were distributed across life periods.

The distributional analysis of life-span memories foregrounds time as the major organizational factor in memory and neglects other forms or levels of organization. To appreciate fully the character of self-narratives and their link to autobiographical memory, we have to examine possible relationships between events from different life periods as well as differences in the salience of specific life periods. One approach for assessing relationships among memories is thematic analysis. Some memory theorists have emphasized the importance of thematic organization (e.g., Barclay & Hodges, 1988; Conway, 1992; Conway & Rubin, 1993), but most of the pertinent research has been done by personality researchers (e.g., Demorest & Alexander, 1992; McAdams, 1982; Singer & Salovey, 1993). Narrative life histories have been widely used to study personality and development across the life span (e.g., Csikszentmihalkyi & Beattie, 1979; McAdams, 1993). Typically, investigators can identify in those histories enduring concerns that carry through many years or periods of development. Enduring concerns are themes. They provide coherence and continuity in self-definition. Superficially diverse experiences distributed over time can share an underlying affective or motivational significance that unifies them and helps to integrate large chunks of one's life. We did not undertake a full-scale analysis of thematic elements in the life stories of our participants. However, we discuss two cases in some depth to demonstrate the importance of this type of organization.

One of the most interesting claims of narrative theorists is that the narrative form of life stories is as important as the narrative content. Genres are prototypical narrative forms. As children we are exposed to many of them through fairy tales and television. In later years we encounter more types of tales and more complex renderings of them in literature, biography and autobiography, and popular culture. Several researchers (e.g., Bruner 1987, 1992; Bruner & Weisser, 1991; M. Gergen, 1992; K. Gergen & M. Gergen, 1986) have discussed the ways these prototypical forms are assimilated and adapted in both the formal and informal autobiographies of individuals and groups. Genres are analogous to cognitive schemas: They comprise patterns that operate in a top-down manner to influence the selection and reconstruction of memories and the ways they are arranged in life stories. There are some striking instances of genre-based accounts of significant experiences in the life stories we obtained. We review two different examples to illustrate this type of organization.

METHOD

Fourteen women, 40 to 55 years of age ($X = 46$ years) were asked to tell about their lives. They did this twice although they were not aware there would be a second telling. Our volunteers were a diverse group, varying widely in education, socioeconomic background, marital status, and adult occupation. A few had difficult and unstable lives. For the first telling, the women were told that we were interested in "how people think about the pattern of their lives." They were asked to talk about their life experiences and how they felt they fit together. The sessions were conducted individually. Participants talked into a tape recorder without the experimenter present for about 20 minutes. After that, they were asked to review their lives once more but to focus on the disruptions, detours, surprises, choices, and turning points, both good and bad, that may have occurred. They were again left alone to talk into the tape recorder for another 20 minutes. The discontinuity task was administered as the second task to maximize the opportunity to assess continuity biases. If participants had first identified disruptive events, it would have been hard for them to ignore or omit those events in a second rendering of their lives and that would have defeated a major purpose of the study.

Several weeks after the narrative session, participants were sent a questionnaire asking them to describe four vivid memories. The instructions defined a vivid memory as one that is exceptionally clear and detailed. Three hypothetical memories were described to clarify the criterion of vividness and to indicate that there were no restrictions on either age of memory or type of experience. Participants used 7-point scales to rate their memories for pleasantness, original importance, vividness, and life impact. They also identified point of view for each memory indicating whether they saw themselves in their memory image (the observer perspective), or if they reexperienced the scene as they would have originally (the field perspective). Participants dated their memories either by reporting their age at the time of the event or by giving a calendar date. Eleven of the fourteen women returned this questionnaire. Memories were collected after the life story session rather than in counterbalanced order because we were concerned about priming effects. We wanted the narratives to be spontaneous. If the memory task had come first, participants would have already thought about their lives and identified some salient experiences and might feel that the narratives should also be organized around those recollections. There was a risk that by putting the memory task last participants would think we were implicitly asking for different life events than they had already reported. We tried to offset such assumptions by explicitly stating in the instructions that memories could but did not need to be related to information in the narratives.

Verbatim transcripts of the two life story episodes were obtained from a professional transcription service. The two episodes are referred to as first and second tellings in the following discussion. The transcriptions were coded by the two investigators and a third assistant who was blind to the purpose of the study. Interrater agreement was high, averaging 90% across the various analyses.

THE DISTRIBUTIONAL APPROACH

Comparison of Narrative Topics and Vivid Memories

Participants provided extended narratives ($X = 2,768$ words) in their first tellings. Most of the women gave chronological accounts of their lives beginning with childhood, parents, and family life, and proceeding up to the present. A few women used different strategies. One woman organized her remarks around two broad categories, relationships and jobs. Another used places where she had lived or worked as a plan. Only one woman did not give a coherent narrative. Her transcript is an associative chain of topics and comments. These differences may reflect individual differences in the organization of autobiographical memory or optional retrieval strategies.

The transcripts of each telling were separated into topical units. Topic is a more inclusive category than event, and for life history material a more appropriate level of analysis. Topics varied in length and level of specificity. Three classes of topics were identified. *General topics* summarized extended experiences such as a job, family relationships, and marriage. *Specific topics* were narratives about a specific event. *Mixed topics* consisted of both general and specific information. The number of topics identified in first tellings ranged from 15 to 30 with a mean of 24. Seventy-five percent were general, 16% were mixed, and 9% were specific. Topics were assigned to one of five life periods: early childhood, childhood (essentially the elementary school years), adolescence, early adulthood (post-high school to the early 30s), and middle adulthood. Ten percent of topics did not refer to any life period (e.g., a summary discussion of one's personality) or included material from more than one life period. They were omitted from the following analyses.

The mean proportion of topics per life period is shown in Fig. 8.1. The distribution pattern for topics resembles the pattern obtained in many other studies of autobiographical memory. There is a clear recency component, a second concentration of topics analogous to the reminiscence bump, and a paucity of topics from early childhood. The main discrepancy between these data and that of other studies is the location of the bump. Our respondents mentioned more topics from the childhood and preadolescent period and very few from the adolescent years per se. This was consistent across participants.

Vivid memories were assigned to life periods according to ages reported by participants. The mean proportion of memories per life period is also shown Fig. 8.1. The sawtooth pattern of the distribution of vivid memories is quite similar to the pattern reported by Fitzgerald (1988). Two features should be noted. First, the bump occurred in the same life period for topics and memories. Second, consistent with Fitzgerald's studies, there was a strong recency effect for topics but not for vivid memories. The memories were highly vivid ($X = 6.63$). More were pleasant (52%) than unpleasant

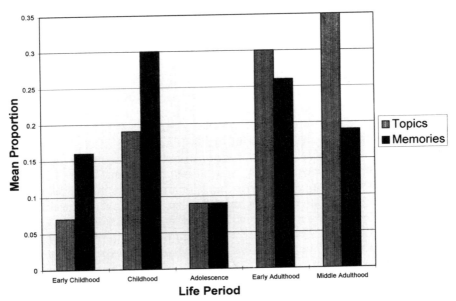

FIG. 8.1.   Mean proportion of narrative topics and vivid memories per life period.

(39%). Remembered events were regarded as highly important ($X = 5.77$) when they occurred but judgments of subsequent life impact ranged widely ($X = 4.66$). Age was an important factor. Significant positive correlations of importance and impact with age (.42 and .52, respectively) indicate that although early experiences can produce vivid, enduring, and meaningful memories, the experiences of later years tend to be seen as more important and as having greater impact.

Two other aspects are noteworthy. First, a few memories (27%) were of extended events or repeated events. Most of these related to childhood experiences (summer vacations, friendships, recurrent nightmares after a bad experience), but a few concerned recent adult experiences such as treatment for cancer. Second, many (37%) were observer memories. Field and observer memories were reported equally often for events in the earliest three life periods, but field memories predominated for adult experiences. This is consistent with previous reports that recent memories are more likely to be field memories (Nigro & Neisser, 1983; Robinson & Swanson, 1993).

Vivid memories were sorted into three categories: *same* if the memory duplicated a topic in either of the two narratives; *related* if the memory clearly referred to a topic mentioned in either narrative although the particular event(s) had not been discussed; and *different* if there was no mention of the memory event or related topics in either narrative. Only 17 of the 44 memories (39%) overlapped with information in the narratives, and 27 referred to other experiences. However, two interesting features were noted. First, overlapping memories came from different life periods than nonoverlapping memories. Seventy-six percent of overlaps pertained to adult experiences, whereas 74% of nonoverlaps pertained to childhood and adolescent experiences. Second, the overlaps from adulthood all pertained to events associated with significant changes in the women's lives. For example, a newly ordained minister recalled her first sermon; a divorced woman remembered moving with her young son to a new locale and job; a professional woman recalled a surprise request to take over her former boss' job; several women described the birth of their first child; memories of abuse, illness, and suicide were also reported. In contrast, the nonoverlapping memories were heterogeneous. There was no predominant type of experience among these memories. The results of these comparisons of memories and narratives indicate that people have vivid memories of experiences that are not central to their life stories, and that many experiences and concerns that are central are not represented in vivid memories. This is an intriguing finding consistent with the proposition that self-narratives are not simply the sum of a person's memories (cf. Bruner & Weisser, 1991; McAdams, 1993). Of course, it is possible that many of the nonoverlapping memories could be shown to have thematic significance or other roles in a life story if more detailed life histories were available.

Collecting vivid memories and life narratives from the same participants proved productive. The representations of life periods in these two memory samples were quite similar to each other and resembled the patterns obtained in many other studies: There was a strong recency effect, a paucity of early childhood memories, and a reminiscence bump for both narrative topics and vivid memories. Also, the recency effect was not as pronounced for vivid memories as for narrative topics, which is comparable to findings of other studies contrasting ordinary and vivid autobiographical memories. This replication is especially interesting because most of the datable topics were summaries of extended events and general memories rather than specific events. It suggests that the reminiscence bump reflects a feature of autobiographical memory at all levels of its hierarchical structure. The main difference between our findings and previous studies was that the bump was located at the childhood and preadolescent years. In most other studies it occurred between 11 and 30 years of age.

We consider two interpretations of this divergence between our findings and other studies. One possibility is that the earlier bump is an artifact of retrieval and report strategies unwittingly favored by our tasks. We noted earlier that most women told their stories in chronological order. That could have favored taking a disproportionate amount of time to talk about early life and then, as the women realized time was running out, have prompted them to skip over adolescent memories in order to cover adult life in the time remaining. However, this argument does not explain why the bump occurred in the same life period for vivid memories, as we found no indication of a chronological retrieval strategy for those memories. Moreover, when we arranged participants' memories sequentially and performed a series of one-way analyses of variance (ANOVAs) on the various ratings, we found no significant differences related to order of recall including age of memory. Finally, overlapping memories were distributed across recall order and were not clustered adjacent to each other.

A second argument is that the bump is due to certain basic memory processes and is only tangentially related to self-definition. Jansari and Parkin (1996) reported comparisons of different age groups on a cued recall task that also yielded a bump in the range of 6 to 15 years rather than later in life. They proposed that the bump results from two factors: a long-term primacy effect for early, especially first-time experiences, and schematization of much of adult memory owing to the repetitive character of adult experience. Our data are only partially consistent with this hypothesis. Several of the vivid memories in our data were of first-time experiences, but just as many were memories of adult events as of childhood events. Robinson (1992) proposed that first-time experiences may be represented in two different structures of autobiographical memory. One is categorical representing a class of similar experiences. First times may anchor these categories and be preserved in greater detail than subsequent instances. The other structure is thematic. First times can organize a sequence of related events that occurs over time. The birth of one's first child is both a unique event and the starting point of a continuing story. In our sample, memories of first experiences from adulthood were all thematic and those from preadult life were predominantly categorical.

We also examined narrative topics to see whether those from the bump period were more specific than those from other eras but did not find any differences. The fact that there were proportionally fewer vivid memories than narrative topics for the most recent life period may indicate that midlife is more routinized and fits with Cohen and Faulkner's (1988) suggestion that fewer vivid memories are formed later in life. However, a review of narrative topics, especially those added in the second telling (discussed later) cautions against supposing that there are fewer new significant experiences in midlife than in younger years. Many midlife experiences can be forecast and people often have a long time to prepare themselves for their eventual occurrence. Furthermore, many by their nature extend over lengthy periods. Both characteristics may attenuate the encoding and rehearsal factors that are associated with the formation of vivid memories.

Thus, although we obtained a reminiscence bump at an earlier life period than has typically been reported, we see no basis for attributing it either to a reporting bias or solely to a combination of distinctiveness and schematization of memories. It is worth emphasizing that both narrative topics and vivid memories showed a bump in the same early life period. There was not much overlap between topics and memories from that period, but the concordance indicates that there is a rich body of autobiographical information available from the bump era.

THE NARRATIVE PERSPECTIVE

Comparison of First and Second Tellings: Continuity Bias

We asked participants to focus on discontinuity experiences in their second tellings in order to assess how many experiences of this type had been omitted from their first life stories. Omissions are one indication of continuity bias in life stories. The transcripts of second tellings were coded for topics in the same way as was done for first tellings. Second tellings were shorter than first tellings (means of 1,942 words and 12.78 topics) and tended to be unordered sequences of discrete topics rather than chronological narratives. Topics were sorted into two categories: *referenced,* if a previously mentioned topic was repeated in either an abbreviated or an elaborated manner; and *new,* if there had been no mention of it in the first telling. Thirty-nine percent of topics referred to similar topics in first tellings; 61% were new. Every woman discussed several new topics ($X =$ 7.78). Thus, asking the women to review their lives again and to focus on a specific class of experiences increased the total number of topics reported in both tellings by 32%.

Because participants were asked to focus on experiences that interrupted or redirected their lives, it is interesting to see how the topics discussed were distributed across life periods. As shown in Fig. 8.2, the distributions of topics for first and second tellings were quite similar through early adulthood. However, proportionally more topics derived from the most recent life period in second tellings than in first tellings. The concentration of topics in the current life period is even more evident among new topics, as shown in Fig. 8.3. There are several possible explanations of the recency emphasis for the new topics. It may be easier to search recent memories than older memories, or there may simply be more instances of discontinuity in middle adulthood than other life periods. The wide variety of new things mentioned by the women (e.g., deaths, separations, illnesses, tran-

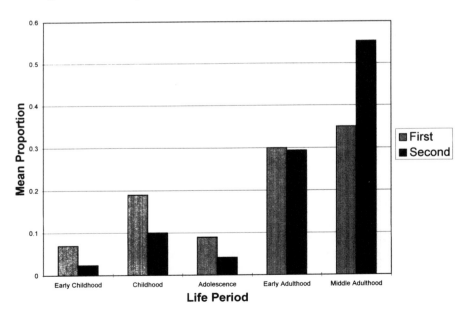

FIG. 8.2. Mean proportion of narrative topics per life period for first and second tellings.

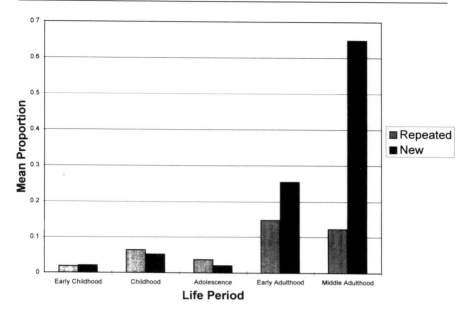

FIG. 8.3. Mean proportion of new versus repeated narrative topics per life period in second tellings.

sitional situations with children or aging parents, new ventures underway) supports the latter explanation. Although it seems plausible that there are a greater number of potentially disruptive life experiences in adulthood, it is just as important to take into account that disruptions are defined by reference to goals and plans. It need hardly be said that adults have more and better defined goals and plans than children or adolescents. Conway (1996) proposed that goal representations are used to organize autobiographical memory and can be used to direct retrieval of information associated with the goals. If the development of goal representations varies across life periods then there would be differences among life periods in the number of events indexed as disruptive of goals. This may explain why illnesses and separation experiences of adult life were added in second tellings, whereas childhood illness or separation from childhood friends were rarely added.

Second tellings were often more elaborate and self-revealing, but a majority of women presented a consistent perspective in both tellings. In a few cases, however, new information came out that substantially altered our impression from the first telling. One woman spoke of her children with affection and pride in her first telling. In her second telling she added that she had not wanted children but had complied with her husband's desires. In another case we learned that a failed love affair had been a major factor in what was initially presented as a simple decision to relocate for more education. When we planned the study it seemed clear to us that changes of this kind along with disclosure of other significant experiences would indicate a tacit continuity bias. Now, however, we are less certain. Perhaps the women simply felt more comfortable confiding in us by the second round. The reactions of the participants were also informative. When we told them of our interest in possible continuity bias some were very receptive and felt they had tried to highlight continuity in their own stories. However, others did not agree. From their perspective, things happen, and there was no point in artifically smoothing one's life history.

Focusing on discontinuities had other effects. It elicited more reflective commentary and modulated the emotional tone of the comments. There were indications of ambivalence, anger, and regret in second tellings that were not as apparent in first tellings. Another shift was apparent in the ending segments of each telling where the women commented about their current situation and their outlook on the future. There was a greater sense of the fragility of plans and prospects in some of the second closings than had been voiced in the first closing. For example, one woman concluded her first telling this way:

> I really feel pretty happy at this time in my life. I feel pretty carefree. I can't imagine why except that I don't feel responsible for anybody else's happiness right now. Susan is grown up now, my other kids are grown up . . . and I'm really enjoying my life.

The second telling closed with a long discussion of her concerns about a son who, unlike his siblings has been a steady worry, and then continues:

> It was really a jolt each time one of the kids would leave home. When Ted left to go to college—my first son—it was really hard . . . and when Joe left, that was really hard. So I have a hard time making adjustments when things change.

Reviewing life from another perspective occasionally produced some surprises too: One woman said she had not realized that her involvment with religious observance and community had lapsed so much until she began thinking about what had changed in her life.

In summary, the results of comparisons of first and second tellings demonstrate two important points about remembering. First, certain kinds of experiences and concerns can be underrepresented when the task favors continuity. Second, emotional perspectives on past, present, and future can shift when the task elicits information about disruptive experiences. Both indicate that narrative accounts provide essential information about life experience that is not readily obtained when people are asked just to report discrete events in their lives.

Thematic Organization. Every woman's story had themes. The same themes that have been noted repeatedly in the literature on personality, development, and women's lives were very much in evidence in these stories. Belonging, intimacy, attachment, separation, and competence headed the list. As noted earlier we did not attempt a full-scale analysis of themes. We discuss two cases in detail to illustrate the value of such analysis. Although in each case themes were apparent in first tellings, information that reiterated, clarified, or elaborated the themes often emerged in second tellings. Following established practice in narrative analysis, our discussion departs from what Mishler (1990) called the "order of telling" and synthesizes information from both first and second tellings.

Paula (a pseudonym) is a nurse. Even though she was an accomplished singer, nursing exerted the stronger pull. She worked in hospitals as a teenager and then went to college and studied nursing. That her interest goes back so far and superceded another area of talent is an important part of the story. It implies that she could have been successful at other things and underscores that nursing was a personal preference and a deliberate choice, not simply something she ended up doing. The first time Paula took her licensing exam she failed it. She explains that she knew she was a good clinical nurse, but had always done poorly on tests. After a major effort she passed with high marks and settled into her career. The experience made her very sympathetic to other fledging nurses who fail the exam. Paula's interpretation of the experience becomes an important theme in her life: *Failing is not a sign of incompetence.* This theme emerges again later on as she discusses doing her dissertation and her current faculty responsibilities. Research is hard for Paula. Her natural strengths are in clinical nursing. However, she had to do it for her PhD. Once again she "passed the test" by completing her dissertation. But Paula now sees herself as again facing possible failure and renewed threats to self-esteem because she must continue to do research as part of her job. Paula is pretty sure she is not going to fail, but research will never be her passion. If she never makes a reputation in research it will not mean she is a failure. She is still a terrific nurse and teacher.

We infer from Paula's various remarks that she regards her career in nursing as a recurrent struggle to preserve her primary interest in clinical nursing in the face of pressure to expand her competencies and responsibilities into other areas of nursing practice. She presents a career narrative marked by recurrent crises and successful resolutions all of which center on tests of competence. One of Paula's vivid memories overlapped with this career theme: She describes the moment when she was asked to take on some administrative responsibilities after her supervisor left for another job. She was surprised, flattered, and apprehensive. Here was another test. Her reactions were quite natural, but they show that themes not only help structure memory, they also influence perception (cf. Demorest & Alexander, 1992).

Christine's (also a pseudonym) story was organized around two themes that spanned her entire life. The first is abandonment. Her mother walked out when she was very young, leaving Christine with grandparents and a father who was emotionally distant. The way she talked about the event made it seem like it was yesterday. Christine, on the other hand, appears to have devoted herself to her children. She is proud of their accomplishments and feels proud of herself. Now that her children are grown she has successfully extended her role as caregiver into a new career in day care. However, there have been complications. One son neglects and abuses his children. Christine faced the abandonment theme again in her efforts to compensate for this son's behavior. She surmounted this the same way she did in her own life: She took his children into her home and cared for them as long as she could.

The other theme is freedom. In Christine's eyes, her mother was a joyous, uninhibited woman who could make others happy. Christine envies this and speculates whether she might have been a different person if her mother had not left. This theme is rooted in childhood memories that are likely to be idealized, but it has been a constant companion. The two themes are subtly tied together in passing remarks about her own marriage. Christine married young, and she seems to think impulsively, just as she believes her parents did. Moreover, her husband has abandoned her emotionally. It appears that Christine chose the same kind of man to marry as her mother did, but because of her own experience of abandonment probably did not feel she had the same choice to leave the marriage. The dualities of duty versus freedom and of love versus abandonment organize Christine's life story.

Two of Christine's vivid memories directly reflected the abandonment theme. The two memories span her life and address the abandonment theme in contrasting ways. One is a memory from childhood of recurrent nightmares after her mother left. The nightmares seem to be rather direct expressions of the violent reaction Christine had to this event and her wish for retribution. The second memory is from midlife and concerns her hospitalization for cancer. Christine must have many memories relating to this experience but the one she reported is how she felt cared for at a time when she desperately needed it. The steady, compassionate concern of her nurses bolstered her spirit and gave her confidence in her recovery.

Mishler (1990) argued that conventional thematic analysis of life stories ignores the very features that make them narratives and fails to capture the distinctive role of narrativity in organizing a life. If all one does is to code and count instances of themes we would agree. But themes can also be treated as a type of narrative structure. Experiences that are superficially different and separated in time can form a meaningful sequence when they embody recurrent life tasks. This is apparent in both Paula's and Christine's narratives. Themes are elements of plots. Although he was discussing reading, Brooks' (1985) remarks about plot and memory seem as valid for life stories. He said, "a plot must be 'of a length to be taken in by the memory' " (p.11). The themes of life stories seem to have the same economical character. They are plot capsules that are used to organize experience, retrieve and reconstruct memories, and compose life stories. Themes also are a resource for managing discontinuity. Themes create repetition, and repetition, even if unpleasant, imparts familiarity and a degree of coherence to a life. Part of the success in coping with instability in a life is to find the angle of view that allows you to see constancy in change (Bateson, 1994).

Genres. We noted earlier that there are many kinds or genres of stories. Genres are a resource we may use to select, condense, organize, and interpret the stream of daily experience in order to construct a large-scale portrait of our lives. The cultural stock of story types is one source of these models, but individuals can be quite creative in devising appropriate narrative forms. Events that come to be regarded as turning points may be particularly fruitful cases for genre analysis (cf. Bruner, 1994). One striking example in our study is Beth's (a pseudonym) story. She is an ordained minister who started her career in social work so it is natural that she would use religious imagery to portray her life. The major change in her life was the decision to study for the ministry. Beth tells a dramatic story that is a variant of the conversion narrative (Bateson, 1994). Interestingly, this version did not emerge until the second telling. Her use of the plot is convincing and unforced. Conversion stories divide a life into periods before and after some pivotal experience. In such stories the narrator has resisted a change, but then in a dramatic encounter gives up the struggle and accepts a new role. Beth's associates urged her to become a minister. She kept saying no, but they kept pressing her. She began to have trouble sleeping and had vivid dreams about the matter. The pivotal event that brought the story to a climax came one exhausting night when she defiantly capitulated, "Out of sheer desperation in the early hours of the morning, I just yelled out to God, okay, okay, I'll go. And then it was a very strange experience; it was like I was very calm, and I was able to sleep once I had made that decision." Beth's narrative combines a major change with a continuing commitment to service, and incorporates a secondary theme of sacrifice. That her account mirrors a central story of the New Testament is surely no coincidence. What should be emphasized, however, is that Beth's use of the model story of resistance and conversion has helped her comprehend and validate her life even though it has brought changes that have made her unhappy.

There are other forms of narrative structure that are not easily categorized (cf. Riessman, 1991). We have noticed an antiphonal structure in some narratives. This pattern consists of a narrative sequence punctuated periodically with a refrain that brings in another topic and creates a kind of counterpoint linking two separate strands of the story. Christine's story is a good example. A sequential discussion of each of her children alternates with comments about her husband. The segments on the children convey her love for them and pride in their accomplishments, whereas the refrain describes her husband's chronic absence from the home and underscores the abandonment theme we mentioned earlier. This antiphonal structure is a creative solution to the narrative problem of expressing the parallel realities of Christine's married life. The pattern of her married life could have been expressed in other ways. For example, she could have discussed her children as one story and her relationship with her husband as a separate story. However, Christine's choice of story form exemplifies the enduring role lifelong concerns with love, abandonment, and freedom have played in her life. Notably absent from her story are any occasions of intimacy. It may be that they were few and far between, but it may also be that Christine has developed a story of her life that deemphasizes and even excludes those occasions from her self-narrative. To the extent that is the case, narrative structures of theme and genre have helped Christine compose a coherent and persuasive account of her life, albeit a selective one.

CONCLUSION

Our study compared two sources of information about autobiographical memory from the same participants—vivid memories and life narratives. We found a reminiscence bump in both sets of data that coincided in time, but was located earlier in life than previous studies have found. From a methodological perspective our results are important because they corroborate Fromholt and Larsen's (1991) demonstration that a bump can be obtained from narrative reports of life-span experiences. We have no compelling explanation of why the reminiscence bump appeared at an earlier life period than has usually been found, but it could be that memory researchers have been too single-mindedly wedded to one theory of development. Perhaps, a theory such as McAdams' (1993), which postulates that the various constituents of self-narratives develop at different stages of life, would be more useful than the assumption that adolescence and early adulthood are the only pivotal points in self-definition. In any case, it seems to us that the overlap data are as important theoretically as the distributional patterns. Commenting on Fitzgerald's (1988) study, Neisser (1988) indicated that it would be important to find out whether all vivid memories are part of a self-narrative. Our comparisons indicated that some are and some are not. People have vivid memories of experiences that appear to be peripheral to their self-narratives, and their self-narratives include many general memories of salient experiences, few of which are associated with particular vivid episodes.

Our results reinforce the claim that autobiographical memory is organized at several levels (e.g., Barclay & Hodges, 1988; Conway, 1992; Linton, 1986; Neisser, 1986; Robinson, 1976; Schooler & Herrmann, 1992; Singer & Moffitt, 1991–1992). The majority of narrative topics were general memories, although some specific memories were also reported. General memories predominated in all life periods. Fitzgerald (1988) noted that some vivid memories were general rather than specific and we found this as well. Themes were identified that linked experiences both within and across life periods, providing additional evidence of multiple forms and levels of organization. Self-narratives may be another type of organization within autobiographical memory. These narratives may not exist as separate chunks of memory. Rather, the constitutents could be distributed throughout the various components of autobiographical memory but be coded in ways that relate them to a central story (cf. Conway, 1992; Robinson & Swanson, 1990). The fact that new information was added in second tellings is consistent with this scheme. Many have asserted that there is no single life story, that every telling is different (e.g., Gergen & Gergen, 1988; Shotter, 1993). Certainly, our results confirm that what is told is influenced by the teller's situation or perceived task. However, it overstates things to imply that the only stability or continuity in life narratives derives from recurrent features of task and circumstance. It is hard to account for any overlap between memories and narratives obtained at separate times by such an assumption. This is not to say that self-narratives never change, only that at any given time there is some select subset of experiences that is regarded as most relevant to one's identity.

Finally, our preliminary exploration of themes and genres convinced us that a narrative perspective is indispensable for understanding both autobiographical memory and self-narratives. Much needs to be learned about the interplay between narrative forms and memory construction. We have found the analogy of genres to cognitive schemas helpful in trying to meld cognitive and narrative perspectives. There are significant disagreements between adherents of narrative and cognitive approaches to memory, yet these should not be allowed to become doctrinaire divisions. Both approaches are needed.

REFERENCES

Barclay, C. R., & Hodges, R. M. (1988). Content and structure in autobiographical memory: An essay on composing and recomposing the self. In *Acts du Colloque European: Construction et functionement de'l identite* (pp. 205–212). Aix-en-Provence, France: University of Provence.

Bateson, M. C. (1994). *Peripheral visions.* New York: HarperCollins.

Brooks, P. (1985). *Reading for the plot.* New York: Vintage.

Bruner, J. S. (1987). Life as narrative. *Social Research, 54,* 1–32.

Bruner, J. S. (1992). The narrative construction of reality. In H. Beilin & P. Puffal (Eds.), *Piaget's theory: Prospects and possibilities* (pp. 229–248). Hillsdale, NJ: Lawrence Erlbaum Associates.

Bruner, J. S. (1994). The "remembered self." In U. Neisser & R. Fivush (Eds.), *The remembering self: Construction and accuracy in the self-narrative* (pp. 41–54). New York: Cambridge University Press.

Bruner, J. S., & Weisser, S. (1991). The invention of self: Autobiography and its forms. In D. R. Olson & N. Torrance (Eds.), *Literacy and orality* (pp. 129–148). New York: Cambridge University Press.

Cohen, G., & Faulkner, D. (1988). Lifespan changes in autobiographical memory. In M. M. Gruneberg, P. E. Morris, & R. N. Sykes (Eds.), *Practical aspects of memory: Current research and issues: Vol. 1. Memory in everyday life* (pp. 277–282). New York: Wiley.

Conway, M. A. (1992). A structural model of autobiographical memory. In M. A. Conway, D. C. Rubin, H. Spinnler, & W. A. Wagenaar (Eds.), *Theoretical perspectives on autobiographical memory* (pp. 167–194). Dordrecht, The Netherlands: Kluwer Academic.

Conway, M. A. (1996). Autobiographical knowledge and autobiographical memories. In D. C. Rubin (Ed.), *Remembering our past: Studies in autobiographical memory* (pp. 67–93). New York: Cambridge University Press.

Conway, M. A., & Rubin, D. C. (1993). The structure of autobiographical memory. In A. F. Collins, S. E. Gathercole, M. A. Conway, & P. E. Morris (Eds.), *Theories of memory* (pp. 103–138). Hillsdale, NJ: Lawrence Erlbaum Associates.

Csikszentmihalkyi, M., & Beattie, O. V. (1979). Life themes: A theoretical and empirical exploration of their origins and effects. *Journal of Humanistic Psychology, 19,* 45–63.

Demorest, A. P., & Alexander, I. E. (1992). Affective scripts as organizers of personal experience. *Journal of Personality, 60,* 645–663.

Fitzgerald, J. M. (1988). Vivid memories and the reminiscence phenomenon: The role of a self narrative. *Human Development, 31,* 261–273.

Fitzgerald, J. M. (1992). Autobiographical memory and conceptualizations of the self. In M. A. Conway, D. C. Rubin, H. Spinnler, & W. A. Wagenaar (Eds.), *Theoretical perspectives on autobiographical memory* (pp. 99–114). Dordrecht, The Netherlands: Kluwer Academic.

Fromholt, P., & Larsen, S. F. (1991). Autobiographical memory in normal aging and primary degenerative dementia. *Journal of Gerontology, 46(3),* 85–91.

Gergen, K. J., & Gergen, M. M. (1986). Narrative form and the construction of psychological science. In T. R. Sarbin (Ed.), *Narrative psychology: The storied nature of human conduct* (pp. 22–44). New York: Praeger.

Gergen, K. J., & Gergen, M. M. (1988). Narrative and the self as relationship. In L. Berkowitz (Ed.), *Advances in experimental social psychology* (Vol. 21, pp. 19–56). San Diego, CA:

Academic Press.

Gergen, M. M. (1992). Life stories: Pieces of a dream. In G. C. Rosenwald & R. L. Ochberg (Eds.), *Storied lives: The cultural politics of self-understanding* (pp. 127–144). New Haven, CT: Yale University Press.

Jansari, A., & Parkin, A. J. (1996). Things that go bump in your life: Explaining the reminiscence bump in autobiographical memory. *Journal of Psychology and Aging, 11,* 85–91.

Linton, M. (1986). Ways of searching and the contents of memory. In D. C. Rubin (Ed.), *Autobiographical memory* (pp. 50–67). New York: Cambridge University Press.

McAdams, D. P. (1982). Experiences of intimacy and power: Relationships among social motives and autobiographical memory. *Journal of Personality and Social Psychology, 42,* 292–302.

McAdams, D. P. (1993). *The stories we live by.* New York: Morrow.

Mishler, E. G. (1990). Validation in inquiry-guided research. *Harvard educational Review, 60*(4), 415–442.

Neisser, U. (1986). Nested structure in autobiographical memory. In D. C. Rubin (Ed.), *Autobiographical memory* (pp. 71–81). New York: Cambridge University Press.

Neisser, U. (1988). Commentary on "Vivid memories and the reminiscence phenomenon: The role of a self-narrative." *Human Development, 31,* 271–273.

Nigro, G., & Neisser, U. (1983). Point of view in personal memories. *Cognitive Psychology, 15,* 467–482.

Riessman, C. K. (1991). Beyond reductionism: Narrative genres in divorce accounts. *Journal of Narrative and Life History, 1,* 41–68.

Robinson, J. A. (1976). Sampling autobiographical memory. *Cognitive Psychology, 8,* 578–595.

Robinson, J. A. (1992). First experience memories: Contexts and functions in personal histories. In M. A. Conway, D. C. Rubin, H. Spinnler, & W. Wagenaar (Eds.), *Theoretical perspectives on autobiographical memory* (pp. 223–239). Dordrecht, The Netherlands: Kluwer Academic.

Robinson, J. A., & Swanson, K. L. (1990). Autobiographical memory: The next phase. *Applied Cognitive Psychology, 4*(4), 321–335.

Robinson, J. A., & Swanson, K. L. (1993). Field and observer modes of remembering. *Memory, 1,* 169–184.

Rubin, D. C., Wetzler, S. E., & Nebes, R. D. (1986). Autobiographical memory across the lifespan. In D. C. Rubin (Ed.), *Autobiographical memory* (pp. 202–221). New York: Cambridge University Press.

Schooler, J. W., & Herrmann, D. J. (1992). There is more to episodic memory than just episodes. In M. A. Conway, D. C. Rubin, H. Spinnler, & W. Wagenaar (Eds.), *Theoretical perspectives on autobiographical memory* (pp. 241–262). Dordrecht, The Netherlands: Kluwer Academic.

Shotter, J. (1993). *Conversational realities: Constructing life through language.* Thousand Oaks, CA: Sage.

Singer, J. A., & Moffitt, K. H. (1991–1992). An experimental investigation of specificity and generality of memory narratives. *Imagination, Cognition and Personality, 11,* 233–257.

Singer, J. A., & Salovey, P. (1993). *The remembered self: Emotion and memory in personality.* New York: The Free Press.

9

Remembering the Past in the Present: Verb Tense Shifts in Autobiographical Memory Narratives

David B. Pillemer
Amy B. Desrochers
Caroline M. Ebanks
Wellesley College

Effective communication about the past requires the use of culturally shared, canonical forms of narrative expression. For example, when people recount their memories of emotionally salient life experiences, they commonly provide information about who, what, when, where, and why (Brown & Kulik, 1977; Chafe, 1990; Neisser, 1982); they adhere to the temporal ordering of event sequences (Bruner, 1990); and they tell their stories in the past tense, using the present tense to offer current commentary on the meaning of remembered episodes (Bruner, 1990). Narrative conventions for memory sharing are acquired in part through parent–child talk about the past, beginning in the early preschool years (Fivush, 1991; Hudson, 1990; Nelson, 1993; Pillemer & White, 1989).

Patterned violations of canonicity in the narratives produced by mature members of a culture may provide special insight into the psychological structures or processes underlying autobiographical memory. One such violation involves verb tense or, more precisely, a dramatic shift from the past to the present tense at the emotional high point of a memory narrative. For example, as part of an extended oral history of his World War II experiences, Hoffman (Hoffman & Hoffman, 1990) recounted a life-threatening event that occurred decades earlier (present tense verbs are in italics):

The next thing I knew, the lieutenant *says,* "All right. Now we're going to prepare for the attack." And I'*m* thinking, this *is* crazy. We *can't* possibly be

145

going to make an attack. In the meantime the 88s *are* over there to the right of us, and they *haven't* realized that the tank *has been* knocked out . . . this colonel *is* kind of walking up in front, getting everybody up there, getting ready to make this attack across this wheat field. . . . Somebody spotted him, and all four of those 88s *come* around like this [gesturing] and *come* pointing at us, and then all of a sudden, boom! boom! boom! boom! boom! And those 88s *are* shooting directly at us. . . . That's the only time in the whole career that I've been in the army when I saw guys leave their rifles. Anything that wasn't nailed down they dropped and ran . . . *I'm* running through the woods with a radio on my back, wishing I didn't have it. (p. 119)

The use of the present tense suggests that the narrator is no longer simply recounting an episode—he is reliving some salient aspect of it (Pillemer, 1992). In this example, and in the illustrations that follow, the present tense is not used to provide a detached commentary on the current meaning or ramifications of a past event. Rather, the speaker shifts abruptly and temporarily into the present at an emotionally momentous point in the memory itself—in this instance, at a point at which his life was in grave danger.

In an earlier case study, Harvey (1986) analyzed several examples of "danger of death" narratives collected by herself and by Labov and Waletzky (1967). Harvey observed that the present tense was used at the point in the narratives when the speaker's life was in danger. For example, a war veteran described sitting in a small boat when it fell unexpectedly from a troop carrier into the water:

Then I remember falling . . . and there's all kinds of debris around . . . and the debris was closing in . . . and there was . . . water all around and I'm under water . . . there is ripping, crashing . . . say something hit me on the head as I'm . . . lurching about falling and then . . . there's sort of things closing in on me, debris and then the debris is jo/it's wet so it's water and debris and foam bubbles and I'm under water. (pp. 158–159)

Harvey concluded that "the use of the present tense is not to make the *audience* relive the event, but that the *narrator* is reliving an intensely personal experience with the use of the historical present as an unconscious signal or cue to the audience that this is the crucial part of the story—the reason why it is being told" (p. 156).

A shift into the present tense need not be unconscious or unintentional. A narrator can purposefully tell stories in the present tense in order to enhance their vividness and impact on the listener. According to novelist John Updike (1990), the present tense communicates intensity and feeling: "Instead of writing 'she said and he said' it's 'he says and she says,' and not 'he jumped' and some past moment, but 'he jumps,' right now in front of you. Action takes on a wholly different, flickering quality; thought and feeling and event are brought much closer together" (p. 1). Similarly, Capps and Ochs (1995) observed that the "use of the present tense . . . brings temporally remote events into a present time vividness. . . . This usage is characteristic of good storytellers who involve interlocutors in the story realm by dramatizing events as if they are taking place in the here-and-now" (p. 417).

In contrast to the carefully crafted presentations of effective writers and storytellers, many of the present tense accounts analyzed in this chapter have an unintentional, spontaneous, unrehearsed quality. Spontaneous verb tense shifts may occur when underlying feelings and perceptual images accompanying a memory are strong enough to influence the mode of narrative presentation: The speaker momentarily relives the event, and this mental reliving accounts for the unplanned use of the present tense.

In this chapter we extend the analysis of verb tense shifts in autobiographical memory narratives in several new directions. First, a diverse collection of memory narratives illustrates that although verb tense shifts regularly occur at emotional high points, present tense accounts are by no means limited to instances in which the speaker's life was in immediate danger. Second, an extended, book-length oral history (Hoffman & Hoffman, 1990) is analyzed systematically for intrusions of the present tense into the narrative flow, and potential psychological underpinnings of verb tense shifts are identified. Third, theoretical, practical, and research implications of verb tense shifts for psychology and related disciplines are explored.

CASE ILLUSTRATIONS

Memories that contain a verb tense shift frequently involve a *threat to the self.* The wartime memory presented in the introduction of this chapter vividly illustrates the use of the present tense to describe a near-death experience. Astronauts who flew the ill-fated *Apollo 13* mission to the moon in 1970 had similarly harrowing encounters with danger. The spacecraft malfunctioned during its journey, and the astronauts returned safely to Earth only after heroic and extremely risky measures were taken by the individuals in the command station and by the astronauts themselves. Years later, astronaut James Lovell described the moment in space when he discovered what had gone wrong:

> I'*m* in the lunar module with a camera and I *tell* Jack, not once, not twice, but three times, I said, "Jack, we're jettisoning the service module, not the lunar module." . . . He *jettisons* the service module and I *pull* the command

module and the lunar module together away and then *maneuver* a little bit to see if I *can* see the service module . . . it *comes* into view and as it *rotates* very slowly, one whole side of that panel was, was blown off. (Buckner & Whittlesey, 1994)

Verb tense shifts are also evident in children's memories of danger. Psychiatrist Lenore Terr (1990) interviewed an 8-year-old kidnapping victim 5 years after his abduction. The boy vividly remembered the trauma:

There were regular footsteps on my stairs. I thought it was my dad coming home early from work. I just woke up to see Dad. And it *is* another man! I was frightened . . . [the final rescue] He had me in a blanket. He took me in the car and said he'd take me somewhere. I *have* a blanket on. It *is* a short ride. The man stopped, said nothing, and *pushes* me out of the car — a light push. I walked. Ran. Didn't see anybody I know. Still had on the blanket. Saw two ladies. They asked me my name. . . . She picked me up and the FBI came. (pp. 6–7)

A particularly compelling example of a present tense intrusion into a memory narrative at a danger point was provided by a female psychiatric patient in her 20s (Gee, 1991). As part of a clinical assessment, the woman recounted a lengthy (over 800 words) description of her childhood activities, one of which was riding horses. The speaker described a past event in the present tense at only one point in the entire narrative:

Then finally we got to ride one day. And maybe this was about a week or 2 later and we got to ride some horses. And so we uh the first horse that I got on, he *starts* backing up on me and *gets* on his hind legs, you know. I'*m* scared out of my wits. I *don't* know what, I *don't* know what's happening. It'*s* unbelievable. So I got off the horse and I got, I got off the horse and I brought him back to the barn because I was too scared to ride him. (p. 19)

In addition to perceived threats to the self, the present tense is frequently used to describe *threats to others*. While on a reconnaissance patrol with another soldier in southern France, WWII veteran Hoffman witnessed a close call involving a civilian:

He went up to the house and had me cover for him. I in the back, with my rifle or carbine, and he'*s* up in the front. He went through the yard, and he was now on the back porch of this house. When I *look* down the street, I *see* coming down the street a girl. I thought to myself, what am I going to do? I better *warn* him since I *don't* want him to shoot the girl. So I *slap* on my rifle and he *looks* up at me like that and I *point* to the road, whereupon he *gets* his gun at ready and he *puts* his back up against the wall like he'*s* just going to leap out and start firing. I *slap* on my rifle again and *go* like this—shaking my head from right to left meaning "no"—and he *lifts* his hands in the air, indicating "What do you mean?" and finally I made the sign for a girl, which was kind of waving my hands in a sort of a figure eight or hourglass to indicate that it*'s* a girl and not a German, at which point he nodded his head. (Hoffman & Hoffman, 1990, pp. 96–97)

Sy Liebergot, the Command Module Systems Controller for the *Apollo 13* space mission, was monitoring computer screens when the explosion in the spacecraft occurred. Liebergot searched desperately for the cause:

I was thinking that it was solvable, and then I was coming to the conclusion that I couldn't solve it. And that wasn't a good feeling . . . Kranz *is,* you know, the flight director, *is* pressing me, and, to the left of my console *is, is* the capcom console, and Jack Larsman *is* the capcom and he*'s* responsible for keeping the crew informed, and he*'s* feeling that *we're* not as forthcoming as we *can* be. For a very good reason we *aren't* forthcoming, *we're* still trying to figure out what the hell*'s* going on . . . I must tell you, I have never felt in all my life as alone as I felt. This is not to denigrate the support I was getting, but I didn't have the answers and I*'m* sitting there and I felt alone. (Buckner & Whittlesey, 1994)

Verb tense shifts are not limited to negative episodes; moments of *intense positive excitement* are also recounted in the present tense. Astronomer David Levy was interviewed by television journalist Charlie Rose about the collision between the comet Levy codiscovered and the planet Jupiter. Rose asked, "What's been, David, while I still have you, the most exciting moment for you after the discovery?" Levy replied:

The most exciting moment was Saturday night when we were getting ready for the NASA press conference. We were just practicing sitting down in the chair. Meantime, Hal Weaver from the space telescope, *comes* down, *walks* calmly over to Gene, *whispers* something to Gene. Gene just *leaps* out of his chair and said, "You mean they saw the plume!" And the three of us were just absolutely as—flabbergasted. (Rose, 1994)

During an interview, vocalist Helen Ward reported a memory of a marriage proposal she received decades earlier from renowned bandleader Benny Goodman:

I remember my date taking me to the Brown Derby and we*'re* sitting there talking and Benny *leans* over to Bill—that was my date's name—and *says,* "You know I'm going to marry that girl." And I*'m* sitting there like this. And my friend *looks* at me—What the heck*'s* going on there? Bill took me home.

Before I knew it, there's a ring at the doorbell. And it's Benny. And I let him in. And I'll never forget this. I'm, I'm sitting on the couch and Benny's standing in front of me and he's saying, "I want to marry you." And now no prelude, no inkling, no, out of left field, "Want to marry you." He convinced me to go East with him." (Jacoby, 1986)

Other memories recounted in the present tense are not easily categorized as positive or negative, but they are obviously infused with strong feelings and vivid imagery. When president Bill Clinton broke his leg as a kindergartener, his friend Joe Purvis came to visit. This led to a follow-up incident years later that was both embarrassing and flattering:

I remember my mom made me take flowers out to him which years later Virginia [Clinton's mother] used to embarrass the living fool out of me. I was working for Bill as his assistant attorney general and one day I saw his mom in the office and she smiled and said, "How are you?" Well, the next thing I *know*, people *are* coming out of the coffee room giggling. Virginia had tacked up a photograph on the bulletin board of Bill with his leg up at almost a 90-degree angle—a 45-degree angle at least. But the worst thing *is* there's this kid wearing a jughead beanie, a three little pigs T-shirt, and a pair of blue jeans holding a little bouquet of posies, and it's me. Boy, did Bill and Virginia ever get revenge on me but Bill was just a good guy. (Gallen, 1994, p. 27)

ANALYSIS OF AN EXTENDED ORAL HISTORY

Although a diverse set of case examples points to a connection between verb tense shifts and the emotional and sensory content of remembered episodes, detailed analyses of extended oral histories are necessary to ascertain whether present tense verbs are used primarily when the speaker or writer is describing emotionally and perceptually salient episodes rather than more mundane happenings. In *Archives of Memory: A Soldier Recalls World War II* (Hoffman & Hoffman, 1990), Howard S. Hoffman was interviewed twice, in 1978 and in 1982, by his wife Alice M. Hoffman, a prominent oral historian. His charge at both interviews was simply to tell about the war, with only occasional requests to clarify or expand on his memories. During the 4-year time interval between interviews, Hoffman tried to "avoid situations that might stimulate him to rehearse or further explore his memories of World War II" (p. 5).

Hoffman's first interview is published in full in *Archives of Memory*. The oral history is divided into four parts: stateside experiences (23 pages of text), the Italian campaign (12 pages), from Southern France to the Elbe (36 pages), and the war's end (3 pages). In addition, Hoffman's Time 2 recall of the Italian campaign is published in full. The entire second interview was not published because "it was nearly identical to the first recall document even though it was conducted four years later" (p. 7).

Verb Tense Coding

We independently examined Hoffman's description of the Italian campaign and then jointly discussed the various functions served by present tense verbs. The entire document was then coded by the second and third authors, with ambiguous cases resolved through discussion with the first author. In order to qualify as an instance of the present tense in an autobiographical memory, Hoffman had to employ one or more present tense verbs when offering a firsthand description of an event that he experienced in World War II. Present tense verbs were not included in this analysis when Hoffman (a) described a "timeless" procedure in the present tense, such as how a gas mask works; (b) offered a general explanation or narrator comment, such as how diagnostic testing is done or how officers behave on the battlefield; (c) reported a fact, such as identifying which troops captured a particular city ("That's who took Cassino"); or (d) used a present tense verb within a verbatim quote.

Memory Content

Analysis of the entire first recall document revealed 18 instances in which at least one present tense verb was used to describe some aspect of a past event or a closely related series of events. The number of present tense verbs used in the event descriptions ranged from 1 to 33. Memories containing present tense accounts were assigned to three content categories: threat to self, threat to other people, and miscellaneous; memories that included threats both to the self and to others were assigned to both content categories. Assignments were made jointly by the three authors. Most of the remembered events (15 out of 18) involved a threat to life. In 11 instances the speaker's own life was endangered, whereas in 14 cases another person's life was endangered. All present tense accounts of potentially life-threatening events involved immediate danger, with one exception: Hoffman described a change in the weather in the present tense ("it *is* now getting very cold, and the snow *has* started to fall"). The harsh weather was potentially life-threatening; Hoffman was "becoming very, very edgy about the possibilities of surviving" (Hoffman & Hoffman, 1990, p. 102) under frigid weather conditions.

The three instances of present tense descriptions involving activities other than threats to life also appeared to be affectively charged: Hoffman getting his orders, and hoping for a particular assignment ("I'*m* just hoping they'*re* going to send me down to Penn State"); Hoffman getting "very, very high" by (illicitly) drinking ether while being treated for malaria ("I said, 'What the hell is that?' He *says,* 'Ether.' I said, 'You can't drink ether.' "); and Hoffman walking in the dark over what turned out to be German bodies ("So I started walking down the road—I'*m* the first one—and I *see* all these clumps of dirt in the road . . . I thought to myself, 'I have the eerie feeling that these are bodies . . . ' ").

The distribution of present tense event descriptions across the four book sections also supports the connection between use of the present tense and heightened emotional responsiveness. Hoffman shifted into the present tense to describe an event only twice in his lengthy description of stateside experiences, whereas the remaining 16 shifts occurred in his account of dangerous and stressful experiences when fighting in Europe. No present tense accounts occurred during Hoffman's brief report of the war's end.

Second Recall Document

Hoffman's second account of the Italian campaign contained four instances of present tense descriptions of wartime events, the same number as in his first recall. Three of these Time 2 events also were recounted with present tense verbs at Time 1. The one new Time 2 event involved an embarrassing public inspection for venereal disease ("What made this so memorable was . . . there'*s* this line of fifty-sixty guys going by and there, not twenty or thirty feet away, *is* a whole row of Italian women standing there, watching and pointing and laughing as we went by.").

THEORETICAL IMPLICATIONS

Autobiographical memory narratives representing diverse topics contain abrupt shifts from the past tense to the present tense. Some people (such as fiction writers or adolescents in conversation with their peers) may intentionally use the present tense when recounting past events, in order to engage the listener or reader. In contrast, the present tense accounts examined in this chapter do not appear to be part of a deliberate presentational style, in which a speaker uses the present tense as an oratorical device. Rather, the occurrence of verb tense shifts appears to be influenced by underlying psychological characteristics of the original event and the speaker.

Emotionality

All of the present tense narratives examined in this chapter described episodes that appeared to be infused with strong emotions — threat to the speaker's well-being or the well-being of other people, scientific discovery, unexpected romantic engagement, or public embarrassment. Use of the present tense when describing emotional high points suggests that affectively based memory representations momentarily infuse the process of ongoing narrative production with a sense of immediacy; the speaker shifts from measured retelling to engaged reexperiencing.

Although highly emotional memory content and present tense descriptions regularly co-occur in our data, heightened affect by itself is not sufficient to produce a verb tense shift; Hoffman's oral history contained several exclusively past tense accounts of extremely stressful events. Identifying the full complement of factors that trigger a present tense intrusion into the recounting of a past episode is a task for future research.

Imagery

Present tense accounts in autobiographical memory narratives frequently provide a lucid description of sensory or perceptual experiences; the speaker uses the present tense to recount what was seen, heard, or felt. The description has a perceptually live quality, as in Boston Red Sox baseball player Ken Ryan's report of how he learned unexpectedly that another player had cancer: "I found out last night. I was lying in bed. The TV was on, but the sound was down low because the baby was sleeping. I *look* at the screen and I *see* John hitting a home run. Then I *see* his picture. Then the word 'cancer.' By the time I turned the sound up, they were on to another story" (Ryan, 1994, p. 41). This account suggests that Ryan was actively reperceiving the television image as he constructed his memory narrative.

Rivka, a holocaust survivor, also used the present tense to recount precisely what was seen and heard during a momentous event at the end of World War II, when escaping Nazis left a group of Jews alone in a forest:

> On this night there was a dreadful downpour, with thunder and lightning. It was as though the heavens were opening up, and the Germans grabbed their dogs, who were barking, and ran away, leaving us on our own . . . I was lying on the ground . . . I put my ear to the ground and I *hear* things moving. The earth *is* reverberating. . . . There was a terrifying flash of lightning and we *see* tanks with men. . . . We *are* lying there and we *hear* speech, and what we hear *is* not German. A Dutch woman doctor lying next to me *says,* "I think I hear English." She *lifts* her head and I *push* it down. She *says,* "No, no, these are

not Germans." . . . Someone ran to me and I was in such a state of ecstasy
that I had froth on my lips and they thought I had epilepsy. A soldier *runs* up
to me and *wipes* my mouth and he *says* in Yiddish, "Shush, ikh bin a Yid.
There are Jewish soldiers here and I am a rabbi, an American." (Richmond,
1995, pp. 392–393)

People who are facile visualizers and imagers may be especially likely to
give present tense accounts of perceptually vivid past experiences. The
ability to activate sensory images clearly or to visualize past experiences
varies across individuals (Kosslyn, 1994; Marks, 1983). According to Alice
Hoffman (Hoffman & Hoffman, 1990), Howard Hoffman "is a visual
rememberer . . . he calls up a scene and then describes it" (pp. 144–145).
Many of Hoffman's present tense accounts suggest that he was revisualizing
past events as he described them verbally. In one instance, he shifted into
the present tense just when the Germans came abruptly into view: "I
remember all of a sudden, we were kind of crawling over the crest of the hill
and looking down the other side, and there on the other side of the hill *are*
the Germans and there*'s* a whole battalion of them, I guess" (p. 97). In
another instance, Hoffman commented directly on the picturelike quality of
his memory: "I remember when we were back standing on the road itself, I
can picture the scene, and standing there looking down at him, and he*'s*
already had some morphine so he*'s* not feeling too bad, and thinking, I wish
it was me" (p. 102). Sometimes auditory images accompanied Hoffman's
vivid visual perceptions: "All of a sudden, not more than fifty-sixty feet
away, I *see* machine-gun fire, I *see* pistol fire, shooting, you know, it*'s* just
the edge of darkness, a bunch of Germans over there, shooting at
us . . . there*'s* still sporadic sounds coming from outside and shooting and
explosions . . . I *can hear* on the radio, these guys *are* calling for mortar
fire" (pp. 120–121).

In these instances, vivid sensory images appeared to provide a template
for present tense event descriptions. Nevertheless, it would be a mistake to
assume that present tense accounts are necessarily more accurate than
conventional retellings. The initial event may have been perceived incorrectly (Terr, 1990), or the memory image may become distorted as a result
of misleading postevent information (Loftus, 1993).

Rehearsal

When spontaneously told in the present tense, autobiographical memories
have a live, intense, unrehearsed quality. Speculatively, one might expect
the perceptually raw, relived character of emotional episodes, including
unintentional use of the present tense, to diminish with repeated retellings

and the corresponding conversion to conventional narrative form. Howard Hoffman's present tense accounts were for the most part unrehearsed, at least overtly. According to Alice Hoffman, Howard had rarely if ever spoken about his shocking wartime experiences: "In fact he felt some disdain for those who talked about the war, a sense that it was somehow unmanly to burden others with the true stories of the horrors of war. . . . It was only after he decided to engage in this project that he told most of these stories. Hence it was as if he was telling those stories not told before" (Hoffman & Hoffman, 1990, p. 81). Similarly, Rivka, the holocaust survivor whose memory of being rescued by Americans was presented earlier in this chapter, had not rehearsed her wartime memories: "So much for a person to endure. I had to tell you about this. I have not told it to anyone before" (Richmond, 1995, p. 393).

Hoffman used present tense verbs in both his first and second recall of several events from the Italian campaign; some episodes may retain their vivid sensory and affective character despite repeated retellings. Nevertheless, Hoffman was asked to refrain from rehearsing his wartime experiences between his Time 1 and Time 2 recalls. Examining records of repeated remembering over extended time periods, such as psychotherapy or eyewitness testimony transcripts, would provide a stronger test of the impact of multiple tellings on use of the present tense.

Multiple Levels of Representation in Autobiographical Memory

Unintentional shifts into the present tense at emotionally and perceptually salient points of a memory narrative support the idea of multiple levels of representation in autobiographical memory. White and Pillemer (1979; Pillemer & White, 1989) proposed that autobiographical memory is composed of two functionally independent systems. The first system is "present from birth and operational throughout life. . . . The memories are expressed through images, behaviors, or emotions" (Pillemer & White, 1989, p. 326). The second, narrative memory system emerges during the preschool years, partly as a result of adult–child conversations about the past (Nelson, 1993). Theoretical models in clinical psychology and psychiatry (Terr, 1988, 1990), psychoanalysis (Spence, 1982), evolutionary theory (Donald, 1991), personality psychology (Epstein, 1994), and cognitive psychology (Brown & Kulik, 1977) are consistent with the existence of an imagistic, perceptually based level of memory representation alongside, and in interaction with, a higher order, language-based, narrative level of memory representation.

Verb tense shifts in memory narratives point to the existence of functionally distinct but interacting representational systems. Present tense autobiographical accounts may occur when unusually strong affective and imagistic representations intrude into ongoing, purposeful narrative processing. Attentional focus shifts fleetingly to the upswell of perceptual images and feelings, and these sensations are actively described, in the present tense, as part of the story.

CLINICAL IMPLICATIONS

Present tense event descriptions in autobiographical memories may provide a link between normal and atypical cognition. Janet (1925) described a depressed patient who was "tormented by an obsession which presents itself in the form of a visual image with an almost hallucinatory intensity" (p. 144). The memories were "all of an extraordinary and ridiculous precision" (p. 144) and had a "peculiar mark of the present" (p. 145), including the use of present tense verbs to describe past events. More recently, symptoms evidenced by patients suffering from posttraumatic stress disorder (PTSD) include "re-experiencing the traumatic event" (McNally, 1992, p. 229). Patients have flashbacks that are "associated with the involuntary activation of a disturbing episodic memory" (McNally, 1992, p. 239). According to Terr (1990), "psychic trauma victims are cursed with an unstoppable tendency to 'see' their traumas" (p. 140). Similarly, Janoff-Bulman (1992) observed that memories of trauma come to mind involuntarily, and that these "intrusions in daily thoughts are typically visual memories and images of the traumatic event" (p. 108). Present tense accounts occurring at emotional peaks of autobiographical memory narratives may provide an everyday analogue to these violent, psychopathological intrusions of the past into the present.

Actively reexperiencing the past is an important component of several forms of clinical intervention. Hypnotic suggestibility is related to the ability to visualize or reinstate the sensory quality of past episodes (Hilgard, 1979; Wilson & Barber, 1983). Excellent hypnotic subjects often have extremely vivid personal memories: "When they are asked to recall a past experience, they do not merely remember it, they also seem to reexperience and relive it" (Wilson & Barber, 1983, p. 356).

Some models of psychotherapy also emphasize the importance of reactivating past events, including retelling life stories in the present tense and elaborating on visual and sensory details: "The therapist, while permitting and encouraging the expression of feelings, also explores and enlarges on other structural details—visual, behavioral, conceptual—how old are you in this scene? in what room of the house does the scene take place? who else is there? what is mother wearing? how do you feel about what your brother is doing?" (Kantor, 1980, p. 158). Within the psychotherapeutic dialogue, the client's spontaneous production of present tense accounts may signal to the therapist that the memory content has special emotional meaning. For example, psychiatrist Terr (1990) commented on the psychological significance of verb tense shifts in her analysis of a child's abduction narrative: "Alan breaks into the present tense here because his release by the kidnapper still stirs up vivid feelings, feelings of immediate danger" (p. 6).

The exaggerated forms of sensory and affective reinstatement that characterize psychological disorders such as PTSD, and clinical interventions such as hypnosis and traumatic event reenactment in psychotherapy, appear to be structurally similar to the momentary reliving of emotional episodes that punctuates normal autobiographical remembering. In each instance, imagistic and affective forms of representation may temporarily assume a position of heightened influence in autobiographical memory compared to higher order, conventionalized, narrative forms of representation.

RESEARCH IMPLICATIONS

The main theoretical claim of this article is that verb tense shifts occur when sensory and affective memory representations are strong enough to exert a direct influence on purposeful narrative processing. If this claim is true, then events recounted in the present tense should be highly emotional and perceptually vivid. Although numerous case examples indicate that present tense memory accounts are associated with strong emotions and vivid imagery, the roles played by emotion and imagery need to be examined more systematically. Memories of highly emotional and relatively unemotional events could be elicited directly from the same group of people, and the incidence of present tense accounts could be compared. For example, the incidence of present tense accounts should be higher when eyewitnesses to a crime are asked to describe the frightening incident itself than when they are asked to describe what they were doing prior to the crime, or to describe a different, relatively benign event. Another research strategy involves analyzing extended oral histories or psychotherapy transcripts to determine if present tense intrusions occur primarily at emotional high points, as was the case for Hoffman's account of World War II.

The role played by imagery could be examined further by obtaining measures of imagery vividness from research participants (e.g., Marks, 1983). If perceptual representations serve as templates for present tense oral reports, then people who have ready access to clear and vivid mental images should produce a higher frequency of present tense accounts than people whose images are relatively unclear and impoverished.

What are the relative contributions of emotion and imagery to the production of present tense memory accounts? Teasing out the independent contributions of strong affect and vivid imagery will be difficult because they frequently co-occur: Heightened emotion often serves as a trigger for the formation of detailed and persistent memory images. Ratings of memory vividness or clarity are positively associated with ratings of affective intensity (Pillemer, 1984; Reisberg, Heuer, McLean, & O'Shaughnessy, 1988; Rubin & Kozin, 1984). Clinical observations also support the interconnectedness of strong feelings and vivid imagery. For example, Terr (1990) stated that "traumatic occurrences are first recorded as visualizations" (p. 182), and Janoff-Bulman (1992) commented that intrusive recollections of trauma usually are "visual memories and images" (p. 108). According to Horowitz and Reidbord (1992):

> The more the person experiences stages of extreme terror during an event, the more likely the imagery of that event will be inscribed in the same sensory modalities of memory as the perceptions. These memory inscriptions tend to return to conscious representation in that same modality and, because of their vividness, to re-evoke the same emotions as the original experience. (p. 347)

Sudden shifts into the present verb tense will often be attributable to the combined influence of strongly felt emotions and intense perceptual imagery.

Another topic for future research involves evaluating the accuracy of memories that are spontaneously recounted in the present tense. For example, an eyewitness to a bank robbery in Cambridge, Massachusetts gave this account to television reporters while still at the scene of the crime:

> I heard a person saying "Stop! Robbery! Stop! Robbery!" And the next thing I *know* we *turn* around to see these people running down this way. And all of a sudden there's someone's . . . they're firing return firing shooting back and forth at each other. . . . Most of us got down on the ground. And the Brink's man *is* shooting in this direction and this man *is* standing facing him and he's got this outlandish disguise on—like frizzy fake hair like Groucho Marx, mustache, eyeglasses, fake like safety glasses. And they kept firing. There was about 15, 20, 30 shots going down. (WBZ News, Boston, 1995, March 1)

The physical act of recounting was animated and dynamic; the eyewitness' eyes darted and his hands waved as he broke into the present tense. The listener is led to believe that the witness was actively reexperiencing sensory and affective aspects of the original episode during the retelling.

Although present tense eyewitness accounts are not immune to distortion, the possibility exists that the use of the present tense is a marker of authenticity. Statement validity assessment (SVA; Raskin & Esplin, 1991) is a controversial procedure for evaluating eyewitness statements. Validity in this context refers to "accounts that are based on personal experience, even though some details of the statement may be inaccurate, as distinguished from invalid accounts that are invented by the child or are the consequence of influence by others" (p. 266). The eyewitness interview is analyzed for the presence of characteristics that are indicative of actual rather than invented memory. These include presence of specific details, reproduction of speech in the form of direct quotes, and descriptions of superfluous as well as central events. Supporters of SVA propose that "only a person who actually experienced an event is likely to incorporate certain types of contents into a statement that describes the experience. For example, it is assumed that persons who invent an account are unlikely to speak as if they are reexperiencing the episode, such as describing actual speech by one or more participants" (p. 280). Spontaneous use of the present tense at the emotional high point of a memory narrative may be another indication that the witness is reporting an event experienced firsthand rather than a fabrication constructed after the fact.

The success of SVA in distinguishing between veridical and false memories has yet to be established convincingly. In any case, a demonstrated relationship between memory accuracy and memory characteristics such as use of the present tense would be probabilistic (Kihlstrom, 1994): A sudden shift into the present tense may increase the likelihood that a memory is authentic, but it would not by itself be a compelling indicator of veridicality. As discussed earlier, the subjective experience of reliving or reperceiving in no way guarantees that the memory is true to the original circumstances. If the initial event was misperceived, the persistent imagery may be a "visual illusion" rather than a veridical record (Terr, 1990). In addition, memory images may become distorted as they are translated into verbal reports and discussed with other people (Loftus, 1993; Terr, 1990).

Although the use of the present tense does not guarantee an accurate memory, present tense accounts may be more believable and more persuasive than memories recounted in the canonical past tense (Pillemer, 1992). Bell and Loftus (1989) identified "trivial persuasion in the courtroom" (p. 669): the presence of extraneous details in eyewitness accounts, such as seeing a customer buy and then drop "a box of Milk Duds and a can of Diet Pepsi" rather than "a few store items" (p. 672), increased the persuasive force of testimony. Similarly, a witness who abruptly breaks into the present tense at an emotional high point of a memory narrative may be viewed as more credible than a witness who gives a dispassionate account. Simulated studies of eyewitness testimony could determine whether verb tense shifts contribute to the persuasiveness of a memory.

Other more fundamental research issues focus on the organization of autobiographical memory rather than on verb tense shifts per se. Spontaneous present tense accounts in autobiographical memory narratives are consistent with the view that memory is composed of separate but interacting imagistic and narrative subsystems. Recent research in cognitive neuroscience supports the existence of multiple memory systems (McKee & Squire, 1993; Tulving & Schacter, 1990). According to Tulving and Schacter (1990) "many researchers have adopted the hypothesis that memory consists of a number of systems and subsystems with different operating characteristics. The problem of what these systems and their properties are, and how they are related to one another, now occupies the center stage in research on memory" (p. 301). The functional duality between image and narrative described in this chapter provides one potential framework for examining the systemic organization of autobiographical memory.

ACKNOWLEDGMENTS

This research was supported by awards from the Louise Overacker Fund and the Ford Foundation, administered by Wellesley College. Blythe Clinchy, Jane Pillemer, and Paul Wink offered valuable comments on an earlier draft. This chapter is dedicated to the memory of friend and colleague Michel Grimaud, who provided invaluable insight and encouragement on this project.

REFERENCES

Bell, B. E., & Loftus, E. F. (1989). Trivial persuasion in the courtroom: The power of (a few) minor details. *Journal of Personality and Social Psychology, 56,* 669–679.

Brown, R., & Kulik, J. (1977). Flashbulb memories. *Cognition, 5,* 73–99.

Bruner, J. (1990). *Acts of meaning.* Cambridge, MA: Harvard University Press.

Buckner, N., & Whittlesey, R. (Co-Producers and Directors). (1994). *Apollo 13: To the edge and back* [Film]. Princeton, NJ: Films for the Humanities and Sciences.

Capps, L., & Ochs, E. (1995). Out of place: Narrative insights into agoraphobia. *Discourse Processes, 19,* 407–439.

Chafe, W. (1990). Some things that narratives tell us about the mind. In B. K. Britton & A. D. Pellegrini (Eds.), *Narrative thought and narrative language* (pp. 79–98). Hillsdale, NJ: Lawrence Erlbaum Associates.

Donald, M. (1991). *Origins of the modern mind.* Cambridge, MA: Harvard University Press.

Epstein, S. (1994). Integration of the cognitive and the psychodynamic unconscious. *American Psychologist, 49,* 709–724.

Fivush, R. (1991). The social construction of personal narratives. *Merrill-Palmer Quarterly, 37,* 59–82.

Gallen, D. (1994). *Bill Clinton: As they know him.* New York: Gallen Publishing Group.

Gee, J. P. (1991). A linguistic approach to narrative. *Journal of Narrative and Life History, 1,* 15–39.

Harvey, A. D. (1986). Evidence of a tense shift in personal experience narratives. *Empirical Studies of the Arts, 4,* 151–162.

Hilgard, J. R. (1979). *Personality and hypnosis* (2nd ed.). Chicago: University of Chicago Press.

Hoffman, A. M., & Hoffman, H. S. (1990). *Archives of memory: A soldier recalls World War II.* Lexington: The University Press of Kentucky.

Horowitz, M. J., & Reidbord, S. P. (1992). Memory, emotion, and response to trauma. In S.-A. Christianson (Ed.), *The handbook of emotion and memory: Research and theory* (pp. 343–357). Hillsdale, NJ: Lawrence Erlbaum Associates.

Hudson, J. A. (1990). The emergence of autobiographical memory in mother–child conversation. In R. Fivush & J. A. Hudson (Eds.), *Knowing and remembering in young children* (pp. 166–196). New York: Cambridge University Press.

Jacoby, O. (Producer and Director). (1986). *Benny Goodman: Adventures in the kingdom of swing* [Film, not available for distribution].

Janet, P. (1925). Memories which are too real. In C. M. Campbell, H. S. Langfeld, W. McDougall, A. A. Roback, & E. W. Taylor (Eds.), *Problems of personality* (pp. 141–150). New York: Harcourt, Brace & Company.

Janoff-Bulman, R. (1992). *Shattered assumptions.* New York: The Free Press.

Kantor, D. (1980). Critical identity image: A concept linking individual, couple, and family development. In J. K. Pearce & L. J. Friedman (Eds.), *Family therapy: Combining psychodynamic and family systems approaches* (pp. 137–167). New York: Grune & Stratton.

Kihlstrom, J. F. (1994). Hypnosis, delayed recall, and the principles of memory. *The International Journal of Clinical and Experimental Hypnosis, 42,* 337–345.

Kosslyn, S. M. (1994). *Image and brain.* Cambridge, MA: MIT Press.

Labov, W., & Waletzky, J. (1967). Narrative analysis: Oral versions of personal experience. In J. Helm (Ed.), *Essays on the verbal and visual arts* (pp. 12–44). Seattle: University of Washington Press.

Loftus, E. F. (1993). The reality of repressed memories. *American Psychologist, 48,* 518–537.

Marks, D. F. (1983). Mental imagery and consciousness: A theoretical review. In A. A. Sheikh (Ed.), *Imagery: Current theory, research, and application* (pp. 96–130). New York: Wiley.

McKee, R. D., & Squire, L. R. (1993). On the development of declarative memory. *Journal of Experimental Psychology: Learning, Memory, and Cognition, 19,* 397–404.

McNally, R. J. (1992). Psychopathology of post-traumatic stress disorder (PTSD): Boundaries of the syndrome. In M. Basoglu (Ed.), *Torture and its consequences: Current treatment approaches* (pp. 229–252). Cambridge, UK: Cambridge University Press.

Neisser, U. (1982). Snapshots or benchmarks? In U. Neisser (Ed.), *Memory observed* (pp. 43–48). San Francisco, CA: Freeman.

Nelson, K. (1993). The psychological and social origins of autobiographical memory. *Psychological Science, 4,* 7–14.

Pillemer, D. B. (1984). Flashbulb memories of the assassination attempt on President Reagan. *Cognition, 16,* 63–80.

Pillemer, D. B. (1992). Remembering personal circumstances: A functional analysis. In E. Winograd & U. Neisser (Eds.), *Affect and accuracy in recall: Studies of "flashbulb" memories* (pp. 236–264). New York: Cambridge University Press.

Pillemer, D. B., & White, S. H. (1989). Childhood events recalled by children and adults. In H. W. Reese (Ed.), *Advances in child development and behavior* (Vol. 21, pp. 297–340). San Diego, CA: Academic Press.

Raskin, D. C., & Esplin, P. W. (1991). Statement validity assessment: Interview procedures and content analysis of children's statements of sexual abuse. *Behavioral Assessment, 13,* 265–291.

Reisberg, D., Heuer, F., McLean, J., & O'Shaughnessy, M. (1988). The quantity, not the quality, of affect predicts memory vividness. *Bulletin of the Psychonomic Society, 26,* 100–103.

Richmond, T. (1995). *Konin: A quest.* New York: Pantheon.

Rose, C. (Producer and Host). (1994, July 19). *Comet Shoemaker-Levy 9* [television interview by Charlie Rose, WGBH, Boston].

Rubin, D. C., & Kozin, M. (1984). Vivid memories. *Cognition, 16,* 81–95.

Ryan, B. (1994, March 11). Kruk's misfortune is a large dose of real life. *The Boston Globe,* pp. 41–42.

Spence, D. P. (1982). *Narrative truth and historical truth.* New York: Norton.

Terr, L. (1988). What happens to early memories of trauma? A study of twenty children under age five at the time of documented traumatic events. *Journal of the American Academy of Child and Adolescent Psychiatry, 27,* 96–104.

Terr, L. (1990). *Too scared to cry.* New York: Basic Books.

Tulving, E., & Schacter, D. L. (1990). Priming and human memory systems. *Science, 247,* 301–306.

Updike, J. (1990, August 5). Why Rabbit had to go. *The New York Times Book Review,* pp. 1, 24–25.

White, S. H., & Pillemer, D. B. (1979). Childhood amnesia and the development of a socially accessible memory system. In J. F. Kihlstrom & F. J. Evans (Eds.), *Functional disorders of memory* (pp. 29–73). Hillsdale, NJ: Lawrence Erlbaum Associates.

Wilson, S. C., & Barber, T. X. (1983). The fantasy-prone personality: Implications for understanding imagery, hypnosis, and parapsychological phenomena. In A. A. Sheikh (Ed.), *Imagery: Current theory, research, and application* (pp. 340–387). New York: Wiley.

10

What Is It Like to Remember?
On Phenomenal Qualities
of Memory

Steen F. Larsen
University of Aarhus

"What is it like to remember?" This question paraphrases the title of a classic paper by the philosopher Nagel (1974), "What is it like to be a bat?" Nagel gave a contemporary formulation to the age-old philosophical problem of other minds; that is, whether and to what extent we can get valid knowledge of the conscious experience of another being. Nagel's question is a tough one in a typical philosopher's way: No human being ever tried being a bat, and no one ever will, so the imagination is free to roam, unhampered by drab reality. In contrast to being a bat, everybody knows what it is like to remember. Still, understanding the conscious experience of remembering raises analogous questions, as we shall see.

In philosophical terminology (cf. Gregory, 1987), the word *qualia* (singular: *quale*) denotes the felt or experienced character of mental states and events, such as the experience of redness, the experience of pain, the experience of being angry, or the experience of familiarity. Because the intention of this chapter is not to unravel the philosophical problems of qualia, the term *phenomenal qualities of remembering*, or just *memory qualities*, is used instead of qualia. (Some researchers use the expression *phenomenal experience*. To me, this has an unfortunate tautological ring, as I equate phenomenal with experiential.)

In the following, I begin by discussing two sets of issues that I think lie behind the de facto ban on conscious experience in the history of memory research: an epiphenomenalist view of consciousness and the other minds

163

problem. Next, a conceptual framework is proposed that distinguishes three logically different classes of phenomenal qualities of memory: content qualities, appearance qualities, and process qualities. Finally, an experiment is presented that investigates the contribution of stored information (memory traces) to the appearance quality of memory vividness, over and above the vividness that can be generated by pure imagination.

EPIPHENOMENALISM IN MEMORY RESEARCH

The primary inspiration for dealing with this topic comes from a series of papers by Brewer. He argued forcefully that it is necessary to account for the conscious experience of remembering on an equal footing with memory performance in behavioral terms (Brewer, 1986, 1992, 1996; Brewer & Pani, 1983). Brewer (1992) concluded a review of the history of research on the phenomenal aspects of memory as follows:

> The history of the study of memory has been a dramatic roller coaster ride from the position that the only interesting aspects of memory are those that are consciously experienced to a position that denied or ignored any consciously experienced aspect of memory. However, now there is a small, (and I hope) growing group of researchers who think that the proper study of memory includes a treatment of memory in terms of both behavior and conscious experience. (p. 36)

I consider this succinct summary quite accurate, and I share the hope that more researchers will join in exploring the conscious experience of remembering. There are indeed promising signs. Johnson and her associates (e.g., 1983, 1988; Johnson & Hirst, 1993) have carried out an extensive research program on reality monitoring, which she explicitly termed a *phenomenological approach*. Gardiner (e.g., in press; Gardiner & Java, 1993) and his coworkers have developed what they call an experiential approach (or first-person perspective) to the study of recognition. And Conway (1992; Conway & Rubin, 1993) has proposed a separate experiential level of autobiographical memory called *event-specific knowledge* or a *phenomenological record*.

Why have memory researchers been slow and reluctant to put these problems of the experience of remembering on the agenda of their field? Methodological problems with research on consciousness are clearly one reason. I think an additional reason may be a basic adherence to epiphenomenalist assumptions that is common to seemingly quite different theories of memory.

Associationism and Ebbinghaus

Ebbinghaus and Watson are the obvious villains of the piece of history Brewer (1992) summarized in the preceding quote. Before Ebbinghaus and behaviorism, as Brewer noted, it was common to regard genuine or true memory as equivalent to conscious recollection, including an awareness that the event belonged to a particular time and place in the person's past. This was the dominant view in continental introspectionism (Wundt), of course, but also in American functionalism (James). How, then, could the single voice of Ebbinghaus (1885/1964), speaking well before the advent of behaviorism, almost completely block out consciousness from the study of memory for 100 years?

In his own lifetime, Ebbinghaus did not seem to succeed. He was not promoted to full professor at Berlin, after which he left to work in less prestigious places, and he had no students or school of importance. Ebbinghaus' inventiveness was methodological and his theoretical discussions were rather rudimentary. But the reason his rejection of a functional role for consciousness in memory did not stir attention was that it was not really new. It agreed with and continued the epiphenomenalism introduced by Hobbes and Hume in the 17th and 18th centuries. According to these empiricist philosophers, the content or phenomenal appearance of associations did not matter to the laws of the mind, although analyses of conscious content could be used as a means for studying such laws. This epiphenomenalist view was also widespread in 19th-century philosophy, and it was an important background for the principles of association proposed by Hartley, Herbart, and Mill (cf. Boring, 1950).

The Würzburg School

The primary reason for the downfall of introspectionism, and thus for abandoning the study of consciousness, is usually claimed to be the methodological problem that introspective reports proved to be utterly unreliable. This problem came to the fore in the dispute between Wundt's Leipzig school and the Würzburg school of Küpe, Ach, and Bühler on the existence of imageless thought (e.g., Boring, 1950). When introspecting on processes of thought, including attempts to remember, the Leipzigers reported images of the things and concepts that were thought about—the contents of thought. The Würzburgers, on the other hand, reported properties of mental acts—experiences of doubt, hesitation, belief, conviction, interests (determining tendencies), and the like. This striking difference of observations served to undermine confidence in the introspective method that was common to both schools. Perhaps the difference was more a matter of emphasis than a real contradiction—an emphasis on content in the Leipzig school versus an emphasis on the process of thinking in the Würzburg school. Nevertheless, the topic of Wundtian introspective psychology, the contents of consciousness, was discredited as being purely epiphenomenal, whereas the study of the processes of thinking appeared less problematic. This process orientation also dominated American functionalism and is continued by cognitive psychology.

Psychoanalysis

The work of Freud bears further evidence to the strength of epiphenomenalism around the turn of the century. Because Freud was centrally concerned with the causal influence of childhood experiences on adult personality, it might be supposed that psychoanalysis would take the conscious appearance of autobiographical memories very seriously. It is not easy to give an adequate picture of Freud's prolific thinking. It seems fair to say, however, that associationism was deeply engrained in Freud, at least in his early works (see Ross, 1991). He considered consciousness to be unimportant, essentially epiphenomenal, although it could be useful as a window onto the functionally decisive unconscious processes—albeit a distorting window, unlike the "royal road" of dreams. Thus, the phenomenal appearance of memories, such as their intensity or perspective, might have symptomatic value for understanding the unconscious, but it had no inherent interest.

An additional example of Freud's epiphenomenalist position is provided by his view of memory for emotions. He claimed that the conscious experiences of emotions and affects simply are not remembered—they are generated anew in each situation by remembering traces of the past situation, activated by unconscious drives (Ross, 1991). This epiphenomenalist view is very similar to the James–Lange theory of emotions (although the psychoanalytic idea of unconscious drives does not figure in that theory, of course).

Gestalt Psychology and Bartlett

Given this pervasive epiphenomenalist background, it is not really surprising that behaviorism met with little resistance when it demanded that introspection and phenomenal experience be excluded from scientific psychology. However, behaviorism is not the whole story. Gestalt psychology did, to some extent, maintain the concern about conscious experience during the reign of behaviorism. The major opponent of behaviorist memory psychology, Sir Frederic Bartlett, tends to be cited only for his reconstructive schema theory of memory. Bartlett (1932) put an equal weight on the role of *images* in memory, however. He regarded images of particular things or scenes as "a device for picking bits out of schemes" (p. 219) so that they can be manipulated independently. Images are thus crucial for that turning around upon one's schemata that in his view was the essence of consciousness. Images were also seen as responsible for providing the outstanding details around which memories were reconstructed. Nevertheless, Bartlett did not attempt to explain how the images are themselves remembered, perhaps because this might have blunted the attack on associationist trace theories that was his main purpose. Later researchers in Bartlett's tradition have by and large ignored his notion of memory images.

One further aspect of phenomenal experience was important in Bartlett's account of memory, namely, the rememberer's *attitude* toward the past situation. Bartlett left the attitude concept even less developed than images, but it does seem to bear some similarity to the notion of determining tendencies of the Würzburg school.

Cognitive Psychology and Reductionism

The assumption of computational functionalism, which is commonly held in cognitive psychology and cognitive science, entails that individual mental states can be reduced to physical events (e.g., to computations or brain events) that are universally comprehensible independent of the experiencing subject (cf. Gregory, 1987). This assumption makes explicit the epiphenomenalist view: Experience is surface appearance, physical events are the ultimate and only reality. The combination of epiphenomenalism and reductionism in effect renders issues of conscious experience irrelevant to a scientific understanding of the mind.

Nagel's (1974) bat paper reacted to the reductionist claim of computational functionalism by taking it to its extreme. He asked how something that is by definition specific to someone's point of view — namely, what it is like to be that someone — can be reduced to something that is comprehensible independent of any particular point of view; that is, to a description in terms of physical processes and states. The force of Nagel's argument is that cognitive reductionism is impossible: The qualia of another being cannot be reduced to a perspective-free level and thus be exhaustively understood.

GETTING THROUGH THE OTHER MINDS PROBLEM

But even if a nonreductionist stance is taken, a number of conceptual or metatheoretical obstacles to empirical research on phenomenal qualities of memory remain. The first pitfall is that relinquishing the possibility of full understanding may lead to doubts about the existence of other minds; that is, solipsism. As Nagel (1974) pointed out, in return for getting out of epiphenomenalism, we must accept that there are limits to the understanding of other beings. The limits are quite narrow for bats, because bats are very dissimilar from any human being, but much wider for the understanding of other humans.

Memory Accuracy as Correspondence

Let us therefore assume that it is indeed possible to understand and describe, if only in part and with approximation, another person's experience of remembering. However, the question about remembering has a recursive character because for something to be a true or accurate memory, it must correspond to something in the past. To understand the experience of someone who is remembering an event from his or her past therefore raises a second question, analogous to Nagel's original one: Is it possible for the rememberer at the present time to achieve, through memory, the same experience that was had at the time the event occurred? That is, we need to consider whether the present experience of a past event corresponds to what it was like to be in that event originally.

The problem is, of course, that the rememberer is only nominally the same person now as in the past; some changes will have taken place, be they transient or permanent ones. If we agree with Nagel that it is impossible to know fully what it is like to be a bat or another person, we also have to accept, as a logical implication, that it is impossible to know fully what it was like to be ourselves in the past—being a child, being a young and untried researcher, or even being about to start reading this chapter (cf. the comments on Nagel's paper by Hofstadter & Dennett, 1982).

This problem of memory accuracy, and the various factors that affect accuracy, have so far consumed most of the research into memory by psychologists and philosophers alike (see Brewer, 1996). For the psychologist, the philosophical problem raised by Nagel can be dealt with in the same manner as the other-minds problem; that is, by acknowledging that there must, in principle, be limits to memory accuracy. Instead of phrasing the accuracy question as a problem of whether correspondence between present and past experiences is possible in principle, it can then be conceived as an empirical issue: To what extent do the present and past experiences correspond?

The question is less straightforward than it looks, however. Koriat and Goldsmith (1996) put a similar emphasis on the correspondence question. They argued that there is a fundamental metatheoretical difference between what they call a storehouse metaphor, which focuses on retention and reproduction of memory items, and a correspondence metaphor, which focuses on the accuracy of memory in representing the past. Koriat and Goldsmith were not concerned with subjective experience, though, only with the correspondence that obtains between the person's memory and the past event as it objectively occurred. For real-life purposes, such as eyewitness testimony, this objective accuracy is clearly the ultimate interest. But even in laboratory settings, where the presentation of events to participants is strictly controlled, it is evident that the functional stimulus as perceived by the participant may differ from the objective or nominal stimulus as viewed by the experimenter (cf. studies of subjective organization in recall; e.g., Tulving, 1962). To prevent processes of perception and encoding of the original event from confounding the assessment of memory, we must get at the correspondence between the original experience and the present recollection. Such subjective correspondence is, paradoxically, the more objective and pure measure of memory accuracy.

Propositions, Images, and Feelings

To assess memory accuracy, then, we have to obtain a description of the original experience from the participant, to be compared with a description of his or her recollection. This procedure is applied in diary studies and by using questionnaires, for instance, in studies of flashbulb memories (e.g., Conway et al., 1994; Winograd & Neisser, 1992). The propositional format of such descriptions cannot be taken as a property of the memories themselves, of course. On the contrary, Brewer (1986, 1992, 1996) argued that, in the case of recollective and autobiographical memories, remembering is essentially experienced as having a mental image. This sounds relatively simple. However, it raises all the complicated issues of imagery research: the nature of images, their dimensions and features, how to assess them, and so on (e.g., Richardson, 1980).

Moreover, what about the things that we seem to remember but that are hard or impossible to have images of: abstract thoughts, meanings and intentions, and bodily experiences, such as pain, hunger, nausea, and pleasantness? It seems quite reasonable to suppose that I can perceive a knife and a roast in the same way as you do. But can I experience your hunger when you see and smell the roast or your pain when you accidentally cut your finger? As for memory, can I remember my own hunger from this morning and the pain at my last visit to the dentist? I might remember the fact that I had these feelings, but the question here concerns the feelings themselves.

A tempting solution to these difficulties is to disregard the phenomenal

qualities and treat memory for feelings and emotions in the same way as
memory for words, descriptions, and propositional facts. This is the
solution adopted by the tradition of verbal memory research (e.g., Bower,
1981), to the extent that memory for feelings and emotions is studied at all.
To get beyond this factual or propositional bias, we should attempt to
develop descriptive tools and taxonomies that heed the distinction between
perceptual qualities and propositional content. And two coding formats,
verbal and imaginal (Paivio, 1986), are probably not enough.

Memorial Attitudes

Finally, a taxonomy of phenomenal memory qualities must reflect that the
present experience of remembering includes qualities that do not correspond to something in the past. For example, a memory must somehow
include the quality of pastness, as Locke pointed out 300 years ago. If the
quality of pastness were lacking, it would be age regression or hallucination
rather than remembering. Thus, there is more to remembering than an
accurate image of the past. Some present evaluations or attributions
concerning the memory must be included, too, similar to the propositional
attitudes that philosophers distinguish sharply from qualia on logical
grounds and to the attitudes toward the past described by Bartlett (1932).
    Propositional attitudes are mental states that take other mental states
(conceived as propositions that may be either true or false) as their objects.
The typical example is the attitude of belief, such as the belief that the
proposition P is true, where P might be "this object is a roast." In the case
of remembering, the proposition P is a memory, for instance of a certain
roast, which can of course be true or false in terms of correspondence to the
past experience of the roast. Now, a number of memorial attitudes
predicated on the information given by this memory can be identified. For
instance, the experience of confidence in the accuracy of P, the experience
that "this P is familiar," remember versus know experiences about P,
feeling-of-knowing a missing P, and so forth.
    Vividness is in some respects similar to memorial attitudes: Vividness
judgments concern the present appearance of the memorial content and
have no corresponding quality in the past. Of course, the original perception is often taken as a point of reference—as 100% vividness—when
participants are asked about vividness (is the memory as vivid as the original
experience?). However, a judgment of 60% vividness has no counterpart in
the original situation. The accuracy of the judgment thus cannot be a matter
of correspondence to the past.

PHENOMENAL QUALITIES OF MEMORY:
THREE CATEGORIES

As a framework for organizing research on phenomenal memory qualities, the preceding discussion suggests that it might prove useful to distinguish three classes of qualities. I call them content qualities, appearance qualities, and process qualities. The phenomenal qualities in these three categories are argued to be fundamentally different in terms of their logical status—what they are qualities of as well as their conditions of veridicality. Content qualities are about the past experience itself, appearance qualities are about the present experience and evaluation of these content qualities, and process qualities are exclusively about the present, concerning how content and appearance qualities are produced cognitively. In contrast to content qualities, appearance qualities and process qualities have no counterparts in the past and, consequently, their accuracy or truthfulness cannot be evaluated in terms of correspondence to past reality. Some examples and tentative subcategories are listed in Table 10.1.

Speaking historically, content qualities were focused on by the Leipzig school of Wundt, process qualities by the Würzburg school of Külpe and Selz, and appearance qualities—in some measure, at least—by Bartlett. Quite recently, Gardiner and his coworkers (e.g., Richardson-Klavehn & Gardiner, 1995) have suggested a similar classification by separating memorial awareness (remember/know experiences) from volitional awareness (consciousness of retrieval processes); these two categories obviously presuppose a third one, experience of the memory content itself.

Content qualities make up the memory itself, so to say, and they are distinct because they purport to represent what was actually the case in the past. For a present phenomenal quality to belong to the content of a memory, it must at least in principle be possible that it corresponds to a quality of the original experience. For content qualities, we can therefore legitimately and meaningfully ask the accuracy question—that is, to what extent does the present experience map onto the original experience—and the accuracy can potentially be checked against evidence of that past experience. In contrast, appearance qualities and process qualities have no counterparts in the past situation and, therefore, their accuracy or truthfulness cannot be evaluated in terms of correspondence to the past.

Appearance qualities may easily be confused with content qualities because they have the content of memories as their object and thus, in an indirect sense, refer to the past. However, it is obvious that the present experiences of vividness, pastness, familiarity, or confidence logically cannot correspond to anything in the original experience; originally, the event was not seen as more or less vivid, as past, as familiar, or as

TABLE 10.1
Three Categories of Phenomenal Qualities in Memory, With Subcategories and Examples

Main Categories and Subcategories	Examples
Content qualities	
Perceptual qualities	Visual: spatial (size, distance), perspective, color, core/context, movement)
	Auditory: pitch, timbre, intensity, paralinguistic fetures
	Olfactory
	Gustatory
	Tactile
	Kinaesthetic
	Somatic/visceral
	Order/duration
Reflective qualities	Thoughts, meanings, verbal content
	Plans, intentions, causality
	Evaluations, preferences
	Emotion, affect, mood
	Self-awareness
	Temporal location
Appearance qualities	
Surface qualities	Vividness, clarity
	Richness of detail
	Coherence, completeness
	Stability of image
Belief qualities	Pastness
	Familiarity
	Know/remember
	Feeling-of-knowing
	Confidence
	Reality status
Process qualities	Processing fluency
	Retrieval effort, accessibility
	Retrieval strategy
	Voluntary/involuntary
	Reconstruction, inference

recollected with confidence. These qualities refer to the way that a certain memory content appears right now — the present impression of the past. The question of correspondence is therefore devoid of meaning for appearance qualities, although we can ask about the validity of such qualities as indicators of content accuracy.

Process qualities denote conscious experiences of the course and conduct of memory search, retrieval, and reconstruction: intention and effort to remember, search strategies, inferences, and so forth. All of these experiences refer entirely to current, ongoing mental events and do not, more or less accurately, map or refer to corresponding experiences that the participant had when the original event occurred in the past. Process qualities are considered accurate to the extent that these mental processes actually can be shown to take place here and now, independently of whether the objects and the outcomes of the processes are truthful memories or not.

Figure 10.1 summarizes how the three proposed classes of memory qualities are assumed to relate to the original experience, to observable descriptions of past events and memories, and to some constructs of memory theory. The single and double arrows distinguish between presumed causal influences and relations of symbolic, intentional reference. The relations depicted are greatly simplified; for instance, the strategic use of memory traces and generic knowledge for cyclic retrieval is hidden in the memory process box. The overlapping of circles (denoting phenomenal entities) and rectangles (denoting material entities, whether observable or hypothetical) indicate mappings assumed to be nonexhaustive; that is, not every feature of the original event is included in the experience of the event, nor is every feature of memory processes reflected in the phenomenal process qualities. It is also indicated that different relations between these entities are addressed by, respectively, the theoretical question of memory accuracy and the operational question of consistency between successive descriptions.

The proposed classification of phenomenal qualities is based on logical grounds of truth conditions and domains of reference, as I mentioned earlier. Does it have any empirical substance, that is, can it be helpful for organizing (and maybe even generating) research questions? Consider a few of the examples in Table 10.1 more closely.

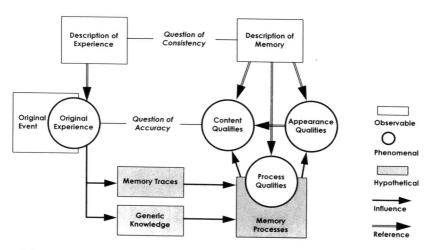

FIG. 10.1. Some suggested relations among phenomenal qualities and pertinent notions in memory theory.

Content Qualities

Following Locke (and, more recently, Johnson, 1983, 1988), the phenomenal content of memories may be divided into perceptual and reflective qualities. The distinction is not entirely clear cut; for instance, emotions certainly have perceptual components and self-awareness may be in part perceptual, as Neisser (1988) argued. It also glosses over a number of basic theoretical issues, for example, whether perception is equally constructive as thinking and whether verbal comprehension is perceptual rather than reflective. The scheme simply attempts to distinguish memory qualities that should correspond to external, sensory information from qualities corresponding to internally generated information.

Perceptual qualities can obviously be divided according to sensory modalities. The term *memory imagery* is commonly used to refer to the perceptual qualities in general, although it tends to connote vision and audition at the expense of the other modalities. In the study of Brewer (1988), which attempted to cover all sensory modalities, vision was indeed found to be the dominant modality in everyday memories. A similar conclusion was suggested by Johnson, Foley, Suengas, and Raye (1988). Inasmuch as the generality of this result is not known, however, it is important to keep the whole range of sensory modalities in mind—what I term the *modality profile* of memories.

To the extent that significant dimensions of perception are identified, the modalities may be further subdivided. This mapping of the domain of memory content could continue ad absurdum. It therefore needs to be motivated by considerations of the relevance of each dimension for memory theory. For instance, the small group of studies of perspective of observation in memories have the clear theoretical motivation that the original experience could not possibly have had the perspective of an outside observer (Nigro & Neisser, 1983; Robinson & Swanson, 1993). Size, distance, and weight in childhood memories might be studied with a similar reasoning, namely, that the experiencing child must have been smaller and weaker than the remembering adult. Further, the distinction between core and context (or central and peripheral information) in memories has been applied, with different theoretical reasons, in studies of the effect of emotional arousal (Christianson, 1992b; Heuer & Reisberg, 1992) and in flashbulb and news memory research (Conway et al., 1994; Larsen, 1992; Larsen & Thompson, 1995).

Order and duration are listed here as perceptual qualities, although it is not clear if they are represented perceptually or are reconstructed from causal and schematic knowledge (see Anderson & Conway, 1993; Friedman, 1993; Larsen, Thompson, & Hansen, 1996). Also, there is virtually no research on the extent to which dynamic features, such as movement, appear in memories — whether memories are experienced more like movies or more like snapshots (but see the use of photograph series by Burt, Mitchell, Raggatt, Jones, & Cowan, 1995).

Reflective qualities were assumed by Johnson (1983) to be internally generated and to bear evidence of the cognitive operations from which they originated. In Table 10.1, it is suggested that not only pure thoughts, but also intentions, emotions, interpretations of linguistic meaning, and self-awareness are predominantly reflective. Although they usually have a basis in sensory impressions, reflective qualities at least to some extent "go beyond the information given," and they are not tied exclusively to any one sensory modality. The difference between remembering the sensory impression and the propositional fact of an emotion illustrates the intended distinction.

Assessment of the accuracy of memory for reflective qualities is complicated by the fact that, often, the reflections could equally well be reconstructions from schematic knowledge at the time of remembering (with the attendant risk of hindsight bias; cf. Ross & Buehler, 1994). For example, recent research has shown that judgments of time in the past depend critically on reconstructions from temporal schemata (Friedman, 1993; Larsen & Thompson, 1995; Larsen et al., 1996). The relatively high accuracy of such judgments therefore cannot be taken as evidence that time, as it was perceived originally, is remembered. Note that this view does not deny that memory for perceptual information, such as day or night and weather, is important as a clue to the time of events.

Appearance Qualities

Although the appearance qualities of memories cannot be accurate in the sense of correspondence to the past, some of them can be justified (or, conversely, be mistaken) whereas to other qualities this distinction does not apply. Vividness belongs to the nonjustifiable group, and so do things like the stability and coherence of a memory image. If the participant thinks a memory is vivid and stable and coherent, he or she cannot be mistaken: This is how the memory appears at recollection, its phenomenal surface quality. It is a purely subjective quality, we may say.

On the other hand, we can meaningfully talk about the correctness or validity of a familiarity experience or a confidence judgment. That is, am I justified in believing that I have met this person before? Am I justified in believing that I remember so well? In this sense, familiarity and confidence conform better to the philosophical concept of propositional attitudes than vividness: They are beliefs about a correspondence between the present experience and the past. As beliefs, they may be right or wrong, depending on whether the believed correspondence obtains or not. Note that this is a kind of second-order accuracy, distinct from memory accuracy proper.

Among *surface qualities*, vividness is the most commonly investigated. For instance, Brown and Kulik (1977) used high vividness, close to a reliving of the past experience, to define so-called flashbulb memories, and Rubin and Kozin (1984) studied vivid autobiographical memories more generally. The basis for memory vividness is not clear, however. If a theory of memory traces is adopted, it is easy to see that memories can be more or less detailed, but how can they vary in vividness? Does vividness reflect trace strength or amount of detail? The strength interpretation might suggest that high vividness indicates memory accuracy, as Brown and Kulik (1977) seemed to assume. Later research has indeed shown fair correlations between vividness and memory accuracy (Brewer, 1988), but also that memories may turn out to be inaccurate or completely false despite their vivid appearance (cf. Neisser & Harsch, 1992). On the amount of detail interpretation, ratings of vividness are just a convenient way to assess richness of phenomenal content, and it is perhaps less tempting to assume that the details are also accurate.

Vividness is often treated as purely or mainly visual, but the distinction of content and appearance qualities should help to remind us that it applies to the other modalities of content as well (e.g., somatic and tactile qualities of emotional and painful memories). Indeed, it should be of interest to study the conditions that affect how vividness varies across content modalities, as attempted in the experiment in the next section.

Belief qualities have enjoyed more attention from theorists than any other category of phenomenal qualities. Pastness and familiarity were extensively discussed by early psychologists (e.g, Höffding, 1885/1891; James, 1890/1950). More recently, Johnson's (1983, 1988) notion of the perceived reality status of memories—was it a real event or not?—is a prominent example. Johnson's research has focused particularly on the basis for reality beliefs. Thus, Johnson and Hirst (1993) proposed that there are two major strategies for arriving at reality belief: heuristic strategies based on the content qualities and appearance of a memory (e.g., the presence of sensory detail, vividness) and systematic strategies that check the memory against other memories, generic knowledge, and logical rules. Notice that such strategies are hypothetical mental processes, distinct from the properties of memories that the strategy relies on to decide their reality status. If the person is aware of using a certain strategy for the decision, that experience belongs to the process quality group, not to the appearance qualities of the memory being judged.

The relation between appearance and process qualities is also highlighted by research on remember and know responses in recognition (see, e.g., Gardiner & Java, 1993). The distinction between remember and know responses was introduced by Tulving (1985) and may be seen as a continuation of the emphasis on familiarity in early accounts of memory (in particular Höffding, 1885/1891). Remember denotes recognition accompanied by recollective experience of the past event in which an item was encountered, and know is recognition accompanied solely by an experience of familiarity with the item. Remember and know thus refer to two different experiences that are predicated on a certain memory content, like beliefs predicated on propositions. For either, it can be asked whether it is a valid or justified belief; that is, to what extent memory of the content is accurate. However, the person's choice of remember and know is something that cannot be disputed. It is a matter of the appearance of the remembered content to the consciousness of the rememberer.

The theoretical interpretation of the remember–know distinction is currently being discussed (see Gardiner, in press). In one approach, recollective experience is identified with conscious, voluntary retrieval processes, whereas familiarity is equated with awareness of perceptual fluency caused by nonconscious, involuntary retrieval (Jacoby, Yonelinas & Jennings, in press). That is, remember and know states are seen as memory experiences based on two different retrieval processes – in the present terminology, as process qualities. In contrast, Gardiner and his coworkers argued that the memorial awareness (i.e., appearance quality) indicated by remember–know responses should be kept apart from the volitional awareness of retrieval processes because the two kinds of awareness can be dissociated empirically (Richardson-Klavehn & Gardiner, 1995). The present framework converges with the latter position, although for reasons of conceptual clarity rather than on empirical grounds. Further, the distinction between appearance and process qualities may serve to prevent accounts of hypothetical processes from being confused with the experience (or nonexperience) of such processes.

Process Qualities

As we have just seen, theories of the underlying processes that cause certain memory phenomena may lead to confusion of appearance and process qualities. But even if recollective experiences have voluntary retrieval processes as causal antecedents, the experience of this retrieval can only be an index of the processes. As such, process qualities provide evidence to constrain functional theories that account for memory accuracy, as well as for content and appearance qualities. However, this supplementary role has not encouraged really systematic research, and the examples given in Table 10.1 are therefore rather few and not exhaustive.

Retrieval strategies, including the distinction between voluntary and involuntary remembering, are the most frequently investigated type of process qualities. Such strategies are typically studied by think-aloud methods (Brown, 1990; Read & Bruce, 1982; Williams & Hollan, 1981) or retrospective reports (Friedman & Wilkins, 1985; Thompson, Skowronski, Betz, & Larsen, 1995). The methodological problems pertaining to such methods, as well as procedures to handle them, are well known and should not be so grave as to impede research (Ericsson & Simon, 1984). The more serious issue is to specify theoretically interesting relations between process qualities and other features of memory. For instance, does retrieval effort correlate with vividness and with accuracy of content qualities? Do memories experienced as being involuntary differ in content from voluntary ones (e.g., Berntsen, in press; Spence, 1988)? Do experiences of one's own memory processes furnish the material from which metamemory knowledge is developed?

MEMORY MODALITIES AND VIVIDNESS: AN EXPERIMENT

Brewer (1996) stated that remembering of autobiographical memories — what he calls recollective memory — is essentially experienced as having a mental image, most frequently a visual image, of the memory content. When perceptual content qualities are considered, it is tempting to think in terms of a copy or trace theory because the format of the memory appears to coincide with the original experience. Brewer himself maintained a partly reconstructive memory theory in which an important role is assumed for stored traces in a perceptual or image format (rather than an interpreted, propositional format). Similarly, Conway's (1992; Conway & Rubin, 1993) notion of event specific knowledge represents fairly raw traces of the person's original experiences.

However, it is certainly possible for the cognitive system to generate purely imaginary experiences that possess vivid perceptual qualities, such as dreams. And influential imagery theories, such as Kosslyn's (1980), claim that all imagery is generated from abstract representations. Therefore, even highly vivid memory imagery could be reconstructed from a propositional format, or from schematic knowledge, instead of reflecting retrieved perceptual traces.

Can it be shown that memory imagery is not entirely generated? That is, do stored memory traces make a contribution to imagery that renders memory images different from generated images? It seems reasonable to assume that if memory traces are available in a perceptual format, a corresponding image can, within a set time, achieve higher vividness than if such traces are less likely to be drawn on. The basic idea of the present experiment is to use purely imagined events as a baseline for evaluating the contribution of memory to the vividness of imagery. One group of participants was told to remember events that had actually happened to them in the past. Another group was told to imagine similar events that might happen at some time in the future but had not happened to them in the past. Thus, the aim was that the two sets of events should be comparable in terms of their content. If memory of the event contributes to enhancing imagery in any way, beyond what can be accomplished by unconstrained imagination, the vividness of imagery in the remember group should exceed that of the imagine group. This strategy is similar to that of Bruce and Van Pelt (1989), who obtained estimates of the imagined likelihood of certain events from native Scandinavians as a baseline for evaluating memories of particular events from a tour of that area.

A further purpose of the experiment was to study whether the dominance of visual imagery that is claimed by Brewer holds true generally. Brewer (1988) found support for this thesis in his study of memory for autobiographical events selected randomly by a beeper, and Johnson et al. (1988) reported similar findings for self-selected autobiographical memories. However, it is conceivable that highly emotional events would show a less vision-dominated modality profile. Various theories of emotion disagree in many respects, but they do agree that internal modalities of perception — visceral, kinaesthetic, and tactile — are indispensable for typical emotional experiences to occur (e.g., Strongman, 1987). Therefore, emotional events, both positive and negative, were employed in the experiment, and the hypothesized superiority of the remember group was studied in terms of both the overall vividness of imagery and the modality profile of the imagery. That is, separate vividness ratings were obtained for each of the major sensory modalities.

Incidentally, memory for emotions has been relatively little researched. Thus, in the *Handbook of Emotion and Memory* edited by Christianson (1992a), the vast majority of work discussed concerns the effect of emotional variables on memory. Memory for emotions is referred to only occasionally in the context of classical conditioning (Christianson, 1992b; LeDoux, 1992) and implicit memory (Tobias, Kihlstrom, & Schacter, 1992), not conscious or explicit memory. This seems like tacit endorsement of the view of Freud and James that emotions are not stored and retrieved from memory, but are rather re-created at recollection by remembering the situations that elicited them originally:

> The revivability in memory of the emotions, like all the feelings of the lower senses, is very small. We can remember that we underwent grief or rapture, but not just how the grief or rapture felt . . . [However,] we can produce, not

remembrances of the old grief or rapture, but new griefs or raptures, by summoning up a lively thought of the exciting cause. (James, 1890/1950, p. 474)

James held that visual and auditory qualities (being commonly regarded as "higher senses") enjoy superior memory, whereas somatic, kinaesthetic, tactile, and perhaps taste and smell qualities require the further work of a lively imagination to be recreated and thus give rise to emotional reexperiencing. If this is so, visual and auditory vividness should show more of an effect of the remember–imagine factor than other modalities.

Whereas the revival of "lower" sense impressions was seen as unlikely by James, it is interesting to note that he took for granted the existence of a propositional memory for the emotion—that we underwent it. In a lengthy review of the literature, Brewer (1996) still considered it an open issue whether emotions can be represented in memory in perceptual/image format or only propositionally—as reflective qualities.

Method

The participants in the study numbered 55, with 28 in the remember group and 27 in the imagine group. All were second-year Danish psychology students, more than two thirds were women, and most were in their 20s. The experiment was conducted in one session for each group. Both groups were instructed that their task was to imagine certain events in their mind and to rate the vividness of imagery afterward. Note that the Danish words for imagine and imagery (*forestille, forestillinger*) do not carry any visual connotations, like the English terms; they can rather be rendered as *represent* and *representations*, respectively. Care was taken to explain the use of the six 5-point imagery scales, one global vividness scale followed by five scales for visual, auditory, olfactory-gustatory, tactile, and somatic-kinaesthetic vividness, respectively.

The remember participants were instructed to think in every case of particular past events they had experienced. The imagine participants were told that they should think of events that had not happened to them in the past but conceivably could happen at some future time. One warm-up event and 12 experimental events, assumed to be characterized by different emotions, were used. The phrases used to describe the events are listed in Table 10.2. The emotions varied on two factors, valence and focus. Six of the experimental events were defined by the presence of emotions with positive valence and six had negative valence. Half of the emotions in each group were described with an internal focus, and half were described by external situations that were likely to generate emotions (although typically

TABLE 10.2
Emotional Events Remembered or Imagined by Participants

Focus	Emotional Valence	
	Positive	*Negative*
Internal	Being joyful	Being afraid
	Being hopeful	Being angry
	Being relieved	Being depressed
External	Holiday breakfast	Exhausting biking
	On beach in sun	Forgetting keys
	Evening at movies	Confusing names

milder ones, presumably). The same random order of events was used in both groups.

In a relaxed state with closed eyes, the participants were given 40 seconds to bring to mind each event and consider its appearance carefully. Time was measured from the point when the event description had been read out loud slowly twice in succession to ensure errorless comprehension. When the end of the period was announced, participants opened their eyes and rated imagery for the event on the six vividness scales in a response booklet. About 2 minutes were provided for the participants to relax again and clear their mind of extraneous thoughts before instructions concerning the next event were presented.

Results

The average overall vividness ratings for each participant were analyzed by a three-way mixed analysis of variance (ANOVA; between-subjects: remember/imagine; within-subjects: internal/external focus, positive/negative valence). The analysis showed small but clearly significant main effects of all three independent variables. Remembered events were more vivid than imagined events, $F(1, 53) = 5.74$, $p < .05$; external focus in events resulted in higher vividness than internal focus, $F(1, 53) = 10.14$, $p < .005$; positive events were more vivid than negative ones, $F(1, 53) = 15.57$, $p < .0005$. In all three cases, the means differed by just above .25 on the 0 to 4-point vividness scale.

These main effects, however, were modified by a significant three-way interaction, $F(1, 53) = 7.95$, $p < .01$, which can be inspected in Fig. 10.2. It is seen that for the internal experience of negative emotions, the superiority of remembered over imagined events was quite marked (means differ by .62, $p = .0005$ by Newman–Keuls test). In the other three

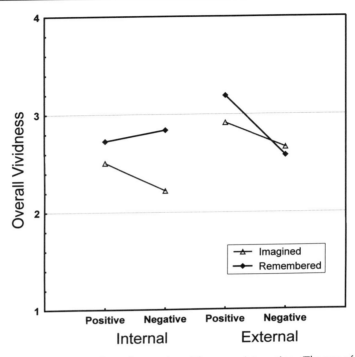

FIG. 10.2. Average overall vividness ratings: Three-way interaction. (The use of line graphs in this and the following figures is solely for ease of comprehension. It does not imply any particular order or continuity along the abscissa.)

conditions, the pairwise comparisons between remembered and imagined events were either nonsignificant or just reached the .05 level.

The *modality profile* was analyzed by entering the average vividness ratings into a four-way ANOVA with the five modality scales as a fourth, within-subjects factor. This replicated the significant main effects from the overall vividness ratings, although at higher levels of significance ($F > 18.85, p > .0001$). Also, the interaction shown in Fig. 10.2 was replicated. More important, however, the five modality scales received highly different ratings, $F(4, 212) = 183.72, p = 0$), but the greater vividness of remembered than imagined events held true in all modalities, as shown in Fig. 10.3 (insignificant interaction, $F < 1$).

The only higher order interaction involving the remember–imagine factor is shown in Fig. 10.4, $F(4, 212) = 3.91, p < .005$. This figure indicates that the visual modality dominated in the externally defined events. These events could be imagined almost as vividly as they could be remembered. On the other hand, somatic and kinaesthetic qualities dominated in the internally defined (and presumably more intense) emotional events. In these events,

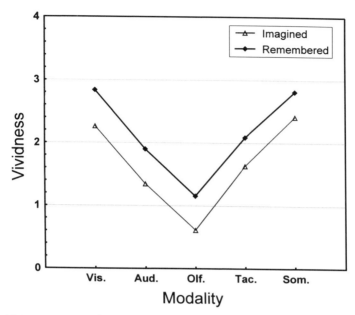

FIG. 10.3.   Average vividness ratings on five modality scales: Vis (visual), Aud (auditory), Olf (olfactory-gustatory), Tac (tactile), and Som (somatic-kinaesthetic).

memory also seemed to contribute more to vividness because they were generally less clearly imagined (except that their somatic qualities could be imagined quite vividly).

Discussion

The results indicated that the vividness of imagery was enhanced in the remember group; this occurred to an equal extent in all five modalities that were studied. This finding is unlikely to be an artifact (caused by the expectancy effects that are a serious concern in imagery research) because the remember–imagine factor was between subjects. Moreover, the difference achieved significance despite the notorious variability of vividness ratings (e.g., Richardson, 1980) and the possible attenuation due to regression toward the mean in each group. It is also noticeable that there were no missing responses in the experiment. Thus, the tasks of retrieving or generating events that corresponded to the 12 descriptive phrases were apparently both quite easy. This observation serves to make it less likely that imagined events received lower vividness ratings because they were generated more slowly than remembered events, which would leave less time

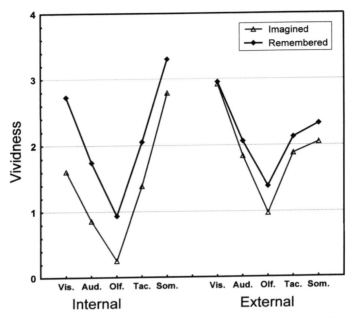

FIG. 10.4. Average vividness ratings on the five modality scales (as in Fig. 10.3): Three-way interaction.

for appreciating their vividness. However, to reject this possibility conclusively, the time for assessing imagery should be measured from the point when participants had identified an appropriate event. This procedure was not possible in the present group sessions.

The superior vividness of remembered events suggests that autobiographical memory images are not entirely generated from generic representations, but that they do — at least to some extent — have a basis in specific, probably perceptual, traces. However, the small magnitude of the difference also suggests that the vividness of memory images is only marginally dependent on memory proper. Thus, the observation of vivid imagery does not guarantee that events are remembered rather than constructed. Unfortunately, a number of other interpretations cannot be ruled out. On the one hand, the advantage of remembered events might derive from other factors than the use of perceptual traces, such as greater embeddedness of remembered events in large-scale knowledge structures. This would imply that the effect of memory traces was less than indicated by the ratings, or entirely nonexistent. On the other hand, the imagined events were undoubtedly not purely imagined but to some extent relied on remembered information, for instance, scenarios from films and books or recombinations of materials from personal experiences. This would imply that the effect of memory traces was greater than indicated by the ratings obtained here. In view of these opposing effects, the most parsimonious interpretation seems to be that, at least, the imagined events were based on memory traces to a lesser extent than the remembered events and, therefore, perceptual memory traces do seem to facilitate imagery production.

The imagined events in the study may be seen as possible memories that the participant feels able to reject as not being real memories. As Brewer (1996) pointed out, such possible but successfully rejected memory errors have not previously been examined and compared to memories that the participant believes to be real and accurate ones (but see Conway, Collins, Gathercole, & Anderson, 1996). The finding of only a small advantage for remembered events suggests that vividness is a pretty unreliable criterion for distinguishing between events believed to be memories and events believed not to be memories. Vividness-based strategies of monitoring memory accuracy (such as the heuristic strategies of Johnson & Hirst, 1993) may thus be of limited use, as also suggested by the study of Johnson et al. (1988, Exp. 2).

The experiment reported here has similarities to a study by Johnson et al. (1988, Exp. 1) in which memory for real events was compared to memory for fictional events imagined in the past. That is, Johnson et al. were concerned with memory for imagery, not with the vividness that can be achieved by present imagination. In their study, moreover, the content of the imagined and the real events was vastly different because the choice of events was left to the individual participant.

A second finding was that positive events were generally imagined more vividly than negative ones (following the "Pollyanna principle" of Matlin & Stang, 1978). Nevertheless, a focus on the internal aspect of clearly negative events was found to produce the largest vividness superiority of remembered over imagined events. A particularly lively memory for the experience of such highly negative events is in accordance with theories of intrusive, traumatic memories (e.g., Horowitz & Reidbord, 1992), and it also agrees with theories of superior retention of flashbulb memories (Brown & Kulik, 1977; Winograd & Neisser, 1992). However, it should be kept in mind that even the most vivid images in this study need not be accurate memories; information was not available to assess memory accuracy.

Unfortunately, emotional intensity and internal–external focus of attention may have been confounded. Thus, the internal-focus emotions are likely to be stronger than the external-focus emotions that were employed (cf. Table 10.2). The finding of higher vividness when the focus was external does speak against an interpretation of vividness differences in terms of emotional intensity, however, because the possibly lower intensity of the external emotions would be expected to result in lower vividness. Still, replication of the results in an unconfounded design is desirable.

The third main finding was that, with emotional events like the present ones, visual imagery dominated only when the participant was asked to focus on the external situation. In contrast, when the focus of defining the emotion was internal (being angry, joyful, or afraid), the vividness of somatic-kinaesthetic imagery dominated. If we are to believe these young students, impressions in "the lower senses" may be imagined and remembered as clearly as visual and auditory ones, contrary to James' (1890/1950) statement. However, this might not be true for older people. Quoting himself as an example, James suggested that, with advancing age, vividness of imagination generally deteriorates, particularly for the lower senses.

The somatic dominance in strongly emotional memories may not be at variance with Brewer's (1988) finding in his beeper study that visual imagery is heavily dominant. The events studied by Brewer were randomly selected and, therefore, they did not include many that were strongly emotional. Furthermore, Brewer's participants quite often failed to record events when the beeper went off, which suggests that a bias toward omitting strongly emotional, and possibly embarrassing, events was present in his study.

More generally, vividness of somatic qualities in the present data seemed to be attained at the expense of the visual components of imagery—when one went up, the other went down (cf. Fig. 10.4). The shape of imagery modality profiles could therefore reflect some kind of capacity limitation on image generation—for instance, the capacity of working memory—in addition to reflecting the content of imagery. Another intriguing finding is the consistently low ratings of olfactory-gustatory vividness, which contrasts with the power that common sense tends to ascribe to smell and taste as memory cues. This underscores the need to extend the very limited research on these modalities (e.g, Rubin, Groth, & Goldsmith, 1984; Schab & Crowder, 1995).

SUMMARY AND CONCLUSIONS

The history of psychological research on the conscious experiences, or phenomenal qualities, that occur in autobiographical and laboratory remembering was briefly considered, arguing that an epiphenomenalist view of consciousness has been common to most research traditions. It was pointed out that the problems encountered in such research have affinities with the philosophical problem of other minds.

To organize research issues in this area, a conceptual framework was proposed, consisting of three logically distinct categories of memory qualities: content qualities, appearance qualities, and process qualities. Only content qualities can map onto corresponding experiences in the past, more or less accurately; they include sensory qualities, temporal and spatial qualities (e.g., perspective), emotions and thoughts, and so on. Appearance qualities did not exist in the original experience but rather refer to the manner in which memory content is currently perceived (e.g., vividness, familiarity, confidence, remember vs. know judgments). Process qualities are entirely concerned with the present; they include awareness of retrieval effort and strategies, reconstructions, inferences, and the like. Although based on logical considerations of truth conditions, this classification should be useful to remind us of the variety of subjective experiences behind the conventional measures of memory performance. Moreover, the classification underscores that different types of questions are appropriate for the different categories. Thus, for content we may ask if it is a true memory, in terms of correspondence to past experience; for appearance qualities like vividness and familiarity, we can only ask if they are predictive of true memories — they have no objective truth; and for process qualities, truthfulness is a matter of their correspondence to present cognitive activities.

The most commonly investigated appearance quality of memories is vividness, usually reported to be predominantly visual. An experiment explored vividness profiles across several sensory modalities in memories of events, compared to imagined events with similar content. The results suggest that the phenomenal qualities of memories are not entirely generated or reconstructed from generic representations. In emotional memories, furthermore, somatic imagery may challenge the ordinary dominance of visual imagery, and perceptual content seems particularly well retained in strongly negative memories. The experiment illustrates one virtue of the classificatory scheme by showing that behind an overall judgment of vividness, there may be widely different vividness profiles. One image may be vivid because of its visual content, another because of somatic qualities. Vividness profiles are apparently determined both by the nature of remembered content and by the cognitive processing of the rememberer. Intriguingly, the results suggest that there may be a trade-off between vividness in different modalities, such as visual and somatic-kinaesthetic imagery.

ACKNOWLEDGMENTS

This chapter was in part prepared during a stay at the Department of Psychology, University of Bristol. The experiment builds on pilot work conducted in collaboration with Bobby Zachariae in Aarhus. The final revision of the chapter benefited significantly from extensive and challenging comments by Dorthe Berntsen, Bill Brewer, Darryl Bruce, Martin Conway, and Don Read.

REFERENCES

Anderson, S. A., & Conway, M. A. (1993). Investigating the structure of autobiographical memories. *Journal of Experimental Psychology: Learning, Memory, and Cognition, 19*, 1178–1196.

Bartlett, F. C. (1932). *Remembering: A study in experimental and social psychology.* Cambridge, UK: Cambridge University Press.

Berntsen, D. (in press). Voluntary and involuntary access to autobiographical memory. *Memory.*

Boring, E. G. (1950). *A history of experimental psychology* (2nd ed.). New York: Appleton-Century-Crofts.

Bower, G. H. (1981). Mood and memory. *American Psychologist, 36*, 129–148.

Brewer, W. F. (1986). What is autobiographical memory? In D. C. Rubin (Ed.), *Autobiographical memory* (pp. 25–49). New York: Cambridge University Press.

Brewer, W. F. (1988). Memory for randomly sampled autobiographical events. In U. Neisser & E. Winograd (Eds.), *Remembering reconsidered: Ecological and traditional approaches to the study of memory* (pp. 21–90). New York: Cambridge University Press.

Brewer, W. F. (1992). Phenomenal experience in laboratory and autobiographical memory. In M. A. Conway, D. C. Rubin, H. Spinnler, & W. A. Wagenaar (Eds.), *Theoretical perspectives on autobiographical memory* (pp. 31–51). Dordrecht, The Netherlands: Kluwer.

Brewer, W. F. (1996). What is recollective memory? In D. C. Rubin (Ed.), *Remembering our past: Studies in autobiographical memory* (pp. 19–66). New York: Cambridge University Press.

Brewer, W. F., & Pani, J. R. (1983). The structure of human memory. In G. H. Bower (Ed.), *The psychology of learning and motivation* (Vol. 17, pp. 1–28). New York: Academic Press.

Brown, N. R. (1990). Organization of public events in long-term memory. *Journal of Experimental Psychology: General, 119*, 297–314.

Brown, R., & Kulik, J. (1977). Flashbulb memories. *Cognition, 5*, 73–99.

Bruce, D., & Van Pelt, M. (1989). Memories of a bicycle tour. *Applied Cognitive Psychology, 3*, 137–156.

Burt, C. D. B., Mitchell, D. A., Raggatt, P. T. F., Jones, C. A., & Cowan, T. M. (1995). A snapshot of autobiographical memory retrieval characteristics. *Applied Cognitive Psychology, 9*, 61–74.

Christianson, S.-Å. (Ed.). (1992a). *The handbook of emotion and memory: Research and theory.* Hillsdale, NJ: Lawrence Erlbaum Associates.

Christianson, S.-Å. (1992b). Remembering emotional events: Potential mechanisms. In S.-Å. Christianson (Ed.), *The handbook of emotion and memory: Research and theory* (pp. 307–340). Hillsdale, NJ: Lawrence Erlbaum Associates.

Conway, M. A. (1992). A structural model of autobiographical memory. In M. A. Conway, D. C. Rubin, H. Spinnler, & W. A. Wagenaar (Eds.), *Theoretical perspectives on autobiographical memory* (pp. 167–194). Dordrecht, The Netherlands: Kluwer.

Conway, M. A., Anderson, S. J., Larsen, S. F., Donnelly, C. M., McDaniel, M. A., McClelland, A. G. R., Rawles, R. E., & Logie, R. H. (1994). The formation of flashbulb memories. *Memory and Cognition, 22*, 326–343.

Conway, M. A., Collins, A. F., Gathercole, S. E., & Anderson, S. J. (1996). Recollections of true and false autobiographical memories. *Journal of Experimental Psychology: General, 125*, 69–95.

Conway, M. A. & Rubin, D. C. (1993). The structure of autobiographical memory. In A. F. Collins, S. E. Gathercole, M. A. Conway, & P. E. Morris (Eds.), *Theories of memory* (pp. 103–137). Hove, UK: Lawrence Erlbaum Associates.

Ebbinghaus, H. E. (1964). *Memory: A contribution to experimental psychology.* New York: Dover. (Original work published 1885)

Ericsson, K. A., & Simon, H. A. (1984). *Protocol analysis: Verbal reports as data.* Cambridge, MA: Bradford Books/ MIT Press.

Friedman, W. J. (1993). Memory for the time of past events. *Psychological Bulletin, 113,* 44–66.

Friedman, W. J., & Wilkins, A. J. (1985). Scale effects in memory for the time of past events. *Memory and Cognition, 13,* 168–175.

Gardiner, J. M. (in press). On consciousness in relation to memory and learning. In M. Velmans (Ed.), *The science of consciousness: Psychological, neuropsychological, and clinical reviews.* London: Routledge.

Gardiner, J. M., & Java, R. I. (1993). Recognising and remembering. In A. F. Collins, S. E. Gathercole, M. A. Conway, & P. E. Morris (Eds.), *Theories of memory* (pp. 163–188). Hove, UK: Lawrence Erlbaum Associates.

Gregory, R. L. (Ed.). (1987). *The Oxford companion to the mind.* Oxford, UK: Oxford University Press.

Heuer, F., & Reisberg, D. (1992). Emotions, arousal, and memory for detail. In S.-Å. Christianson (Ed.), *The handbook of emotion and memory: Research and theory* (pp. 151–180). Hillsdale, NJ: Lawrence Erlbaum Associates.

Höffding, H. (1891). *Outlines of psychology.* London: Macmillan. (Original work published 1885)

Hofstadter, D. R., & Dennett, D. C. (Eds.). (1982). *The mind's I.* Harmondsworth, UK: Penguin.

Horowitz, M. J., & Reidbord, S. P. (1992). Memory, emotion, and response to trauma. In S.-Å. Christianson (Ed.), *The handbook of emotion and memory: Research and theory* (pp. 343–358). Hillsdale, NJ: Lawrence Erlbaum Associates.

Jacoby, L. L., Yonelinas, A. P., & Jennings, J. M. (in press). The relation between conscious and unconscious (automatic) influences: A declaration of independence. In J. Cohen & J. W. Schooler (Eds.), *Scientific approaches to the question of consciousness.* Hillsdale, NJ: Lawrence Erlbaum Associates.

James, W. (1950). *The principles of psychology* (Vol. 1). New York: Dover. (Original work published 1890)

Johnson, M. K. (1983). A multiple-entry, modular memory system. In G. H. Bower (Ed.), *The psychology of learning and motivation* (Vol. 17, pp. 81–123). New York: Academic Press.

Johnson, M. K. (1988). Reality monitoring: An experimental phenomenological approach. *Journal of Experimental Psychology: General, 117,* 390–394.

Johnson, M. K., Foley, M. A., Suengas, A. G., & Raye, C. L. (1988). Phenomenal characteristics of memories for perceived and imagined autobiographical events. *Journal of Experimental Psychology: General, 117,* 371–376.

Johnson, M. K., & Hirst, W. (1993). MEM: Memory subsystems as processes. In A. F. Collins, S. E. Gathercole, M. A. Conway, & P. E. Morris (Eds.), *Theories of memory* (pp. 241–286). Hove, UK: Lawrence Erlbaum Associates.

Koriat, A., & Goldsmith, M. (1996). Memory metaphors and the real-life/laboratory controversy: Correspondence versus storehouse conceptions of memory. *Behavioral and Brain Sciences, 19,* 167–228.

Kosslyn, S. M. (1980). *Image and mind.* Cambridge, MA: Harvard University Press.

Larsen, S.F. (1992). Potential flashbulbs: Memories of ordinary news as the baseline. In E. Winograd & U. Neisser (Eds.), *Affect and accuracy in recall: Studies of flashbulb memories* (pp. 32–64). New York: Cambridge University Press.

Larsen, S. F., & Thompson, C. P. (1995). Reconstructive memory in the dating of personal and public events. *Memory & Cognition, 23,* 780–790.

Larsen, S. F., Thompson, C. P., & Hansen, T. (1996). Time in autobiographical memory. In

D. C. Rubin (Ed.), *Remembering our past: Studies in autobiographical memory* (pp. 143–173). New York: Cambridge University Press.

LeDoux, J. E. (1992). Emotion as memory: Anatomical systems underlying indelible neural traces. In S.-Å. Christianson (Ed.), *The handbook of emotion and memory: Research and theory* (pp. 269–288). Hillsdale, NJ: Lawrence Erlbaum Associates.

Matlin, M. W., & Stang, D. J. (1978). *The Pollyanna principle.* Cambridge, MA: Schenkman.

Nagel, T. (1974). What is it like to be a bat? *Philosophical Review, 83*, 435–450.

Neisser, U. (1988). Five kinds of self-knowledge. *Philosophical Psychology, 1*, 35–59.

Neisser, U., & Harsch, N. (1992). Phantom flashbulbs: False recollections of hearing the news about Challenger. In E. Winograd & U. Neisser (Eds.), *Affect and accuracy in recall: Studies of "flashbulb" memories* (pp. 9–31). New York: Cambridge University Press.

Nigro, G., & Neisser, U. (1983). Point of view in personal memories. *Cognitive Psychology, 15*, 467–482.

Paivio, A. (1986). *Mental representations: A dual coding approach.* New York: Oxford University Press.

Read, J. D., & Bruce, D. (1982). Longitudinal tracking of difficult memory retrievals. *Cognitive Psychology, 14*, 280–300.

Richardson, J. T. E. (1980). *Mental imagery and human memory.* New York: St. Martin's.

Richardson-Klavehn, A., & Gardiner, J. M. (1995). Retrieval volition and memorial awareness in stem completion: An empirical analysis. *Psychological Research, 57*, 166–178.

Robinson, J. A., & Swanson, K. L. (1993). Field and observer modes of remembering. *Memory, 1*, 169–184.

Ross, B. M. (1991). *Remembering the personal past: Descriptions of autobiographical memory.* New York: Oxford University Press.

Ross, M., & Buehler, R. (1994). Creative remembering. In U. Neisser & R. Fivush (Eds.), *The remembering self* (pp. 205–235). New York: Cambridge University Press.

Rubin, D. C., Groth, L., & Goldsmith, D. (1984). Olfactory cuing of autobiographical memory. *American Journal of Psychology, 97*, 493–507.

Rubin, D. C., & Kozin, M. (1984). Vivid memories. *Cognition, 16,* 81–95.

Schab, F. R., & Crowder, R. G. (Eds.). (1995). *Memory for odors.* Mahwah, NJ: Lawrence Erlbaum Associates.

Spence, D. P. (1988). Passive remembering. In U. Neisser & E. Winograd (Eds.), *Remembering reconsidered: Ecological and traditional approaches to the study of memory* (pp. 311–325). New York: Cambridge University Press.

Strongman, K. F. (1987). *The psychology of emotions* (3rd ed.). Chichester, UK: Wiley.

Thompson, C. P., Skowronski, J. S., Betz, A. L., & Larsen, S. F. (1995). Long-term performance in autobiographical event dating. In A. F. Healy & L. E. Bourne (Eds.), *Learning and memory of knowledge and skills* (pp. 206–233). Thousand Oaks, CA: Sage.

Tobias, B. A., Kihlstrom, J. F., & Schacter, D. S. (1992). Emotion and implicit memory. In S.-Å. Christianson (Ed.), *The handbook of emotion and memory: Research and theory* (pp. 67–92). Hillsdale, NJ: Lawrence Erlbaum Associates.

Tulving, E. (1962). Subjective organization in free recall of "unrelated" words. *Psychological Review, 69*, 344–354.

Tulving, E. (1985). Memory and consciousness. *Canadian Psychologist, 26*, 1–12.

Williams, D. M., & Hollan, J. D. (1981). The process of retrieval from very long-term memory. *Cognitive Science, 5*, 87–119.

Winograd, E., & Neisser, U. (Eds.) (1992). *Affect and accuracy in recall: Studies of "flashbulb" memories.* New York: Cambridge University Press.

Author Index

A

Abelson, R. P., 54, 66
Adams, S., 91, 100
Aggleton, J. P., 59, 63
Akin, C., 57, 66
Alexander, I. E., 127, 138, 142
Anderson, S. J., 118, 122, 174, 185, 188
Andres, D., 107, 122
Arbuckle, T. Y., 107, 122
Aries, E., 80, 100
Aukett, R., 98, 100
Avertt, C. P., 80, 101

B

Bachevalier, J., 59, 65
Bacon, F., 17
Baddeley, A., 19, 24, 49, 55, 58, 63, 115–117, 122
Bahrick, H. P., 6, 30, 42, 69–72, 74–77
Bahrick, P. C., 4, 42
Balswick, J. O., 80, 81, 101
Balzer, W. K., 70, 78
Banaji, M. R., 19, 25, 29, 43
Banks, W. P., 16, 25
Barber, D., 16, 25
Barber, T. X., 156, 162
Barclay, C. R., 53, 54, 63, 127, 141, 142
Barsalou, L. W., 53, 63, 101, 115, 122
Bartlett, F. C., 70, 77, 166, 167, 170, 171, 188
Bateson, M. C., 139, 142
Beardsall, L., 91, 101
Beattie, O. V., 127, 142
Belenky, M. F., 80, 101

Bell, B. E., 55, 63, 159, 160
Berger, D. E., 16, 25
Berger, S. A., 70, 77
Berntsen, D., 51, 63, 178, 188
Betz, A. L., 32, 36, 39, 43, 74, 78, 178, 190
Black, J. B., 48, 49, 52, 65
Bock, M., 74, 77
Boring, E. G., 107, 165, 188
Bower, G. H., 26, 39, 43, 170, 188, 189
Boyle, P., 91, 100
Bretherton, I., 91, 101
Brewer, W. F., 31, 43, 49, 55, 57, 63, 76, 77, 164, 165, 168, 169, 174, 176, 178–180, 185, 186, 188
Brice, J., 59, 65
Broadbent, K., 115, 123
Brody, L., 90, 99, 101
Brown, G. E., 13, 25
Brown, J., 91, 101,
Brown, N. R., 178, 188
Brown, R., 47, 53, 55, 63,145, 155, 160, 176, 185, 188
Bruce, D., 3, 29, 43, 70, 77, 178, 179, 188, 190
Bruck, M., 30, 43
Bruner, J., 54, 56, 63, 79, 87, 101, 126, 127, 131, 139, 142, 145, 160
Buckner, N., 148, 149, 160
Buehler, R., 175, 190
Bull, M. P., 111, 123
Burke, D. M., 120, 122, 123
Burt, C. D. M., 31, 43, 175, 188
Butters, N., 61, 62, 64

C

Cabeza, R., 59, 65

Cappeliez, P., 107, 123
Capps, L., 147, 160
Cason, H., 37, 43
Ceci, S. J., 6–9, 12, 30, 43
Cermak, L. S., 61, 62, 64
Chafe, W., 56, 64, 145, 160
Chapanis, A., 16, 25
Chase, W. G., 57, 64
Chodorow, N., 80, 101
Christiaansen, R. E., 69, 70, 77
Christianson, S.-Å., 57, 64, 67, 73, 75, 77, 78,
    161, 174, 179, 188–190
Clinchy, B. M., 80, 101
Cohen, G. D., 9, 10, 105, 107, 109, 111, 113,
    118, 120, 122, 133, 142
Cohen, N. J., 61, 67
Collins, A. F., 64, 142, 185, 188, 189
Conrad, F. G., 20, 24, 26
Conway, M. A., 47, 52, 53, 55, 63, 64, 111, 118,
    122, 123, 127, 135, 141–143, 164, 169,
    174, 178, 185, 188, 189
Cook, P., 59, 65
Cornoldi, C., 55, 64
Cowan, N., 79, 94, 101
Cowan, T. M., 31, 43, 175, 188
Craik, F. I. M., 119, 122
Crombag, H. F. M., 54, 67
Crowder, R. G., 19, 25, 29, 43, 186, 190
Csikszentmihalkyi, M., 127, 142
Cutshall, J. L., 16, 27

D

Damasio, A. R., 58, 64
Davidson, G., 79, 94, 101
Davis, M., 96, 101
De Beni, R., 55, 64
Deaux, K., 98, 101
Deffenbacher, K. A., 16, 21, 25, 26
della Sala, S., 118, 122
Demorest, A. P., 127, 138, 142
Denham, S. A., 91, 101
Dennett, D. C., 168, 189, 190
Dippo, C. S., 22, 25
Donald, M., 155, 160
Donnelly, C. M., 188
Dooling, J. D., 69, 70, 77
Dosser, D. A., Jr. 81, 101
Dritschel, B. H., 56, 67
Dunn, J., 91, 101

E

Ebbinghaus, H. E., 69, 77, 165, 189
Edwards, A., 70, 77
Edwards, D., 79, 102
Eisenberg, A. R., 82, 101
Emory, E., 96, 101
Engel, S., 82, 101

Epstein, S., 155, 160
Ericsson, K. A., 57, 64, 178, 189
Esplin, P. W., 159, 161

F

Falk, J., 25, 107, 123
Faulkner, D., 109, 111, 122, 142
Feldman, C. F., 54, 63
Fischoff, B., 72, 77
Fitzgerald, J. M., 52, 54, 64, 107, 122, 125, 130,
    141, 142
Fivush, R., 4, 6, 8–10, 29, 30, 43, 54, 64, 79, 82,
    84, 87, 91, 94, 97, 98, 100–103, 142,
    145, 160, 161, 190
Foley, M. A., 174, 189
Freeman, M., 26, 43, 54, 61, 64, 65, 78, 102,
    123, 161
Freud, S., 36, 40, 41, 55, 70, 77, 166, 179
Friedman, W. J., 79, 94, 102, 161, 174, 175,
    178, 189
Fritz, J., 91, 101
Fromhoff, F. A., 30, 43
Fromholt, P., 140, 142
Fung, H., 54, 65

G

Gallant, L., 117, 123
Gallen, D., 150, 161
Galton, F., 47, 64, 123
Gardiner, J. M., 164, 171, 176, 177, 189, 190
Gathercole, S. E., 64, 142, 185, 188, 189
Gee, J. P., 148, 161
Gergen, K. J., 54, 65, 126, 127, 141, 142
Gilbert, G. M., 74, 77
Gilligan, S. G., 39, 43, 80, 102
Gold, D. P., 26, 107, 122
Goldberg, S., 96, 102
Goldberger, N. R., 80, 101
Goldsmith, D., 49, 52, 66, 186, 189
Goldsmith, M., 70, 77, 168, 169, 190
Golombok, S., 98, 102
Gordon, B., 61, 67
Gordon, K., 73, 77
Graddol, D., 80, 102
Gregory, R. L., 163, 167, 189
Griffin, M., 69, 77
Groth, L., 49, 52, 66, 186, 190
Gruendel, J., 115, 123
Gruneberg, M. M., 14–16, 19–21, 24–26, 122,
    123, 142

H

Haden, C. A., 54, 64, 79, 82, 84, 87, 101–103
Hager, D. R., 20, 24, 26
Hall, J. A., 90, 99, 101

Hall, J. F., 69, 77
Hall, L. K., 30, 42, 70, 77
Halverson, C. F., Jr., 81, 101
Hansen, T., 174, 189
Harsch, N., 30, 43, 176, 190
Harvey, A. D., 146, 161
Hasher, L., 69, 77
Hashtroudi, S., 56, 65
Healy, H., 67, 190
Herrmann, D. J., 13–18, 20–22, 24–26, 141, 143
Hertel, P., 16, 25, 26
Hertzog, C., 16, 25, 26
Heuer, F., 158, 162, 174, 189
Hilgard, J. R., 156, 161
Hirst, W., 54, 65, 164, 176, 185, 189
Hodges, J. R., 61, 62, 65, 127, 141, 142
Höffding, H., 176, 177, 189
Hoffman, A. M., 110, 122, 145, 147, 148, 150–152, 154, 155, 161
Hoffman, H. S., 110, 122, 145, 147, 148, 150–152, 154, 155, 161
Hoffman, R. R., 16, 21, 26,
Hoff-Ginsburg, E., 94, 102
Hofstadter, D. R., 168, 189, 190
Holden, C., 13, 26
Hollan, J. D., 178, 190
Holland, C. A., 24, 27, 107–109, 113, 117, 119, 123
Holmberg, D., 79, 94, 97, 103
Holmes, D. S., 37, 39, 43, 74, 77
Hoogstra, L., 54, 65
Horowitz, M. J., 158, 161, 185, 189
Hudson, J. A., 82, 102, 145, 161
Hunt, R. R., 6, 9–11, 55, 65
Hyde, J. S., 95, 102

I-J

Intons-Peterson, M. J., 17, 26
Isen, A. M., 74, 77
Jacoby, L. L., 177, 189
Jacoby, O., 150, 161
James, W., 147, 165, 166, 176, 179, 180, 186, 189
Janet, P., 156, 161
Janoff-Bulman, R., 156, 161
Jansari, A., 132, 143
Java, R. I., 164, 176, 189
Jennings, J. M., 119, 122, 177, 189
Jersild, A., 74, 77
Johnson, F., 80, 100
Johnson, M. K., 16, 25, 56, 65, 164, 174–176, 179, 185, 189
Jones, C. A., 31, 43, 175, 188

K

Kalamarides, P., 52, 65

Kantor, D., 157, 161
Kapur, N., 59, 61, 65
Ketcham, K., 23, 26
Kihlstrom, J. F., 74, 77, 159, 161, 162, 179, 190
Koch, H. L., 74, 77
Koriat, A., 70, 77, 168, 169, 189
Kosslyn, S. M., 154, 161, 189
Kozin, M., 47, 50, 53, 55, 66, 75, 78, 158, 162, 176, 190
Kuebli, J., 91, 100
Kulik, J., 47, 53, 55, 63, 145, 155, 160, 176, 185, 188

L

Labov, U., 81, 87, 102
Labov, W., 146, 161
Laiacona, M., 118, 122
Lang, D., 59, 65
Lapp, D., 23, 27
Larsen, S. F., 5, 7, 8, 11, 12, 31, 32, 36, 39, 43, 63, 142, 163, 174, 175, 178, 188–190
Law, A. B., 5, 65
Lawrence, R., 43, 64, 66, 67, 102, 122, 142, 190
LeDoux, J. E., 179, 190
Leeper, R., 74, 78
Lever, J., 96, 102
Lewis, M., 96, 101, 102
Lieberman, M. A., 107, 123
Linde, C., 79, 102
Lindsay, D. S., 6, 56, 65
Linn, M. C., 95, 102
Linton, M., 31, 39, 43, 74, 77, 78, 114, 123, 141, 143
Loftus, D. A., 74, 78
Loftus, E. F., 19, 23, 26, 30, 43, 55, 63, 72, 78, 154, 159–161
Logie, R. H., 24, 27, 188
Luh, W. M., 57, 66

M

Mackay, D. G., 120, 123
Major, B., 7, 30, 36, 49, 54, 66, 88, 91, 94, 98, 101, 127, 128, 135, 137, 139, 167, 176, 179
Malamut, B., 59, 65
Mandler, G., 74, 78
Manier, D., 54, 65
Marks, D. F., 137, 154, 157, 161
Marschark, M., 55, 65
Marshall, E., 13, 26
Matlin, M. W., 39, 43, 185, 190
Maylor, E,. 111, 122
McAdams, D. P., 126, 127, 131, 143
McCabe, A., 81, 82, 87, 94, 102, 103

McCarthy, G., 60–62, 65
McCloskey, M., 61, 67, 72, 78
McEvoy, C. L., 16, 22, 25, 26
McKee, R. D., 160, 161
McLean, J., 158, 162
McNally, R. J., 156, 161
Middleton, D., 79, 102
Mill, K., 98, 100, 165
Miller, G., 50, 51, 65
Miller, K., 16, 26
Miller, P. J., 54, 65, 79, 82, 102
Mintz, J., 54, 65
Mishkin, M., 59, 65
Mishler, E. G., 137, 138, 143
Mitchell, D. A., 31, 43, 66, 175, 188
Moffitt, K. H., 141, 143
Morris, P. E., 14, 16, 19, 24–26, 64, 122, 123,
    142, 188, 189
Morton, J., 115, 123
Mullen, P., 79, 94, 102
Mullin, P., 22, 26
Munn, P., 91, 101
Munsterberg, H., 17, 26
Murphy, K. R., 70, 78

N

Nagel, T., 163, 168, 190
Nebes, R. D., 62, 66, 109, 123, 125, 143
Neisser, U., 15, 19, 26, 30, 43, 47, 53, 55, 63,
    65–67, 75–79, 81, 101, 102, 122, 123,
    131, 141–143, 145, 161, 169, 174, 176,
    185, 188–190
Nelson, K., 29, 30, 43, 54, 65, 79, 87, 101, 102,
    115, 123, 145, 155, 161
Nezlek, J., 80, 103
Nigro, G., 131, 143, 174, 190
Norman, D. A., 43, 56, 66, 77, 117, 123
Nyberg, L., 59, 60, 65

O

O'Shaughnessy, M., 158, 162
Ochs, E., 147, 160
Ogden, J. A., 58, 65

P

Paivio, A., 55, 65, 170, 190
Palmisano, M., 22, 25
Pani, J. R., 164, 188
Parkin, A. J., 118, 123, 132, 143
Pascal-Leone, J., 117, 123
Payne, D. G., 20, 24, 26
Pedhazur, E. J., 18, 26
Peterson, C., 17, 26, 63, 81, 82, 87, 94, 102, 103

Petri, H. L., 59, 65
Pezdek, K., 16, 25
Pillemer, D. B., 5, 6, 8, 10, 11, 55–57, 65, 79,
    103, 145, 146, 155, 158, 159, 161, 162
Pines, A., 79, 94, 102
Plude, D., 22, 25
Poon, L. W., 27, 62, 66
Potts, R., 54, 65
Pra Baldi, A., 55, 64
Proust, M., 49–51, 61, 65

R

Rabbitt, P. M. A., 108–110, 113, 117, 123
Raggatt, P. T. F., 31, 43, 175, 188
Rahhal, T. A., 62, 66
Raskin, D. C., 159, 161
Raybeck, D., 14, 17, 18, 20, 21, 24, 25
Raye, C. L., 56, 65, 174, 189
Read, J. D., 3, 6, 12, 43, 178, 181, 190
Reese, E., 54, 64, 79, 82, 84, 102, 103, 161
Reidbord, S. P., 158, 161, 185, 189
Reisberg, D., 158, 162, 174, 189
Reiser, B. J., 52, 65
Revelle, W., 74, 78
Richardson, J. T. E., 169, 171, 177, 183, 190
Richardson-Klavehn, A., 171, 177, 190
Richman, C. L., 55, 65
Richmond, T., 154, 155, 162
Ridgeway, D., 91, 101
Ritchie, J., 98, 100
Robinson, J. A., 9–11, 52, 53, 55, 57, 66, 105,
    123, 125, 131, 132, 141, 143, 174, 190
Roediger, H. L., 29, 43
Rogoff, B., 97, 103
Rose, C., 149, 162
Ross, B. M., 41, 43, 75, 78, 166, 175, 190
Ross, M., 72, 78, 79, 94, 97, 103
Rubin, D. C., 7, 8, 10, 11, 27, 47, 49, 50, 52–55,
    62–67, 75, 78, 102, 109, 122, 123, 125,
    127, 142, 143, 158, 162, 164, 176, 178,
    186, 188–190
Rumelhart, D. E., 43, 56, 66, 77
Ryan, B., 153, 162

S

Safer, M. A., 57, 64
Salovey, P., 126, 127, 143
Schab, F. R., 186, 190
Schacter, D. L., 61, 66, 160, 162, 179, 190
Schafer, R., 54, 66
Schank, R. C., 54, 66
Schmelkin, L. P., 18, 26
Schooler, J. W., 141, 143, 189
Schulkind, M. D., 50, 52, 62, 66

Schwanenflugel, P. J., 57, 66
Scott, J., 115, 123
Searleman, A., 21, 22, 26
Semmer, N., 14, 27
Shallice, T., 117, 123
Shannon, L., 74, 78
Shapiro, L., 82, 102
Sharp, A. A., 70, 78
Sheikh, J. I., 23, 27, 161, 162
Shepard, R. N., 56, 66
Shotter, J., 141, 143
Simon, H. A., 178, 189
Singer, J. A., 126, 127, 137, 141, 143
Skowronski, J. J., 32, 36, 39, 43, 74, 78, 178, 190
Smith, T. S., 53, 54, 63
Spence, D. P., 66, 155, 162, 178, 190
Sperry, L. L., 54, 65, 82, 102
Squire, L. R., 52, 59, 61, 66, 67, 160, 161
Stang, D. J., 39, 43, 185, 190
Stanhope, N., 118, 122
Strongman, K. F., 179, 190
Suengas, A. G., 174, 189
Swann, J., 80, 102
Swanson, K. L., 55, 66, 131, 141, 143, 174, 190
Sykes, R. N., 14, 16, 19, 25, 26, 122, 123, 142

T

Tannen, D., 64, 80, 96, 102, 103
Tarule, J. M., 80, 101
Taylor, S. E., 9, 10, 42, 43, 125, 161
Terr, L., 148, 154–159, 162
Thompson, C. P., 29, 31, 32, 36, 39, 43, 44, 74, 78, 174, 175, 178, 189, 190
Thompson, S., 59, 65
Tobias, B. A., 179, 190
Tollestrup, P. A., 75, 78
Treadway, M., 61, 62, 67
Trivelli, C., 118, 122
Tulving, E., 21, 27, 47, 49, 52, 59, 61, 65–67, 160, 162, 169, 177, 190

U–V

Updike, J., 146, 162
van Koppen, P. J., 54, 67

Van Pelt, M., 70, 77, 179, 188
Vogl, R. J., 36, 44
Vygotsky, L. S., 80, 103

W

Wagenaar, W. A., 31, 39, 43, 54, 63, 64, 67, 74, 78, 122, 123, 142, 143, 188
Waletzky, J., 146, 161
Walker, W. R., 6, 9, 10, 36, 44
Walter, B. M., 118, 123
Wang, P. L., 61, 66
Waters, R. ,74, 78
Webster, J. D., 107, 123
Weisser, S., 127, 131, 142
Wertsch, J., 80, 103
Wetzler, S. E., 62, 66, 109, 123, 125, 143
Wheeler, L., 80, 103
White, R. T., 31, 44
White, S. H., 79, 103, 145, 155, 161, 162
Whittlesey, R., 148, 149, 160
Wilkins, A. J., 178, 189
Williams, D. M., 178, 190
Williams, J. M. G., 56, 57, 61, 67, 114, 115, 118, 119, 123
Wilson, B. A., 22, 27, 58, 63, 115, 117, 122
Wison, S. C., 156, 162
Winograd, E., 43, 47, 55, 63, 65–67, 77, 101, 122, 123, 161, 169, 185, 188–190
Winthorpe, C. A., 108, 109, 123
Wittlinger, R. P., 30, 42
Woodworth, R. 73, 78
Wulf, F., 70, 78

Y

Yarmey, A. D., 6, 111, 123
Yates, F. A., 55, 67
Yesavage, J. A., 23, 27
Yonelinas, A. P., 177, 189
Yuille, J. C., 4, 7, 8, 11, 16, 27, 55, 65, 75, 78

Z

Zahn-Waxler, C., 91, 101
Zaragoza, M., 72, 78
Zola-Morgan, S., 52, 61, 67
Zoller, D., 91, 101

Subject Index

A

Affect, 5–7, 10, 11, 22, 23, 37, 43, 49–53,
   56–58, 65, 67, 70–78, 105, 106, 109,
   153, 158, 161, 162, 168, 176, 189, 190
Aging, 10, 105, 118, 120–123, 135, 142, 143
Amnesia, 30, 48, 59–67, 115, 122, 162
Appearance qualities, 11, 164, 171, 172,
   175–177, 186, 187
Applicable research, 16, 20
Application research, 16
Applied research, 13–18, 20, 24–26, 29
Associationism, 77, 165, 166
Autobiographical memory, 3–12, 29, 30, 36, 39,
   43–45, 48–60, 62–67, 69, 70, 74, 78, 80,
   81, 90, 95, 97, 98, 100–102, 105,
   107–109, 115, 117, 118, 120–123,
   125–127, 129, 130, 132, 135, 140–143,
   145, 147, 151–153, 155–157, 160, 161,
   164, 184, 188–190

B

Basic research, 13–17, 19–21, 24, 25
Belief, 49, 57, 165, 170, 176, 177

C

Clinical implications, 156
Cognitive psychology, 13–15, 17, 20, 25, 26,
   30, 43, 51, 53, 65, 66, 76–78, 143, 155,
   166, 167, 188, 190
Cognitive resource deficit, 117
Cognitive socialization, 80

Collaboration, 14, 15, 17, 20, 21, 23, 24
Common process strategy, 21
Communicative fluency, 95
Confabulation, 63, 111, 112, 122
Confirmations, 84–87
Confounding, 74–76, 169
Content qualities, 11, 164, 171, 174, 176, 178,
   186
Cuing, 50, 51, 58, 66, 190

D

Depression, 61, 67, 97, 107, 115, 117, 123
Diary, 29, 31, 32, 38, 169
Diary memory, 29, 31, 32
Displacement hypothesis, 70–72
Distortions, 4, 5, 69, 72, 75, 76, 78
Distributional analysis, 127
Durability of memory, 30
Dysexecutive syndrome, 116, 117

E

Ecological research, 15, 16
Elaborativeness, 83, 85
Elderly, 22, 27, 107–114, 117, 118, 121–123
Emotion, 6–9, 39, 40, 42, 57, 64, 67, 73, 74,
   77–79, 90–93, 101, 113, 143, 157, 158,
   161, 175, 179, 180, 186, 188–190
Emotional intensity, 7, 37–39, 41, 185
Emotionality, 62, 109, 153
Empathy, 106
Epiphenomenalism, 164–168

197

Everyday memory, 12, 19, 24–26, 29, 30, 32, 43
Eyewitness testimony, 5, 30, 57, 72, 109, 111, 122, 155, 160, 169

F

Fallibility of memory, 30
Feelings, 73, 75, 147, 150, 156–158, 169, 170, 179
Flashbulb memory, 10, 55, 109, 111, 112
Frontal lobe amnesia, 115

G

Gender differences, 6, 9, 10, 79–81, 84, 86, 89–92, 94–103
General knowledge, 107
Genres, 127, 128, 139, 141, 143
Gestalt Psychology, 166

I

Identity construction, 107
Imagery, 5, 7, 8, 11, 22, 49, 51, 52, 54–59, 65, 78, 121, 139, 150, 153, 157–159, 161, 162, 169, 174, 178–181, 183–187, 190
Inferential processing, 70, 76
Interpersonal functions, 106, 121
Intrapersonal functions, 106, 107, 121

L

Life histories, 125–127, 131
Life narratives, 10, 132, 140, 141
Life review, 107
Life stories, 102, 126–128, 131, 133, 138, 139, 142, 156

M

Maintenance of knowledge 30
Memorial attitudes, 170
Memory accuracy, 5, 159, 168, 169, 173, 176, 177, 185
Memory modalities, 178
Memory narrative, 145, 148, 153, 155, 159
Memory narratives, 143, 147, 152, 153, 155, 156, 160
Memory quality, 108, 110
Misleading information, 8, 12, 111
Mobilization-minimization, 42, 43
Mood, 22, 49, 54, 73, 74, 77, 78, 106, 107, 188
Mood regulation, 106

N

Narrative forms, 10, 127, 139, 141, 157
Narrative memory system, 11, 155
Narrative self, 79, 80
Narrative structure, 10, 53, 54, 56, 87–89, 94, 102, 103, 139, 140
Narratives, 5, 9–11, 54, 64, 66, 67, 79–82, 87, 88, 91, 95, 101, 102, 115, 125–127, 129, 131, 132, 134, 138–141, 143, 145–147, 152, 153, 155, 156, 160, 161
Naturalistic approach, 74
Neuropsychology, 51, 57, 58, 61, 62, 65
Node Structure Theory, 120

O

Oral history, 145, 147, 150, 153
Overgeneral memories, 11, 113, 114, 118, 119, 121

P

Perceptual qualities, 170, 174, 178
Personal disclosure, 98
Phenomenal qualities, 5, 11, 163, 164, 167, 171, 173, 176, 186, 187
Pleasantness, 37–40, 44, 78, 128, 169
Post-traumatic stress disorder, 156, 161
Problem solving, 25, 107
Process qualities, 11, 164, 171–173, 176–178, 186, 187
Propositions, 169, 170, 177
Psychoanalysis, 66, 155, 166
PTSD, 118, 156, 157, 161

R

Recollective memory, 49, 63, 178, 188
Reconstructive, 6, 69, 70, 72, 73, 75–77, 167, 178, 189
Reductionism, 143, 167
Reflective qualities, 174, 175, 180
Rehearsal, 8, 22, 53, 56, 108, 110, 113, 121, 133, 154
Reminiscence, 9, 64, 106, 107, 122, 123, 125, 130, 132, 133, 140, 142, 143
Reminiscence bump, 9, 132, 133, 140, 143
Reminiscing, 6, 64, 79, 81, 82, 84–89, 91, 93–100, 102, 103
Replacement hypothesis, 70, 71
Replicative, 69, 70, 72, 73, 75–77
Representation, 8, 11, 55, 66, 101, 125, 132, 155, 157, 158
Repression, 23, 36, 40, 41, 116, 118, 120

Research cultures, 14, 20, 25
Retrieval, 7, 11, 43, 47, 50–53, 58–62, 64, 65,
    69, 70, 74, 116, 117, 119, 120, 129, 132,
    135, 171–173, 177, 178, 187, 188, 190

S

Screen memories, 41, 70
Self-concept formation, 106
Self-disclosure, 106, 121
Self-narratives, 11, 54, 125, 140
Self-concept, 42, 91, 97, 126
Social functions, 107
Social interaction, 79, 80, 103, 106
Spatial memory, 48
Specificity, 21, 67, 98, 110, 111, 113, 114,
    117–121, 123, 129, 143
Statement Validity Assessment, 159, 161
Surface qualities, 176
SVA, 159

T

Temperament, 96

Temporal schemata, 29
Temporal trace, 36
Themes, 3, 5, 94, 127, 137–139, 141, 142
Theoretical implications, 11, 152
Transmission deficit, 117, 120

V

Verb tense shift, 147, 153
Verb tense shifts, 5, 10, 11, 145, 147–150, 152,
    155, 157, 160
Vivid memories, 30, 50, 53, 55, 64, 66, 78, 81,
    109, 111, 125, 126, 128–133, 137, 138,
    140–143, 162, 190
Vividness, 10, 53, 62, 109, 110, 121, 128, 146,
    147, 157, 158, 162, 164, 170, 171, 175,
    176, 178–187
Voice, 80, 101, 102, 165

W

Word cueing method, 109
Würzburg School, 165–167, 171